## EUROPE

**711** Muslim armies enter Spain

**732** Battle of Poitiers checks Muslim expansion into Europe

**768** Charlemagne becomes king of the Franks

**1054** Great Schism: Christianity splits between Roman Catholic and Eastern Orthodox Church

**1066** William the Conqueror establishes Norman kingdom in England

**1088** First European university founded in Bologna, Italy

**1095** Christian Crusades begin

**1215** England's King John signs Magna Carta

**ca. 1300** Beginning of the Renaissance

**1337–1453** Hundred Years' War between England and France

**1347–1351** Black Death kills one-third of Europe's population

**1455** Johannes Gutenberg pioneers use of moveable-type printing press

**1498** Vasco da Gama sails around Africa to India

**1517** Martin Luther sparks the Reformation that divides Europe into Protestant and Catholic lands

**1562–1598** Wars of Religion pit French Catholics against Protestants

**1618–1648** Thirty Years' War

**1689** Great Britain becomes a constitutional monarchy

**ca. 1700** Beginning of the Enlightenment

**mid-1700s** Beginning of the Industrial Revolution

**1789–1799** French Revolution

**1799–1812** Napoleon Bonaparte becomes dictator of France and conquers most of Europe

**1812** Napoleon defeated in Russia, later deposed and exiled to Elba

## ASIA AND THE PACIFIC

**1526** Islamic Mughal Empire established in India

**1557** First European colony in Asia founded at Macau

**1601** First British trading post established in India

**1603** Beginning of Tokugawa shogunate in Japan

**1644** Manchurian invaders topple Chinese Ming Dynasty and establish Qing Dynasty

**1757** Battle of Plessey establishes British dominance over India

**1778** First European settlers arrive in Australia

**1839** First Opium War

**1854** U.S. opens Japan to trade

**1860** Second Opium War

**1868** Beginning of Meiji period in Japan, marked by rapid modernization

**1894–1895** First Sino-Japanese War

**1899** Boxer Rebellion in China begins

**1904–1905** Russo-Japanese War

**1910** Japan annexes Korea

**1911** Revolution topples China's Qing Dynasty

**1928** Chiang Kai-shek unifies China under his rule

**1934–1935** Mao Zedong leads Chinese Communists on "Long March"

**1937** Japan invades China, begins Second Sino-Japanese War

**1940** Japan signs Tripartite Pact supporting Germany and Italy

**1941** Japan attacks U.S. forces at Pearl Harbor, Hawaii, causing U.S. to enter World War II

**1945** U.S. drops atomic bombs on Hiroshima and Nagasaki; Japan surrenders; Korea divided into Soviet-occupied North Korea and Western-occupied South Korea

**1492** Christopher Columbus lands in Caribbean

**1494** Treaty of Tordesillas divides world's unclaimed territories between Spain and Portugal

**1497–1498** John Cabot explores eastern coast of present-day Canada, claiming the land for England

**1500** Pedro Álvarez Cabral claims what is now Brazil for Portugal

**1502** Enslaved Africans reach the Americas

**1521** Fall of Tenochtitlán, capital of the Aztec Empire

**1532** Pizarro conquers Incan Empire in Peru

**1607** Jamestown, Virginia is first permanent English settlement in the Americas

**1620** Mayflower lands at Plymouth Rock

**1754–1763** French and Indian War

**1775** American Revolutionary War begins at Battles of Lexington and Concord

**1776** U.S. Declaration of Independence signed in Philadelphia

**1783** Treaty of Paris of 1783 recognizes American independence

**1804** Haiti becomes world's first independent black state

**1810** Miguel Hidalgo y Costilla, a Mexican priest, instigates revolt against Spain

**1821** Simón Bolívar secures independence for Gran Columbia; Mexico gains independence

**1822** Brazil declares independence

**1825** Bolivia declares its independence

**1838** John Deere invents steel plow

**1846** Mexican-American War begins

**1848** Treaty of Guadalupe Hildalgo ends Mexican-American War

# The Modern World

## Civilizations of Africa

VOLUME 1

# Set Contents

*The Modern World*

Vol. 1: *Civilizations of Africa*

Vol. 2: *Civilizations of Europe*

Vol. 3: *Civilizations of the Americas*

Vol. 4: *Civilizations of the Middle East and Southwest Asia*

Vol. 5: *Civilizations of Asia and the Pacific*

# The Modern World

## Civilizations of Africa

## Volume 1

### GENERAL EDITOR
Sarolta Takács, Ph.D.
*Rutgers University*

MATAWAN-ABERDEEN PUBLIC LIBRARY
165 MAIN STREET
MATAWAN, NJ 07747

## SHARPE REFERENCE
*an imprint of M. E. Sharpe, Inc.*

**DEVELOPED, DESIGNED, AND PRODUCED BY DWJ BOOKS LLC**
Principal Author: Karen H. Meyers

# SHARPE REFERENCE
Sharpe Reference is an imprint of M.E. Sharpe, Inc.

M.E. Sharpe, Inc.
80 Business Park Drive
Armonk, NY 10504

© 2008 by M.E. Sharpe, Inc.

All rights reserved. No part of this publication may be reproduced, stored in a retrieval system, or transmitted in any form or by any means, electronic, mechanical, photocopying, recording, or otherwise, without prior permission of the copyright holders.

Library of Congress Cataloging-in-Publication Data
The modern world / Sarolta Takács, general editor.
    p. cm.
Includes bibliographical references and index.
ISBN 978-0-7656-8096-9 (set: alk. paper)
1. Civilization, Modern—Encyclopedias.
2. World history—Encyclopedias.
I. Takács, Sarolta A.
CB357.M65 2008
903—dc22
2007044253

Printed and bound in Malaysia
The paper used in this publication meets the minimum requirements of American National Standard for Information Sciences—Permanence of Paper for Printed Library Materials.
ansi z 39.48.1984

TI (c) 10 9 8 7 6 5 4 3 2 1

Cover images (clockwise, from top left) were provided by Getty Images and the following: Travel Ink/Gallo Images; Per-Anders; Michael J.P. Scott/Stone; Tilly Willis/The Bridgeman Art Library; Michael Lewis/National Geographic.

# Contents

| | |
|---|---|
| List of Illustrations | vii |
| Topic Finder | ix |
| Preface | xi |
| The Most Diverse Continent | xii |
| Map of Modern Africa | xvi |

| | |
|---|---|
| African Union | 1 |
| Agriculture | 4 |
| Algeria | 9 |
| Apartheid | 10 |
|    **GREAT LIVES:** Nelson Mandela | 13 |
| Art and Architecture | 15 |
| Aswan High Dam | 19 |
| Boer War | 21 |
| British Colonies in Africa | 22 |
|    **GREAT LIVES:** Cecil Rhodes | 25 |
| Civil Wars | 27 |
|    **INTO THE TWENTY-FIRST CENTURY:** Blood Diamonds | 28 |
| Colonization | 30 |
|    **TURNING POINT:** Berlin Conference of 1884–1885 | 33 |
| Communist Movements | 34 |
| Congo | 36 |
|    **GREAT LIVES:** Mobutu Sese Seko | 38 |
| Culture and Traditions | 39 |
| Democratic Movements | 44 |
| Drought | 48 |
| Economic Development and Trade | 49 |
| Egypt | 54 |
|    **GREAT LIVES:** Muhammad Ali Pasha | 56 |
|    **GREAT LIVES:** Gamal Abdel Nasser | 57 |
| Environmental Issues | 58 |
| Eritrea | 62 |
| Ethiopia | 63 |
|    **GREAT LIVES:** Haile Selassie | 65 |
|    **GREAT LIVES:** Menelik II | 66 |
| Famine | 67 |
| French West Africa | 68 |
|    **GREAT LIVES:** Ahmed Sékou Touré | 70 |
| German Colonies | 71 |
| Imperialism | 73 |
| Independence Movements | 75 |
| Italian Colonies | 80 |
|    **TURNING POINT:** The Treaty of Wuchale | 81 |
|    **INTO THE TWENTY-FIRST CENTURY:** Return of the Aksum Obelisk | 83 |
| Language | 84 |
| Liberia | 88 |
|    **INTO THE TWENTY-FIRST CENTURY:** Al-Qaeda in Africa | 89 |
| Literature and Writing | 90 |
| Migration | 96 |
| Nigeria | 97 |
|    **TURNING POINT:** Biafran War, 1967–1970 | 99 |
| Pan-African Movement | 101 |
| Portuguese Colonies | 102 |
| Refugees | 103 |
| Religion | 104 |
|    **INTO THE TWENTY-FIRST CENTURY:** Islamic Politics in Africa | 108 |
| Rwanda | 110 |
| Slavery and the Slave Trade | 113 |
| Society | 116 |
|    **INTO THE TWENTY-FIRST CENTURY:** AIDS in Africa | 117 |
| Somalia | 121 |
| South Africa | 122 |
|    **MODERN WEAPONS:** Nuclear Testing | 125 |
|    **TURNING POINT:** 1994 Free Elections | 127 |
| Sudan | 128 |
|    **INTO THE TWENTY-FIRST CENTURY:** Darfur | 129 |
| Suez Canal | 131 |
| Technology and Inventions | 133 |

Tools and Weapons                              137
    **MODERN WEAPONS:** NeoStead 2000     139
    **MODERN WEAPONS:** The Military Innovations
    of Shaka Zulu                          138

Tutsis and Hutus                               140

Uganda                                         142
    **GREAT LIVES:** Idi Amin              143

## Glossary                                    145
## Selected Bibliography                       149
## Index                                       153

# List of Illustrations

## Time Lines

| | |
|---|---|
| Modern World Time Line | Endpapers |
| Rise and Fall of Apartheid | 12 |
| Modern African Art and Architecture | 16 |
| Communist Movements, 1920–1992 | 35 |
| Democracy in Modern Africa | 45 |
| Independence Movements, 1912–1994 | 76 |
| Landmarks in African Literature, 1845–2006 | 93 |
| African Religions, 1324–2005 | 106 |
| South Africa, 1488–Present | 123 |
| Technology in Africa | 134 |

## Maps

| | |
|---|---|
| Map of Modern Africa | xvi |
| British Colonies in Africa, ca. 1913 | 24 |
| Major Civil Wars, Border Disputes, and Guerilla Activities in Modern Africa, 1960–Present | 29 |
| Africa on the Eve of the Berlin Conference, 1884–1885 | 32 |
| Gross Domestic Product of African Countries | 51 |
| Climate Map of Africa | 59 |
| French Colonies in Africa in the Early 1900s | 69 |
| Official Languages in Modern Africa | 85 |
| The African Slave Trade, 1700–1810 | 114 |
| The Boer War and the Union of South Africa, 1899–1910 | 124 |

## Photos

| | |
|---|---|
| African Union delegates | 2 |
| River Nile and fertile floodplain | 6 |
| Kente Cloth | 18 |
| Aswan High Dam | 20 |
| Mobutu Sese Seko | 37 |
| Initiation rite for tribal youth | 42 |
| Shopping mall in Soweto, South Africa | 52 |
| Pyramids at Giza and Cairo | 55 |
| African elephant killed for ivory tusks | 60 |
| Haile Selassie | 64 |
| Sudanese famine victims | 68 |
| Kwame Nkrumah signing African Charter | 77 |
| Modern African writer Chinua Achebe | 92 |
| Nigerian oil rig | 98 |
| Christian church and Islamic mosque | 107 |
| Paul Kagame, President of the Republic of Rwanda | 111 |
| Nelson Mandela released from prison | 126 |
| Sudanese refugees | 130 |
| Expedition against the Aros of Nigeria | 135 |
| Tutsi refugees from 1994 civil war in Rwanda | 141 |

# Topic Finder

### Civilizations and Peoples
British Colonies in Africa
Colonization
Tutsis and Hutus

### Culture and Language
Agriculture
Art and Architecture
Culture and Traditions
Economic Development and Trade
Environmental Issues
Language
Literature and Writing

### General Topics
Agriculture
Art and Architecture
Colonization
Culture and Traditions
Democratic Movements
Drought
Economic Development and Trade
Environmental Issues
Famine
Imperialism
Language
Literature and Writing
Migration
Refugees
Technology and Inventions

### Notable Figures
Nelson Mandela (*see* Apartheid)
Cecil Rhodes (*see* British Colonies in Africa)
Mobutu Sese Seko (*see* Congo)
Muhammad Ali Pasha (*see* Egypt)
Gamal Abdel Nasser (*see* Egypt)
Menelik II (*see* Ethiopia)
Haile Selassie (*see* Ethiopia)
Ahmed Séiko Touré (*see* French West Africa)
Idi Amin (*see* Uganda)

### Periods and Events
African Union
Colonization
Communist Movements
Democratic Movements
Environmental Issues
Independence Movements
Pan-African Movement
Slavery and the Slave Trade

## Places
Aswan High Dam
Congo
Egypt
Eritrea
Ethiopia
French West Africa
German Colonies
Italian Colonies
Liberia
Nigeria
Portuguese Colonies
Rwanda
Somalia
South Africa
Sudan
Uganda

## Society, Religion, and Way of Life
Agriculture
British Colonies in Africa
Colonization
Communist Movements
Culture and Traditions
Democratic Movements
Economic Development and Trade
Environmental Issues
Religion
Slavery and the Slave Trade
Society

## War and Military Affairs
Boer War
Civil Wars
Tools and Weapons

# Preface

In ancient times, barriers such as mountain ranges and great bodies of water slowed the cultural interaction between peoples. The modern era, however, is defined by the shrinking of frontiers as revolutions in transportation and technology closed distances.

Around the turn of the sixteenth century, European nautical technology allowed the transport of people and goods over distances never before fathomed. The Age of Exploration had begun and with it came the Modern Age. The groundwork for this age had been set in the preceding centuries by the conflicts between two religions, Christianity and Islam. The Crusades, armed Christian campaigns against various Muslim groups from the eleventh century through the fifteenth century, sought to wrest the holy city of Jerusalem from Islamic control. The mustering and marching of crusaders across Europe helped develop trade routes throughout the continent. The interactions in the Middle East, born in conflict, brought to the European market a taste for the products of the Middle East and the Far East. Advances in mathematics, astronomy, and other sciences were also imported from the Middle East to Europe. These advances and an increased economic interest in regions outside Europe led to the explosion of trade and exploration that ushered in the Modern Age.

From the sixteenth through the nineteenth centuries, European commercial powers became colonial powers. The Spanish, Portuguese, French, Dutch, and British established colonies across the globe in order to assure ownership of trade routes. Trading posts guaranteed the continual supply of goods and natural resources, such as spices and precious metals. During this period, the cultures of the colonizers and the colonized would greatly influence each other. Such mutual influences and blending can be seen, for example, in gastronomy; modern Indian cuisine was created when chilies from South America arrived in India and then influenced the tastes of British colonists.

In the twentieth century, former colonies became independent. The struggle for independence was often fierce and the creation of democratic governments hard fought. The endurance and spirit of Nelson Mandela, for example, helped South Africa overcome apartheid. The last century also saw two World Wars, as well as devastating regional conflicts and civil wars. While technological advances have made it possible to explore space, the same advances also have the capability of destroying property and life.

Articles in the five volumes of *The Modern World: Civilizations of Africa*, *the Americas*, *Asia and the Pacific*, *Europe*, and *the Middle East and Southwest Asia* are arranged alphabetically with time lines and cross-references that provide the reader a greater historical context in which to understand each topic. Features expand the coverage: "Turning Points" describe cultural, political, and technological changes that have had a lasting effect upon society; "Great Lives" profile individuals whose deeds shaped a people's history and culture; "Modern Weapons" delivers hard facts on modern warfare; and "Into the 21st Century" provides an introduction to topics that are important for understanding the most recent dramatic developments in world history. Each volume will be your guide in helping you to explore the rich and varied history of the modern world and participate in its future. May this journey offer you not only facts and data but also a deeper appreciation of the changes throughout history that have helped to form the modern world.

Sarolta A. Takács

# The Most Diverse Continent

Africa is a vast continent. The United States could easily fit into the Sahara, and there would still be room on the continent for China, India, New Zealand, Argentina, and half of Europe. It is a place of great ethnic and linguistic diversity. The land is home to several thousand different ethnic groups, and more than 800 languages are spoken there, including Arabic, native languages such as Swahili, Zulu, and Hausa, and European languages such as English, French, Portuguese, and German.

## GEOGRAPHY

Africa is geographically the most diverse of all continents. Because it is on a north-south axis, it has several quite different climate zones, from the dry heat of the Sahara, the world's largest desert, to the humid steam of tropical rainforests, to wide grasslands on which gazelle and zebra graze, to rocky highlands and plateaus where coffee is grown, to coastal areas with Mediterranean climates. Africa is home to more animal species than any other continent, including exotic antelopes such as the ibex and the oryx, and the world's great predators—lions, leopards, wildcats, and cheetahs. In addition, native to Africa is the largest land mammal—the elephant—and the smallest land mammal, the tiny musk shrew.

Of all the continents, Africa is most threatened by global warming. As the temperature rises, many areas of Africa that once had sufficient rainfall to grow crops and sustain grazing are becoming too dry to grow either food or fodder.

## EARLY HISTORY

Africa's history is as complicated and varied as its geography and people. Two of the world's first great civilizations—the Egyptian and the Kush—arose in Africa thousands of years ago. Parts of North Africa and Ethiopia were among the earliest lands to convert to Christianity, and large parts of northern Africa were conquered by Muslim invaders, leading many Africans to convert to Islam. In the Middle Ages, several large empires—such as Mali, Songhai, and Ghana—rose and fell.

## EUROPEAN CONTACT AND THE SLAVE TRADE

Everything changed for Africa when the first Europeans—the Portuguese—arrived on its shores in 1419. They continued to explore southward along the west coast into what is known as sub-Saharan Africa and, by 1441, were buying Africans from African middlemen and transporting them to Portugal as slaves. In the 1470s, they explored what are today the countries of Sierra Leone, São Tomé, and Gabon. By 1502, the first enslaved Africans reached the Americas, and during the next 300 years, more than 10 million natives were taken captive, packed into slave ships under horrendous conditions, and transported to slave markets in the Caribbean, Latin America, and North America. To this day, Africa's population has not rebounded from the devastating theft of its young men and women.

Many European nations engaged in the African slave trade, but the primary slave-trading nations were Portugal, the Netherlands, and Great Britain. Each of these nations established forts and outposts along Africa's coast to defend their access to this lucrative commodity. Most of the interior of the continent was unknown to Europeans, and they referred to it as a *terra incognita* (unknown land). Africa was also called "the dark continent," referring not only to the color of its inhabitants' skin but also to the fact that Europeans did not know what lay beyond the coast.

Denmark was the first nation to ban the slave trade, in 1803, followed by Britain in 1807. Britain outlawed slavery throughout the empire in 1834 and began to interfere actively with the ships of other nations that tried to take slaves from the continent.

## THE SCRAMBLE FOR AFRICA

It was not long before Europe began to take a different kind of interest in Africa—in its vast mineral resources, untouched raw materials, and human capital. In 1871, when Henry Morton Stanley was sent to central Africa to find explorer David Livingstone, and uttered the famous remark, "Dr. Livingstone, I presume," everything again would change for Africa. Stanley and Livingstone together explored some of the vast interior of the continent. In 1874, Stanley returned to continue his explorations, tracing the course of the Congo River to the Atlantic Ocean. It is thought that Stanley helped King Leopold II of Belgium to establish a personal colony in Africa, known as the Congo Free State, even though the inhabitants were brutalized by Leopold's overseers and were anything but free to pursue their own destinies.

To prevent wars among European powers, Otto von Bismarck, chancellor of the newly united nation of Germany, convened the Berlin Conference in 1884 to determine a method for dividing Africa among European powers. The conference was successful—at least for the Europeans. They were able to avoid fighting with one another while they concentrated their efforts on taking over Africa, by peaceful means, by trickery, and sometimes by the sword. Countries with extensive holdings included Germany, Great Britain, France, and Belgium, each adding more and more territory to their original coastal settlements. After the conference, these powers divided the continent with little knowledge of the native peoples and their histories, joining into nations ethnic groups that had hated one another for centuries and splitting unified groups by the imposition of arbitrary borders. As British prime minister Lord Salisbury once remarked in a speech to a London audience, "We have been giving away mountains and rivers and lakes to each other, only hindered by the small impediment that we never knew exactly where they were."

Colonialism brought both good and bad to Africa. The colonial powers built roads, railroads, hospitals, and schools, but they also brought suffering and humiliation to Africa's people. European masters used Africans in much the same way slave masters had used their slaves. They forced Africans to work for much less than their labor was worth, causing many Africans to accept the idea that they were inferior to their European masters. To this day, the marks of colonialism can be found across Africa, not only in place names and languages still spoken but also in failed political systems and ethnic hatreds.

## INDEPENDENCE

*Uhuru* is the Swahili word for freedom, and the 1960s were the uhuru decade for Africa, a time during which more than twenty African nations became independent of their colonizers. The first sub-Saharan nation to gain its independence was Ghana in 1957; the last was Namibia in 1990.

The more than half-century of African independence has been a time of ongoing turbulence and conflict. Long and bloody civil wars have killed tens of thousands in nations such as Liberia, Rwanda, Sierra Leone, Angola, Sudan, Uganda, and the Congo. Some nations that began with the hope of freedom eventually succumbed to ruthless dictators who pillaged national treasuries, murdered thousands of people, and made a mockery of the idea of democracy. Idi Amin of Uganda, Robert Mugabe of Zimbabwe, Omar-al Bashir of Sudan, Muammar al-Qaddafi of Libya, Mengistu Haile Mariam of Ethiopia, and Mobutu Sese Seko of the Congo are just a few of the ruthless dictators—often military men who took over their governments in **coups** and ruled for decades.

During these years, the Soviet Union and the West were enmeshed in a **Cold War** in which each side feared that the other was committed to world domination. While communists did not see potential in Africa for the ideal revolution of the working class against the middle class, the Soviet Union was happy to assist African nations in the hope of recruiting them to their side in the conflict. On the other hand, Western powers often propped up African dictators because they feared Soviet influence more than they objected to the anti-democratic policies of the African strongmen.

### END OF APARTHEID

The year 1994 was a year of triumph for many black South Africans because it marked the first free elections in that nation in which the majority black population was allowed to vote. In that year, the people elected as their president Nelson Mandela, a leader of the African National Congress (ANC) who had been imprisoned for twenty-seven years for his fight against the all-white South African government and its policy of apartheid—the official policy of racial separation. Apartheid became the law of the land in South Africa beginning in about 1948. It forced blacks to carry identification; denied them education, jobs, and the right to vote; and pushed them out of their homes and into ghetto-like areas reserved for blacks only. The all-white government under President F.W. de Klerk eventually realized that it could no longer dominate the black majority in the country and, in 1989, began to talk about free elections.

### CURRENT SOCIAL PROBLEMS

Today, many African nations are dealing with daunting social issues. Africa is the poorest continent on earth. The bottom twenty-five slots on the United Nations' list of the world's poorest countries are filled by African nations; in many countries, the average income is less than $200 (U.S.) a year. While some African economies have done well (Botswana's and South Africa's, for example), others have hovered on the brink of collapse.

Africans have long been plagued by tropical diseases such as malaria and sleeping sickness, but beginning in the late twentieth century, HIV/AIDS ravaged the continent. Millions of people are infected, millions of others have died, and millions of children have lost both parents to the illness. In countries such as Botswana, up to 40 percent of pregnant women have the disease. And while in places like Somalia, only about 1 percent of the population is infected, in Zambia and South Africa nearly 20 percent of all adults are HIV positive.

Rapidly growing cities have created major problems for modern African cultures. Famine, drought, poverty, war, and civil unrest all have driven rural Africans into cities in search of employment and refuge. Many urban centers, however, are overwhelmed by the rapid increase in population and do not have sufficient housing or adequate social services. Consequently, many people in African cities live in squalid conditions without adequate water, sanitation, food, or shelter. Young men who cannot find jobs often turn to crime; cities such as Johannesburg are overrun with armed robbers and rapists.

It is a depressing picture. While there are bright spots, such as rural women succeeding as farmers in cooperatives (in which people pool their resources to buy equipment and do the work) and micro-loans (small loans that help poor people buy things like seed and farm equipment so they can earn a decent living), the problems facing Africa are daunting. The African

Union (AU), an organization that comprises most African nations, has as its goals a common African currency, a common market, and shared judicial system, which it believes will help solve some of Africa's most pressing economic problems.

This huge, rich continent, with all its wealth and diversity, has great potential but faces even greater challenges. It is here that human beings first walked upright, and it is from here that they traveled to populate the earth. Today, the long-suffering people of Africa, the "cradle of humanity," must yet figure out how to govern this vast continent to secure their futures and ensure the legacies of their ancient traditions.

## FURTHER READING

Meredith, Martin. *The Fate of Africa. From the Hopes of Freedom to the Heart of Despair: A History of 50 Years of Independence.* New York: Public Affairs, 2005.

Reader, John. *Africa.* Washington, DC: National Geographic Press, 2001.

———. *Africa: A Biography of the Continent.* New York: Vintage, 1999.

Karen H. Meyers

# Map of Modern Africa

**MAP OF MODERN AFRICA**
Present-day Africa is comprised of fifty-four nations. Some, such as Sudan, are very large in land area, and others, such as Guinea-Bissau, at only 13,948 square miles (36,125 sq km), are tiny. National boundaries in Africa were drawn by colonial powers without consideration of ethnic loyalties or hatreds, leading to many of today's civil wars.

# A

# African Union

An organization of fifty-three African nations formed in 2002 with the goal of fostering political and economic cooperation among African nations, officially replacing the Organization of African Unity (OAU) and loosely based on the European Union (EU). Eventually, the African Union (AU) hopes to implement a common currency, a common economic market, and a greater degree of political unity. Also proposed are a central bank, a court of justice, and an all-African parliament.

The formation of the African Union reflects the developments and changes that have occurred in many parts of Africa in recent years. Among these developments are the growth of democracy and an emerging political philosophy that concentrates less on the battles of the past and more on the need to improve the lives of ordinary people. A major change between the AU and its predecessor is that the principle of state **sovereignty** has been abandoned. One of the aims of the AU is the promotion of "democratic principles and institutions, popular participation and good governance." The AU has the right to initiate a so-called "peer review" of a member country's record, intervene in the event of genocide or war crimes, and impose sanctions. Under the AU's directive, for example, member states have sent troops to Darfur in Sudan to try to end the genocide there.

Other key objectives of the AU include:

- To achieve greater unity and solidarity between the African countries and the peoples of Africa;
- To defend the sovereignty, territorial integrity, and independence of its member states;
- To accelerate the political and socioeconomic integration of the continent;
- To promote and defend African common positions on issues of interest to the continent and its peoples;
- To encourage international cooperation, taking due account of the Charter of the United Nations and the Universal Declaration of Human Rights;
- To promote peace, security, and stability on the continent;
- To promote democratic principles and institutions, popular participation, and good governance;
- To promote and protect human and peoples' rights in accordance with the African Charter on Human and Peoples' Rights and other relevant human rights instruments;
- To establish the necessary conditions that enable the continent to play its rightful role in the global economy and in international negotiations;
- To promote sustainable development at the economic, social, and cultural levels as well as the integration of African economies.

Today, a major concern of the African Union remains how to find the funding it needs to carry out its agenda. Presently, the African Union includes the following financial institutions: the African Central Bank, the African Monetary Fund, and the African Investment Bank. Although the AU relies on membership dues and international sources of funding, many member nations do not pay their dues, a situation that has led to various financial crises. The peacekeeping mission in Darfur, for example, has been seriously hampered due to lack of money.

## ROOTS

Ethiopian Emperor Haile Selassie and President Sékou Touré of Guinea spearheaded

## AFRICAN UNION

In 2004, African heads of state and other African Union delegates met in Addis Ababa, Ethiopia. Delegates represented fifty-three of the fifty-four nations on the African continent. (Simon Maina/Stringer/AFP/Getty Images)

the foundation of the Organization of African Unity (OAU). The organization's charter was signed by thirty-two nations on May 25, 1963, a day still commemorated as "Africa Day." As more African nations became independent, the number of member states grew, so that by the time the OAU was disbanded in 2002, fifty-three of Africa's fifty-four countries were members; only Morocco did not belong. (Morocco had once been a member but withdrew in 1985 when the organization allowed Western Sahara to join as a separate nation. Morocco regards Western Sahara as part of its territory.)

Article II of the OAU charter listed five major goals for the organization: to promote unity, to coordinate efforts to improve the lives of African people, to defend the sovereignty of member states, to eliminate colonialism, and to promote international cooperation.

The OAU was an outgrowth of the Pan-African Movement, which began in 1900 as an attempt to promote the idea that Africans everywhere, whether in Africa, the United States, or the Caribbean, shared similar goals and values. Within Africa, the movement promoted the idea of cooperation among individual nations for the betterment of all.

## PROBLEMS

From the beginning, however, many members disagreed about exactly what sort of organization the OAU should be. Some, such as President Kwame Nkrumah of Ghana, wanted the OAU to be the first step toward a unified Africa. Other nations, enjoying their first taste of independence, did not want to relinquish any power and preferred that the organization be a loose affiliation of independent states. The compromise that the original members made left the OAU without real power to act on its own in many situations.

In the West, some people referred to the OAU as the "dictators' club," because of its firm policy of nonintervention in the affairs of sovereign nations, even when the ruthless leaders of member countries murdered their political enemies and plundered national treasuries. Although the borders of Africa's fifty-four modern states were drawn largely by Europeans with no regard for ethnic and tribal loyalties, the OAU staunchly defended those borders as part of its policy of noninterference.

In addition, member states often disagreed about which side the organization would take in conflicts. The first such incident occurred during the Angolan Civil War (1974–2002). Half of the members of the OAU voted to back one faction and half to back the other. A similar split occurred during the 1977 and 1978 invasions of the Katanga Province in Zaire (now the Democratic Republic of the Congo) by Angola, during the invasion of Ethiopia by Somalia in 1978, and during the conflict between Uganda and Tanzania in 1978 and 1979. The OAU also proved unsuccessful in improving Africa's economy or combating AIDS.

## SUCCESSES

Although ineffective in many situations, the OAU did have some successes. It mediated border disputes between Algeria and Morocco in the mid-1960s and between Somalia and Kenya in the late 1960s. The OAU also provided significant financial support to movements seeking to end Portuguese colonial rule in Guinea-Bissau, Angola, and Mozambique. In addition, the OAU advocated economic sanctions against South Africa, demanding that its policy of apartheid be ended. In 1994 when South Africa ended apartheid, it was, for the first time, allowed to join the OAU.

The OAU had also sent an observer mission to the United Nations (UN). Observers cannot vote but try to influence delegations, much as lobbyists do in the U.S. Congress. In this capacity, the OAU was able to coordinate action among African nations at the UN. It also successfully lobbied to have South Africa barred from the UN because of its policy of apartheid.

## LATER DEVELOPMENTS

The prestige of the OAU was revived in the 1990s, partly because of the election of Tanzania's Salim Ahmed Salim as its secretary general in 1989. Salim was reelected in 1993 and 1997. Under his leadership, the OAU devised the "Method for Conflict Prevention," which made conflict resolution central to its mission. The OAU's policy of nonintervention in the 1970s and 1980s had made it clear to members that failure to act to resolve internal conflicts affected the entire continent, not just the country where the conflict originated. Neighboring countries not only experienced massive floods of refugees in need of food and shelter, they also suffered from armed combatants carrying the conflict across borders. The economic devastation that resulted from years of civil war also crossed borders, affecting entire regions.

Still, over the years, the OAU had lost much of its credibility. According to Delphine Djiraibe, president of the Chadian Association for the Promotion and Defense of Human Rights, the OAU was "a private club for friends." She added that, "It preserves the interests of African heads of state instead of addressing the real problems that are tearing apart Africa. With a few exceptions, the problems are the same across Africa: leaders are not committed to genuine democracy, they organize electoral masquerades to stay in power, they oppress the African people."

In the mid-1990s, Libyan head of state Muammar al-Qaddafi proposed the idea of an African Union as it exists today. In 1999, African heads of state and the government of the OAU issued the Sirte Declaration, which called for the establishment of "an African Union, in conformity with the ultimate objectives of the Charter of our continental Organization and the provisions of the Treaty Establishing the African Economic Community."

## ACCOMPLISHMENTS

The AU has been active for several years in promoting democratic elections in various African nations. In 2005, it put pressure on the government of Togo to hold elections after the death of its leader, Gnassingbe Edayema. He had named his son as his successor, in violation of the Togoan constitution. The AU also suspended Mauritania's membership in 2005 when its military government failed to hold elections as promised. In addition, the AU has sent peacekeeping forces to Darfur (Sudan) and Somalia to help preserve stability in these nations wracked by civil war.

*See also:* Apartheid; Civil Wars; Colonization; Congo; Economic Development and Trade; Pan-African Movement; Portuguese Colonies; Refugees; South Africa; Sudan.

### FURTHER READING

El-Ayouty, Yassin. *The Organization of African Unity After Thirty Years*. Westport, CT: Praeger, 1993.

Murithi, Timothy. *The African Union: Pan-Africanism, Peacebuilding and Development.* London: Ashgate, 2005.

Roberts, Russell. *The Role of the African Union.* Broomall, PA: Mason Crest, 2007.

# Agriculture

Although about 65 percent of all Africans work the land to raise crops and animals for food or cash, an estimated one-third of Africa's people are malnourished. One-fourth of its children are believed to be underweight, and one-third have had their growth stunted from lack of food over a long period of time. Africa is in the midst of an agricultural crisis that threatens to worsen without concerted and coordinated efforts on the part of African governments and donor nations.

## POOR AGRICULTURAL YIELDS

A number of factors have contributed to the failure of African agriculture—depletion of natural resources, inadequate infrastructure to store and transport goods to market, dependence on natural rainfall rather than irrigation systems, failure to aid poor rural farmers, trade barriers, and disease.

### Depleted Natural Resources

In many regions of Africa, planting the same crops in the same fields has led to depletion of the nutrients in the soil. Most African farmers do not use fertilizers, so the soil yields less and less as the years go by. In many rural areas, animals are left to graze rather than being fed fodder, a practice that leaves the land without sufficient plant life to prevent erosion. Most rural Africans depend on wood fires for heat, leading to massive deforestation, which in turn causes more soil erosion. This is clearly a vicious and deadly cycle: as the land produces less, the population continues to grow, leading to starvation.

In the 1950s and 1960s, Asia and Latin America underwent an agricultural transformation known as the "green revolution." Agricultural development programs created new seed varieties that were resistant to disease or produced greater yields. These same programs taught farmers how to rotate crops, as well as methods to halt soil depletion and erosion. As a result, agricultural production doubled and sometimes even tripled in these regions. Unfortunately, the green revolution bypassed Africa, partly because of the variety of growing regions on the continent and partly because of the kinds of crops poor African farmers typically plant.

Many experts believe that a similar revolution is needed in Africa. In particular, African farmers need to use crop rotation and chemical and organic fertilizers to increase yield. They also need access to new seed varieties that are disease or drought resistant.

### Inadequate Infrastructure

Even assuming that farmers were able to grow more, getting crops to market in Africa is a daunting task. Most farmers do not have a place to store surplus grain, nor do they have refrigeration to keep fruits and vegetables fresh after they are picked. In developed countries, farmers who can store grain are able to ride out price fluctuations. If prices are low, they can hold onto the grain until prices rise and the grain can be sold for a profit. African farmers generally cannot wait to do so and must take whatever price they can get at the time. Less profit means less to invest in next year's crop.

Much of Africa lacks the necessary infrastructure to transport agricultural goods to markets where they can be sold. Roads and railroads are either nonexistent or in disrepair, and cars and trucks are in short supply; most goods are taken to market on bicycles or on foot over unpaved roads. To hire a truck to transport goods to market is too costly for most farmers, adding so much to the price of goods that no profit can be made.

### Irrigation

Water is a major problem in Africa. Nearly 300 million Africans do not have access to safe drinking water or adequate sanitation. Moreover, only about 4 percent of all African land that can be farmed is irrigated. Most poor rural African farmers simply rely on nature to provide enough rain, and nature is notoriously unreliable in many parts of Africa. The problem is not that Africa has insufficient water; it is, rather, that the potential for irrigation has not been fully realized.

At least fifty-four rivers in Africa either cross national borders or form the borders

A Landsat satellite image shows the fertile area of the Nile River delta in Egypt. The delta is one of the most fertile regions in North Africa.
(NPA/Stone/Getty Images)

of nations. Few nations have reached agreements on how to share the water effectively or move it to where it is needed to grow crops. Experts believe that cooperation between nations and strategic water-use policies will be necessary to irrigate all the land in Africa that can be used to grow crops. While large-scale water projects, such as the Aswan High Dam in Egypt, have benefited many farmers, many experts believe that there is also a need for small-scale irrigation projects designed to help farmers in isolated areas.

### Failure to Help Poor Rural Farmers

Most farmers in Africa are poor and grow only enough to live on. Many experts believe that helping this group grow more and sell more is the key to Africa's agricultural development. According to the International Food Policy Research Institute, "Since small-scale farms account for more than

90 percent of Africa's agricultural production and are dominated by the poor... growth must be centered on the small farmer." This is a relatively new idea, as most aid and assistance in the past has gone to producers of cash crops such as cotton, coffee, tea, and cocoa, not to poor farmers who grow maize, rice, cassava, and other food crops.

According to the World Bank, about 42 percent of all those involved in agriculture in Africa are women. Despite the importance of women to agricultural productivity in Africa, the laws in many nations of Africa bar them from owning land and obtaining the credit they need to buy seeds and equipment.

### Trade Barriers

Because Africa is home to fifty-four sovereign nations, trade from one country to the other is subject to taxes and restrictions that reduce farmers' profits. More importantly, however, are the barriers to international trade. The United States' African Growth and Opportunity Act (AGOA) and the European Union's Everything But Arms (EBA) initiative allow importation of African products without payment of certain taxes and without quotas. However, even after the passage of AGOA in 2000, only 8 percent of the goods imported into the United States from Africa were agricultural products; rather, the primary imports brought in under AGOA were petroleum and **textiles.** The European EBA does not allow complete exemption from **tariffs** on Africa's most important agricultural exports—bananas, rice, and sugar. Under the initiative, duties on these products would be gradually reduced. Duty-free access was allowed for bananas beginning in January 2006 and was expected to be granted for sugar and rice before the end of the decade.

Moreover, both the United States and Europe pay subsidies to farmers that help to keep prices of **domestic** produce up and make it difficult for African farmers to compete. If the United States and the European Union did away with subsidies and opened their markets to African imports, Africa's total agricultural exports would be expected increase by an estimated 20 percent.

### Disease

Africa's agricultural productivity has been severely affected by disease. Since 1985, more than 7 million farmers have died from AIDS in the twenty-five African nations that have been hardest hit by the disease, including much of south, central, and southeastern Africa. As of 2007, there were more than 25 million Africans with HIV/AIDS, and the number continues to grow. Those most affected by the AIDS epidemic are between fourteen and forty-five years of age, the members of society with the greatest potential for economic productivity.

Malaria is also a killer in many parts of Africa. At least 300 million serious cases of malaria occur worldwide every year, resulting in more than one million deaths. More than 80 percent of these deaths occur in sub-Saharan Africa; most of the victims are young children and pregnant women, whose immune systems are not strong enough to resist the disease. As the continent's population is decimated by disease, fewer and fewer healthy young people are available to farm the land, sharply decreasing productivity. This, of course, constitutes another vicious cycle. Fewer farmers lead to less food, less food leads to more starving people, starving people are more vulnerable to illness.

## IMPACT OF CLIMATE CHANGE

Of all the continents in the world, the one least responsible for the carbon emissions that cause global warming—Africa—promises to be the one most adversely affected by climate change. Global warming has already had a dramatic effect on rainfall in parts of sub-Saharan Africa, leading to severe droughts. The last year in which rainfall was normal was 2002 and many rivers are drying up, ultimately causing more land in Africa to turn into desert.

Moreover, as the climate heats up, an additional 80 million people in Africa may be exposed to malaria. While some areas where malaria is prevalent will see a sharp reduction in the disease, zones that are more **temperate** could experience a sharp rise. This would mean a net increase in instances of the disease, since these more temperate areas are more heavily populated. All in all, climate change could have a devastating impact on agricultural production in Africa, reducing the amount of land suitable for growing crops and reducing the number of farm workers.

### REASONS TO HOPE

As grim as the agricultural situation in Africa is, there are some bright spots. In 1995, in the tiny nation of Burkina Faso, the government established the Soil Fertility Management Unit (UGFS) to develop and implement a national strategy for improving soil fertility. This unit helps train farmers in the proper use of fertilizers, in how to rotate crops to avoid depleting nutrients in the soil, and in how to build bunds (stone or earthen embankments) to slow water runoff. The government has also embarked on a national program to plant trees and encourage conservation of forests. Irrigation projects are also planned to help increase the rice yield.

Throughout Africa, rural farmers are organizing to make their voices heard by governments and to pool their resources to increase crop yield. Today, Africa boasts more than 24,000 cooperative associations with more than 10 million members. In Cameroon, for example, a cooperative of women farmers has been so successful in producing and marketing cassava that they have been able to build a new school, a new library, and a processing plant to make cassava flour. Farmers' groups have also begun many conservation efforts, such as terracing hillsides to prevent runoff and conserving water supplies.

In South Africa, many supermarket chains are now committed to buying produce from African nations rather than importing it from abroad. The Southern African Development Community (SADC), an organization of fourteen nations in southern Africa established in the 1970s, has signed a free-trade agreement that boosts trade between South Africa and many of its smaller and poorer neighbors.

South African researchers have developed genetically modified maize and cotton that resist disease and pests and therefore have higher yields than other varieties. Zambia and Malawi have developed a strain of cassava that better resists both disease and pests. New Rice for Africa (NERIC) is a strain of rice produced from crossbreeding Asian and African varieties that has been introduced in seventeen nations in Central Africa and promises to produce a much higher yield than other varieties.

Thus, while Africa faces many serious problems in growing enough food to feed its people, government and grassroots initiatives hold promise for the future.

*See also:* Drought; Famine; Society; South Africa; Technology and Inventions.

### FURTHER READING

Christiaensen, Luc J., and Lionel Demery. *Down to Earth: Agriculture and Poverty Reduction in Africa.* Washington, DC: World Bank, 2007.

Pallangyo, E.P. *Environmental Concerns and the Sustainability of Africa's Agriculture in the 1990s and Beyond.* New York: Vantage, 1995.

Sayre, April Pulley. *Africa.* Minneapolis: Lerner Books, 1999.

# AIDS *See* Society.

# Algeria

Located in northwest Africa on the Mediterranean Sea and plagued by years of **guerrilla** warfare, the second largest country in Africa after Sudan. Ninety percent of Algeria's population lives on the Mediterranean coast on just 12 percent of the land. Unlike many other African nations, most of Algeria's population shares an ethnic and cultural heritage. Most Algerians are Muslim, and most are Arab, Berber, or of mixed Arab-Berber stock. The Berbers are the **indigenous** people of northern Africa, given the name "Berber" by the Greeks. The Berbers call themselves "Amazigh."

Conquered by Phoenicians, Romans, and Vandals in antiquity, Algeria's culture was most deeply influenced by the Arab conquerors of the eighth through the eleventh centuries, and by the French, who began colonizing the area in the 1830s. The French colonists tended to live separately from the indigenous rural population, and although French colonists were represented in the French National Assembly, the native peoples were not.

On November 1, 1954, an Algerian rebel group known as the National Liberation Front (FLN) began a guerrilla war against the French, in which both sides attacked civilians and used extraordinarily brutal tactics. More than a million Algerians died and 2 million were left homeless. The war ended with the Evian Accords in 1962. The parties agreed to an interim administration until elections could be held. More than a million French citizens who lived in Algeria, known as *pieds-noirs* ("black feet"), fled to France.

Algeria declared its independence from France on July 3, 1962. Its first president, Ahmed Ben Bella, was elected in 1962 but deposed three years later in a bloodless coup led by Colonel Houari Boumédienne, head of the Council of the Revolution. Boumédienne and others who supported the coup felt that Ben Bella had become increasingly **autocratic** and overly focused on foreign policy to the detriment of **domestic** policy.

Boumédienne led the country as head of state from 1965 until he was formally elected to the presidency in 1976. After Boumédienne's death in 1978, Colonel Chadi Bendjedid was elected president, a post he held until 1992. In 1989, Algeria adopted a new constitution that permitted the formation of political parties other than the FLN; among the parties that arose was the militant Islamic Salvation Front (FIS). After years of suppression by the government, the FIS was successful in winning votes and seats in the National Assembly in 1990. The Algerian military, fearful of an Islamist government, dissolved the National Assembly, banned the FIS, and forced Bendjedid to resign. He was replaced by a five-person High Council, which canceled elections and then asked Mohamed Boudiaf, a hero of the war for independence, to serve as president. Islamists responded with violence, and more than 50,000 members of the FIS were jailed. Still, the fighting continued between government forces and the FIS. In 1992, Boudiaf was assassinated by Lembarek Boumarafi on behalf of the Islamists. Years of guerrilla warfare followed.

In 1999, former political exile Abdelaziz Bouteflika was elected president of Algeria and pledged a return to peace and stability. In an effort to put an end to the conflict, he offered amnesty to the rebels, except for those who had committed crimes such as rape and murder. In 2000, this policy, known as the Civil Concord Policy, was approved in a national **referendum.** As many as 80 percent of those who had opposed the government accepted the amnesty.

In 2004, Algeria held its first truly democratic election. (Previous elections were either restricted to one party or manipulated by the ruling party.) Bouteflika was re-elected with nearly 85 percent of the vote. He continued to work toward national reconciliation.

Algeria's economy is largely dependent on its vast supplies of oil. It also exports cotton, figs, dates, and cork. Although the majority of the population lives along the Mediterranean coast, there are still nomadic populations who inhabit the desert regions to the south. Despite oil wealth and fertile soil, Algeria's people are still quite poor by Western standards. In recent years, however, the government has made substantial efforts to diversify the economy and attract foreign investors, including a 2001 treaty with the European Union to lower **tariffs** and increase trade.

***See also:*** Civil Wars; Colonization; French West Africa; Independence Movements; Language.

### FURTHER READING

Hintz, Martin. *Algeria.* San Francisco, CA: Children's Press, 2006.

Horne, Alistair. *A Savage War of Peace: Algeria 1954-1962.* New York: NYRB Classics, 2006.

Mitchell, Peter, ed. *Peoples and Cultures of North Africa.* New York: Chelsea House, 2006.

# Angola *See Portuguese Colonies.*

# Apartheid

A legally sanctioned system of racial discrimination and oppressive government policies in twentieth-century South Africa. Apartheid began to be dismantled in 1990. However, the nation continues the long struggle of freeing itself of its racist policies.

### EARLY DISCRIMINATION

Systematic discrimination against black Africans began with the arrival of the first Dutch settlers in South Africa in 1652. These first settlers took land from some native people without compensation and enslaved others. Over the centuries, German and French Huguenot settlers joined the Dutch settlers. Eventually, these European people lost their national identities and began to consider themselves "Afrikaners."

Beginning in 1795, British settlers moved into South Africa, asserting complete control of the area by 1806. In 1834, the British outlawed slavery throughout the empire, an action that caused more than 12,000 Afrikaner farmers to leave—an exodus called the Great Trek. Members of this group moved north and east and eventually established two **republics**, the Central Orange Free State and Transvaal. The Afrikaans word for farmer, *boer,* was used to refer to these settlers.

The discovery of gold in the Witwatersrand hills in 1886 in what is now Johannesburg eventually led to the Boer War (1899–1902) between the British and the Boers. The British prevailed in 1902, and in 1910 they created the Union of South Africa, a self-governing dominion within the British Empire, by joining the English-speaking and Dutch-speaking areas. The South African Party, an amalgamation of several Afrikaner political groups came into power, and their leader, Louis Botha, became South Africa's first president. Under Botha, a number of repressive measures were enacted, including the Masters and Servants Act, which barred blacks from skilled jobs, and the 1913 Land Act, which reserved 90 percent of the land for whites. In response, the African National Congress (ANC) was formed in 1912 to represent the interests of South Africa's blacks. Founders included John Dube, the son of a minister; Pixley ka Isaka Seme, a Columbia- and Oxford-educated attorney, and Sol Plaatje, who was educated and taught at a mission school.

Blacks were not the only group that suffered under the repressive rule of Botha and his successor, Jan Smuts. Many workers who had come to South Africa from India were discriminated against in housing and employment. Some were subjected to violence. Mohandas Gandhi, the Indian spiritual leader, first used his strategy of nonviolent resistance in the early 1900s in South Africa on behalf of his fellow Indian immigrants. After World War II, the right-wing Nationalist Party, under the leadership of D.F. Malan, won the 1948 election, having campaigned on a platform of apartheid.

## TOTAL SEPARATION

Shortly after the 1948 elections, the South African Parliament enacted a series of laws to enforce total separation between the races. The new laws prohibited mixed marriage and required every individual to be classified as white, black, or colored (of mixed race).

The Group Areas Act of 1950 created a system of urban apartheid, assigning races to particular residential and business districts. Nonwhites were required to carry identity passes when they traveled in white areas. The Separate Amenities Act, passed in 1953, created segregated beaches, buses, hospitals, and schools; virtually every aspect of life was divided along racial lines, and those "amenities" reserved for blacks were all substandard.

Perhaps the most repressive of the apartheid laws were those that established "homelands" for blacks in the most undesirable areas of the country. The irony of the term *homeland*, of course, was that the entire country was the homeland of black South Africans, yet they were herded into certain areas and forbidden from others. The first of these homelands acts was the Bantu Authorities Act of 1951, which created separate governmental structures for blacks. The Bantu Homelands Citizens Act of 1970 went further, stripping blacks living in South Africa of their citizenship, making them citizens of the homelands. Between 1976 and 1981, four such areas, collectively known as Bantustans, were created, forcing 9 million black South Africans to become foreigners in their own country.

From 1960 through the 1980s, the South African government forcibly moved nonwhites into areas set aside for blacks. During this period, 3.5 million people were resettled. Prime Minister P.W. Botha, who served from 1978 to 1984, was an especially strong advocate of apartheid. During his tenure, thousands of black South Africans were detained without trials.

## RESISTANCE

Beginning in 1949, through strikes, civil disobedience, and marches, the ANC resisted apartheid openly. In 1959, some members, who believed that progress toward ending

## RISE AND FALL OF APARTHEID

**1652** Dutch East India Company establishes a settlement at Cape Town, South Africa

**1806** British take over Cape Colony

**1830s** On the "Great Trek," Dutch farmers called Boers migrate to northern and eastern parts of area

**1867** Diamonds discovered at Hope Creek

**1884** Gold discovered in the Boer-controlled Transvaal

**1899** Boer War begins between British and Dutch settlers

**1902** Boer War ends with Treaty of Vereeniging

**1910** Union of South Africa becomes member of the British Commonwealth

**1948** Apartheid—separation of the races—becomes law

**1951** Bantu Homelands Act strips native peoples of South African citizenship

**1953** Preservation of Separate Amenities Act passed

**1958** Nelson Mandela opens first black law office in South Africa

**1960** Sharpeville Massacre, in which South African police open fire on black protestors

**1962** Mandela sentenced to life in prison for plotting to overthrow the government

**1974** South Africa expelled from the United Nations

**1976** Soweto uprising

**1990** Mandela freed from prison

**1991** South African president F.W. de Klerk repeals apartheid

**1994** Mandela elected president of South Africa

---

apartheid was too slow, split from the ANC to form the more radical Pan-Africanist Congress (PAC). This group organized a protest against the requirement that blacks carry identity cards, conducting its initial demonstration in a township called Sharpeville.

During this peaceful protest, on March 21, 1960, white police opened fire against the demonstrators, killing 69 and injuring 186 people. As a result of this demonstration, the government banned both the ANC and the PAC, forcing the resistance movement underground. After the violence at Sharpeville, other protests occurred, leading the South African government to declare a state of emergency, which allowed security forces to arrest and detain people without trial. Among those arrested was Nelson Mandela, leader of Umkhonto we Sizwe, or "Spear of the Nation," the military wing of the ANC. In 1962, Mandela was tried for treason, found guilty, and sentenced to life in prison.

During the 1970s, black South Africans continued to resist the oppressive

## GREAT LIVES

**Nelson Mandela**

Nelson Rolihlahla Mandela was born in Transkei, South Africa, in 1918, the son of a chief of the Tembu tribe. Mandela was educated in law at the University of Witwatersrand. He joined the African National Congress (ANC) in 1942 and began to work against the South African government's policy of apartheid. In 1952, Mandela was elected National Volunteer-in-Chief of the ANC Campaign for the Defiance of Unjust Laws. His goal was to incite civil disobedience and recruit more supporters to the ANC cause. Throughout the 1950s, the government threatened Mandela with arrest, prohibited him from attending certain gatherings, and confined him for a period to Johannesburg. In order to be able to operate freely in spite of these restrictions, he became a master of disguise, sometimes dressing as a chauffeur, sometimes as a laborer, to avoid detection.

At Mandela's recommendation, the ANC formed a military wing, Umkhonto we Sizwe, ("Spear of the Nation"), with Mandela as its commander. This group made a number of guerrilla attacks against government-owned facilities—including a nuclear power plant. Arrested for sabotage in 1961, Mandela was sentenced to five years in prison. While he was still serving this sentence, he was tried for treason and sentenced to a life term. During his trial, Mandela declared,

> I have fought against white domination, and I have fought against black domination. I have cherished the idea of a democratic and free society in which all persons live together in harmony and with equal opportunities. It is an ideal which I hope to live for and achieve. But if needs be, it is an ideal for which I am prepared to die.

Released from prison in 1990, Mandela received the Nobel Peace Prize in 1993. He was elected president of South Africa in 1994. After serving one term as president, Mandela chose not to run for reelection. Since leaving office, he has worked for human rights and to raise AIDS awareness.

government policies. Steve Biko, a medical student, led the South African Students' Organization and was a powerful force behind the Black Consciousness Movement, which promoted black pride and opposition to apartheid. In 1976, students at Orlando West Junior School in Soweto (a segregated township) went on strike to protest the Afrikaans Medium Decree, a law requiring that all education be conducted in Afrikaans, the official language of South Africa. Again, law enforcement authorities countered with violence. When children threw stones, the police responded with bullets, killing 566 children. Violence erupted across the country, and the government reacted by arresting Steve Biko. Biko was beaten so badly in custody that he lost consciousness. Left untreated for three days, Biko died, sparking an angry reaction in South Africa and around the world.

Many South African whites vehemently opposed apartheid as much as their black neighbors did. The liberal Progressive Party was against the policy, but they and other opposition groups were unable to gain a majority in elections. This situation existed partly because of **gerrymandering**, which gave rural voters, who supported apartheid, more power than urban voters, many of whom opposed it. An organization of white women called Black Sash, as well as the South African Communist Party, also opposed apartheid.

### WORLD REACTION

In 1961, South Africa gave up its status as British dominion and declared itself a **republic**. At the same time, South Africa applied to continue as a member of the British Commonwealth, a relationship that gave it a privileged trading status among former British colonies. It soon became clear, however, that many Commonwealth nations opposed continuing South Africa's membership because of apartheid, so South Africa withdrew its application. In 1962, the United Nations General Assembly passed a resolution condemning apartheid. A year later, the United Nations Security Council instituted a voluntary arms embargo against South Africa. After the Soweto massacre in 1976, the arms embargo was made mandatory. Many foreign-based companies that had invested in South Africa began to withdraw, the country's sports teams were banned from international competition, and many tourists opted not to travel to South Africa. Both the United States and Great Britain imposed economic sanctions on South Africa. Sanctions included prohibitions against corporate investment, sales to the police and military, and bank loans.

As South Africa became increasingly isolated from the world community through the 1970s and 1980s, its National Party government implemented a socially conservative system of laws. Gambling and other social vices were outlawed. Movie theaters, liquor stores, and other businesses were closed by law on Sundays, and television was forbidden until 1976. Censorship laws limited public access to information, as police squads continued to crack down on resistance.

### ENDING APARTHEID

In 1990, after decades of economic and social pressure, South African president F.W. de Klerk announced that the ANC and PAC were no longer banned and that all political prisoners would be released, including Nelson Mandela, who had been incarcerated for twenty-seven years. Though a longtime member of the National Party, de Klerk recognized that South Africa could no longer continue its racist policies. Two million of the nation's blacks were unemployed and the economy had been seriously weakened by international economic sanctions. Many white South Africans had left the country, fearful of what the future would bring.

South Africa's first free election, in which black and other citizens of color could vote, was held on April 27, 1994. Nelson Mandela was elected the nation's president. Under his administration, South Africa embarked on a time of healing. In 1993, a draft constitution prohibiting discrimination was published. Mandela's government established a Commission on Truth and Reconciliation to investigate and come to terms with the evils of apartheid. The Commission heard massive amounts of testimony from victims and victimizers, granting many individuals amnesty in return for the truth. It issued a final report in 1998, in which it condemned both the government and anti-apartheid forces for committing atrocities.

While some questioned the Commission's conclusions, especially the lack of punishment, Archbishop Desmond Tutu, a member of the Commission, saw it differently: "Anger and resentment and retribution are corrosive of this great good, the harmony that has got to exist between people. And that is why our people have been committed to the reconciliation where we use restorative rather than retributive justice . . . we are looking to the healing of relationships, we are seeking to open wounds, yes, but to open them so that we can cleanse them and they don't fester; we cleanse them and then pour oil on them, and then we can move into the glorious future that God is opening up for us."

*See also:* Colonization.

## FURTHER READING

Clark, Nancy L., and William H. Worger. *South Africa: The Rise and Fall of Apartheid.* White Plains, NY: Longman, 2004.

Louw, P. Eric. *The Rise, Fall, and Legacy of Apartheid.* Westport, CT: Praeger, 2004.

Matahbane, Mark. *Kaffir Boy: The True Story of a Black Youth's Comng of Age in Apartheid South Africa.* Topeka, KS: Tandem Books, 1999.

Waldemeir, Patt. *Anatomy of a Miracle: The End of Apartheid and the Birth of a New South Africa.* New York: Norton, 1997.

# Art and Architecture

While there is tremendous diversity in the visual arts of Africa—including sculpture, **textiles**, and buildings—there are also some common characteristics among the various forms and **genres**. Throughout most of Africa, for example, there is little art produced merely for art's sake; most of the objects that are admired as works of art also have a practical or religious use. While a Western artist might sculpt a beautiful statue that had no practical use, for example, an African artist might create a sculpture that represents a revered ancestor for use in religious rituals.

Another common characteristic of African art is that many of its forms are determined more by tradition than by the ideas of individual artists. This does not mean that the hand of a particular artist cannot be seen in any given work, but rather that creating something that breaks with tradition in form or material is not usually an important value for the African artist as it might be for a Western artist. African art often has the human figure as its primary subject. Yet most African art works do not attempt to portray people or animals realistically. Instead, they tend to be stylized and abstract.

## SCULPTURE

African sculpture uses a variety of materials, including wood, clay, metal, ivory, and stone. One of the sculptural objects common to nearly all ethnic groups in Africa is the mask, which can cover the face or the entire body, or just be mounted atop the head in the form of a headdress. Masks are used in a number of important religious rituals, including weddings, funerals, and initiation ceremonies. Many African masks represent animals and are believed to connect the wearer with the spirit of a particular creature. The Bwa and Nuna people of Burkina Faso, for example, believe that animal masks protect them from evil. The animals most often represented in their masks are crocodiles, hawks, and buffalo. Like most African masks, these are carved from wood and often decorated in geometric patterns.

Among the Dogon people of Mali, there are more than seventy different types of

## MODERN AFRICAN ART AND ARCHITECTURE

**1100-1400** Great Zimbabwe is constructed

**15th-16th Century** Benin bronzes crafted

**16th-17th Century** Palace in Benin City built

**1871** Europeans arrive at Great Zimbabwe

**1874** Ashante palace in Kumasi destroyed

**1897** British destroy Benin palace; take 1,000 bronzes to England

**1902-1904** Richard Nicklin Hall removes "debris" from Great Zimbabwe

**1906-1907** Great Mud Mosque at Djenné built

**1960** Largest known kente cloth presented to United Nations

**1989** Kenyan artist Shine Tane opens first of several art expositions in East Africa

**1997** Peter Kwangware of Zimbabwe wins the Award of Distinction at the Annual Heritage Exhibit

**2000** Africa Resource Center begins publication of *Ijele*, an online African art journal

**2002-2003** Tanzanian artist Mkumba begins four-month exhibit in Stuttgart, Germany

**2007** Cote d'Ivoire artist Gilbert G. Groud paints "Childsoldier in the Ivory Coast," part of his effort to draw the world's attention to the use of children in warfare

---

masks used in secret religious ceremonies. A common mask among the Dogon is one representing the antelope. The Dogon are farmers, and the antelope is the symbol of the farmer. The mask itself is a rectangle with large horns protruding from the top. The Bamana people, also from Mali, wear elaborately carved antelope headdresses; they too regard the antelope as symbolic of agriculture.

In addition to animals, masks are carved to represent people, either individuals or idealized types. In many ethnic groups, masks are carved to represent that group's idea of female beauty. The Punu of Gabon make masks with arched eyebrows, slightly slanted eyes, and a narrow chin. The face is painted white, which to the Punu represents spirituality, and the mask is topped with black hair. Among the most famous of such masks is Idia's Mask, commissioned in the sixteenth century by Esigie, a king of Benin, in memory of his mother, Idia. This mask, carved of ivory, has a wide forehead and full lips.

Masks in many areas of Africa have exaggerated features that represent certain moral virtues. The Senefou people of Cote d'Ivoire, for example, depict calm and peacefulness by carving masks with eyes partially closed and horizontal lines near the mouth. The Temne of Sierra Leone depict wisdom with highly decorated, prominent foreheads.

Many ethnic groups create human figures of wood, stone, pottery, or metal. Such figures can be freestanding or carved into other objects. The Dan-Ngere of western Africa craft huge rice ladles with handles carved to resemble people. These ladles are used only at the harvest festival.

Freestanding sculptures typically have spiritual significance. A stylized carving of a female figure, for example, could function as a fertility symbol. In some villages, sculptures of heroes and ancestors are kept in a shrine in the center of the village. The Ibibio people of southwestern Nigeria, for example, carve realistic bearded figures, about 4 feet (1.2 m) tall, which represent their ancestors.

The Makonde of Tanzania make highly detailed, 6-foot-tall (1.8 m) carvings from African blackwood. These "Tree of Life" carvings, which resemble a tree trunk covered with carvings, represent the lineage of an extended family, with each generation supporting the next.

Among the most famous of all African sculptures are the Benin Bronzes, a collection of more than 1,000 brass plaques seized by the British in 1897. These plaques, cast in **bas-relief**, depict people, animals, and scenes of life in the court. They were made during the fifteenth and sixteenth centuries using a sophisticated process known as the "lost wax technique," in which the shape is molded in wax, then surrounded in clay. The wax is melted away, leaving a mold into which the metal is poured.

## TEXTILES

In addition to sculpture, African artists are known for their work in textiles. Generally, cloth in Africa is woven by men, though in Nigeria and the Sudan women are also involved. Once the cloth is woven, it can then be dyed using various vegetables and minerals. Cloth is often further embellished by embroidery or appliqué.

Probably the best-known African cloth is kente cloth made by the Ashante of Ghana. Kente is a woven cloth (in fact, its name comes from the word meaning "basket") made on narrow looms. The resulting strips, which are 5 to 6 feet (1.5 to 1.8 m) long and 3 to 5 inches (7.6 to 12.7 cm) wide are then sewn together to make the cloth. The cloth is known for its bright colors and bold designs. It is worn only on very special occasions, and was once worn only by kings. The largest known kente cloth, which measures 12 feet (3.65 m) by 20 feet (6.1 m), was presented to the United Nations in 1960 by the government of Ghana.

## ARCHITECTURE

Outside of Egypt, there is little monumental architecture in Africa. African religions do not tend toward the building of houses of worship, since spirits are believed to dwell everywhere, and many African kings lived in the same sorts of houses their subjects did. Still, some great mosques and palaces are **indigenous** to Africa.

The only well-known African ruins south of the Sahara are those of Great Zimbabwe, located in southern Africa in the the present-day nation of Zimbabwe. Built by native people between C.E. 1100 and 1400, Great Zimbabwe is a large complex that includes a number of stone walls and other structures, including a bee-hive-shaped tower. The wall surrounding the part of Great Zimbabwe known as the Great Enclosure is the largest stone structure south of the Sahara and an architectural marvel. It runs in a winding path for more than 800 feet (244 m), with neither corners nor angles. It was constructed from more than a million blocks of granite, put together without mortar. When Europeans came upon Great Zimbabwe in 1871, they did not believe that such an edifice could have been built by Africans, whom they considered inferior. Between 1902 and 1904, British journalist Richard Nicklin Hall, convinced that someone other than Africans had build Great Zimbabwe, had 12 feet (3.65 m) of deposits removed from the site—deposits he considered mere debris but that contained valuable archeological evidence.

In the nineteenth century, the palace of the king of the Ashante, covered 5 acres (2

Vibrant and colorful Kente cloth is hand woven by the peoples of Western Africa. These examples are from Ghana. (Jacob Silberberg/Getty Images)

hectares) in what is now Kumasi, Ghana. Built of stone, it had more than sixty rooms with steep thatched roofs. The palace was designed to impress visitors with the power and majesty of the king. Unfortunately, the British destroyed it in 1874. The rubble was used to build a fort.

Also destroyed by the British, in 1897, was the great palace of the king of Benin City, Nigeria. Built in the sixteenth and seventeenth centuries, the palace was immense, with an inner area where the king lived and an outer area for other royal family members, as well as artisans and local chiefs. The palace included many courtyards surrounded by buildings with galleries supported by pillars covered with bronze plaques.

The strong influence of Islam can be seen in the mud mosques of western Africa. One of the most famous of these is the Great Mosque at Djenné. The mosque, designed by Ismaila Traoré, was begun in 1906 and completed in 1907. The structure is made of mud bricks plastered over with mud, and the walls are between 16 inches (40.6 cm) and 24 inches (61 cm) thick. From nearly every vertical surface of the huge building, palm wood beams jut out. These serve as supports for workers who reapply mud to the mosque every spring. The mosque sports three huge towers, each topped with a spire and an ostrich egg, symbolizing fertility. Although inspired by Islamic art, the Great Mosque makes use of African materials, such as mud bricks and palm wood.

During the nineteenth century, indigenous architecture was replaced by European models, including Christian churches, often built in the Gothic style. Most African homes, even today, are built of impermanent material, such as grass, wood, animal skins, or clay, and are not intended to withstand the passage of time.

## PAINTING

Only in the twentieth century did painting become a significant art in Africa. Today, many African painters are known throughout the world. In 1989, Kenyan artist Shine Tani opened the first of several art expositions in East Africa. Self-taught, Shine Tani began to work seriously as an artist in 1988. His paintings are brightly colored and representational, but not realistic. He paints scenes of African life, but the figures themselves are exaggerated, bulbous, and stretched into impossible postures.

Peter Kwangware of Zimbabwe won an award at that country's Annual Heritage Exhibit in 2000. A graduate of the Visual Art Studios of the National Gallery in Harare, Zimbabwe, Kwangware also paints scenes of daily life in Africa. Bright colors also abound in his work.

Tanzanian painter Mkumba had a four-month-long exhibit in Stuttgart, Germany, beginning in 2002. Mkumba's work is representational, but the figures depicted are in large, unshaded blocks of color, giving an almost cartoon-like appearance to his work.

In 2007, Cote d'Ivoire artist Gilbert G. Groud created his "Childsoldier in the Ivory Coast," a work that protests the use of children in the military. This artwork, done in crayon, has a pale and ghostlike quality. The face of the child is shown in close up, with the huge helmet completely obscuring the eyes, as if the helmet has stolen his soul.

There are so many exciting young artists in Africa today that an online journal *Ijele* was founded by the African Resource Center in 2000 to allow scholars to discuss African art. The journal focuses both on art produced by Africans from all over the world and on art by non-Africans that uses African iconography and symbolism.

***See also:*** Colonization; Religion; Society; Technology and Inventions.

## FURTHER READING

Baldwin, James. *Perspectives: Angles on African Art.* New York: Harry N. Abrams, 1987.

Finley, Carol. *The Art of African Masks: Exploring Cultural Traditions.* Minneapolis: Lerner, 1999.

Gillon, Werner. *A Short History of African Art.* New York: Penguin, 1991.

Rea, William. *African Art.* New York: Chelsea House, 1996.

# Aswan High Dam

A dam constructed on the Nile River in Egypt between 1960 and 1970 and designed to help control the annual flooding of the river. Constructed to generate power, the Aswan High Dam generates **hydroelectric power** at billions of kilowatt hours annually.

There have been two dams at the city of Aswan in modern times. The first was begun by the British in 1899 and completed in 1902. It was not long, however, before the dam proved to be inadequate, and its height had to be increased twice. When the dam nearly burst in 1946, Egyptian officials decided to build another dam about 4 miles (6.4 km) upriver from the original structure.

When the new dam was complete, it created one of the world's largest reservoirs, Lake Nasser, which covers much of lower Nubia. Before the lake was constructed,

Completed in 1971, the Aswan High Dam in Egypt has controlled the flooding of the Nile River downstream. It has also generated power for the region. (Upperhall Ltd/Robert Harding World Imagery/Getty Images)

the United Nations Educational, Scientific, and Cultural Organization (UNESCO) asked for time to allow archeologists to document the ancient treasures that would be lost when the lake was filled. Even though construction was delayed, not everything could be saved, and many objects and structures have been lost forever under the waters of Lake Nasser.

An entire island, Philae, was lost to the dam, but the Temple of Isis (from the Ptolemaic Period, 332–330 B.C.E.), located on it, was dismantled and moved to the nearby island of Aglika. Thousands of Nubian artifacts were preserved, including ceramics, jewelry, statuary, funerary items, and documents.

The dam was completed in 1970. Measuring 2.3 miles (3.36 km) long and 364 feet (111 m) tall, it is the largest man-made structure in the world. Aswan is a rockfill dam made of granite rocks and sands. It generates more than 10 billion kilowatt hours of electricity per year, and has benefited the people of Egypt in many other ways. Agricultural production has increased greatly, the people have a consistent and reliable source of water for drinking and agricultural needs, and travel on the Nile itself is easier, leading to increased tourism.

The dam has also created many problems for the people living nearby. It traps some of the silt that used to fertilize the land of the Nile Delta, leading farmers along the river to use more artificial fertilizer, which in turn causes chemical pollution. About 12 percent of the water in Lake Nasser evaporates each year, and the standing water in the irrigated fields sometimes breeds disease-bearing mosquitoes. Because of poor drainage, the soil and water are becoming increasingly salty, making the land less fertile and the water undrinkable. Still, most people believe that the benefits of the dam outweigh the drawbacks.

*See also:* Agriculture; Art and Architecture; Egypt.

## FURTHER READING

Mitchell, Peter, ed. *Peoples and Cultures of North Africa.* New York: Chelsea House, 2006.

Parks, Peggy J. *Aswan High Dam (Building World Landmarks).* Farmington Hills, MI: Blackbirch Press, 2004.

# B

# Boer War

A war between the British and Dutch settlers known as Boers (a Dutch word that means *farmer*), in southern Africa fought over who would control the territory now known as South Africa. The Boer War began in 1899 and ended in 1902, resulting in a British victory, but not before the Boers had inflicted many causalities on the more numerous and better armed British.

By the 1890s, the southern third of Africa had been carved up into several colonies by European powers. The west coast was known as German Southwest Africa; the east coast as Portuguese East Africa. The rest of the area was divided into several British colonies and **protectorates**, as well as two states almost completely surrounded by the British-held land, Orange Free State and Transvaal. Both of these states had been founded by descendents of the original Dutch immigrants who had settled southern Africa in the seventeenth century.

In 1885, gold was discovered in Transvaal. Thousands of European prospectors and settlers swarmed into the region in the hope of striking it rich. The Boer government of Transvaal disliked the influx of foreigners, known as *outlanders*, and passed laws limiting their voting rights and imposing taxes on the entire gold industry. Eventually, the British issued an **ultimatum** demanding equality for British citizens in the Transvaal and threatening war if their demands were not met. Most historians believe their real motive was control of the gold fields.

Paul Kruger, president of the Transvaal, responded by issuing his own ultimatum demanding that the British withdraw their troops from the Transvaal border within forty-eight hours. The British press responded to the ultimatum with both anger and amusement. They could hardly believe that this tiny country would dare to defy the might of the British Empire.

As a result, war was declared on October 11, 1899. The British forces were surprised by the immediate and fierce response of the Boers. In the cities of Mafeking, Ladysmith, and Kimberly, British forces and settlers were trapped by the Boers and sustained heavy losses. In February 1900, Field Marshal Lord Roberts arrived with reinforcements and was able to relieve the towns that were under siege. By May, when Mafeking was relieved, there were wild celebrations in Britain.

When the British captured Johannesburg and Pretoria in May and June of 1900, they believed they had won the war. However, the Boers were not ready to give up and continued to fight a **guerrilla** war, in which small groups of soldiers continued to attack the British for two more years, inflicting heavy losses. During this period, the British began to herd Boer women and children, as well as many black Africans, into concentration camps located throughout South Africa. Although there had been such camps in earlier wars, this was the first time the term *concentration camp* was used. The stated purpose of the camps was to prevent Boer families from assisting the guerrillas. Altogether, as many as 27,000 Boers and 14,000 black Africans died of disease and starvation in forty-five camps.

The last of the Boer forces surrendered in May 1902, and the Treaty of Vereeniging was signed in the same month. Altogether about 75,000 people died during the Boer War, including 22,000 British soldiers, most of whom succumbed to disease;

6,000 to 7,000 Boer soldiers; 28,000 Boer civilians; and 20,000 black Africans. The treaty dissolved the states of Orange and Transvaal, and control of all of South Africa fell to the British.

*See also:* Apartheid; British Colonies; Colonization.

**FURTHER READING**

Farwell, Byron. *The Great Anglo-Boer War.* New York: Norton, 1990.

Fremont-Barnes, Gregory. *The Boer War 1899–1902 (Essential Histories).* Oxford: Osprey, 2003.

# British Colonies in Africa

Compared to other European powers, the British were late to begin colonizing Africa. By the beginning of the twentieth century, however, they held the largest amount of territory of any European nation. Although Great Britain had some holdings in Africa before the late eighteenth century, it was the Industrial Revolution that first sparked British interest in colonizing the continent. Possessions there would be both sources of inexpensive raw materials and purchasers of finished goods.

### BRITISH WEST AFRICA

In 1788, the English naturalist Joseph Banks, who had sailed the Pacific Ocean with Captain Cook, founded the Africa Association, whose purpose was to fund exploration of Africa. One of the most important projects of the Africa Association was the Niger River expedition by Mungo Park, which began in 1795 and ended in 1797. The British government sponsored Park's second expedition in 1805 and sent a subsequent expedition to the Ashante capital at Kumasi on the Gold Coast (now Ghana) in 1817. However, the government lost interest in exploring the continent for the next twenty years and left the field to merchants, who established trading posts along the Gold Coast and at the mouth of the Gambia River. Then, in the 1840s, the British established a settlement in the lower Niger Valley for the purpose of producing palm oil, which was used to lubricate many of the machines that made the Industrial Revolution possible. Many settlers died of malaria until the discovery in 1850 that quinine could prevent the disease.

In 1889, after years of conflict and shifting borders, the French granted the British a strip of land about 10 miles (16 km) wide along each side of the Gambia River. This created the Gambia, an oddly shaped possession in the middle of the French colony of Senegal.

British abolitionists founded Freetown in Sierra Leone in 1787, as a haven for freed slaves, and the British government began to administer the colony in 1808. In 1895, the British governor of Sierra Leone was granted the authority to administer all British possessions on the West African coast from Gambia to the Gold Coast. In that same year, the British began to build a railroad into the interior.

Among the riches that drew the British to West Africa was gold. Gold mining in the region was controlled by the Ashante **federation** from its capital at Kumasi. In 1823, the Ashante fought a British force commanded by Sir Charles McCarthy, who had declared war on them. McCarthy was advancing on the Ashante forces when he was killed. The Ashante added insult to injury by converting McCarthy's skull into a drinking cup. This conflict was followed by wars in 1873, 1893–1894, 1895–1896, and a final one in 1900—as the Ashante tried to preserve their **sovereignty** against the incursion of the British.

In 1861, the British made Lagos in southern Nigeria a crown colony. In 1900, British explorer and soldier Frederick Lugard conquered the north and fourteen years later united the two halves of Nigeria. Lugard set up a system of governance there that became the model for most of the British colonies in Africa. This method is called indirect rule, and it contrasts with the methods used by other European nations. Lugard appointed a central governor and a legislative council, but depended on traditional leaders and institutions for local control. Following this model, Sir Gordon Guggisberg, who governed the Gold Coast from 1919 to 1929, restored the title to the traditional Ashante king.

Under the terms of the Treaty of Versailles that ended World War I, the former German colonies of Togoland and Cameroon were divided between Britain and France. British Togoland was administered from the Gold Coast and Cameroon from Nigeria.

## BRITISH EAST AND SOUTH AFRICA

British involvement in east and south Africa began as a way for the empire to protect sea routes to its possessions in India. The colony at Cape Town in South Africa was founded in 1806 to protect British ships as they rounded the Cape of Good Hope on their way to India. After the Boer War (1899–1902), the British **annexed** the Afrikaner territories of Transvaal and the Orange Free State to form the Union of South Africa in 1910.

The Suez Canal, which opened in 1869, allowed ships to travel from the Mediterranean Sea to India without sailing around the Cape, reducing the strategic importance of Cape Town for the British (although the discovery of diamonds and gold nearby gave the territory new importance around the turn of the century). Because the Egyptian government was unstable and unable to guarantee the safety of the canal, the British took over the administration of that nation in 1882. In 1895, the British government sent diplomat and statesman Herbert Kitchener to conquer Sudan, which had previously been Egyptian territory. This action was undertaken because the British wanted to control the Nile River and access to a planned dam at Aswan. Kitchener succeeded in 1898 at the Battle of Omdurman, in which 11,000 Sudanese died.

In the 1860s, British explorers searching for the source of the Nile forged into the region north of Lake Victoria. After annexing a number of nearby territories, the British unified them in 1894 and gave the name "Uganda" to the newly formed colony. In 1888, the British East Africa Company began to move away from the coast and explore the interior of the territory that is now Kenya. This company also built the Kenya-Uganda railway between 1895 and 1905.

Cecil Rhodes, a British-born South African businessman who grew rich in the diamond fields of Kimberly and who, from 1890 to 1896, had been prime minister of Cape Colony, believed that Britain's holdings in Africa should stretch from South Africa to Egypt, and he wanted to build a railroad from Cape Town to Cairo. Rhodes's company, the British South Africa Company (BSAC), began in 1890 to acquire territory to the north of South Africa, eventually founding the colony of Rhodesia. Britain achieved its goal of controlling contiguous territory from Cape Town to Cairo after World War I when the German colony that was later called Tanzania was ceded to the British.

## INDEPENDENCE

The British government had long envisioned a time when the colonies would be independent. In order to prepare its colonies for

## BRITISH COLONIES IN AFRICA

**BRITISH COLONIES IN AFRICA, CA. 1913**

The British emerged from what is known as the "Scramble for Africa" with a large portion of the continent's landmass. One goal of colonists in Africa was to move goods easily from one area to another. Clearly, the British succeeded, with colonies side-by-side nearly all the way from South Africa to Egypt.

## GREAT LIVES

### Cecil Rhodes

Cecil Rhodes was born in Hertfordshire, England, in 1853. Because of his delicate health, his parents sent him to Natal in South Africa, hoping that the milder climate would be beneficial. There, young Cecil worked on his brother Herbert's cotton farm.

In 1871, Rhodes and his brother gave up farming and traveled to the diamond fields of Kimberley, where they staked a mining claim. Rhodes's brother eventually returned to the farm, but Cecil continued to manage their claim. He returned to England in 1873 to complete a degree at Oxford University while still managing his interests at Kimberley. In 1880, he founded the DeBeers diamond company. He also began a political career, and in 1890 became prime minister of Cape Colony at the southern tip of Africa. Rhodes had an interest in overthrowing the Afrikaner Boer government of the Transvaal and in 1895 supported an attack on Transvaal known as the Jameson Raid. That attack, led by British statesman Leander Starr Jameson, was intended to encourage British workers in Transvaal to rebel; they did not and the raid was a failure. Rhodes was forced to resign.

Rhodes had tried many times to obtain the right to mine in Matabeland (in what is now Zimbabwe) from Lobengula, king of the Ndelbele. In 1888, Rhodes deceived Lobengula into signing a treaty of friendship, which effectively gave Rhodes complete power over Lobengula's territory. In 1889, he received a charter from the British government for his British South Africa Company (BSAC) to rule all territory from the Limpopo River to the great lakes of Central Africa. In 1895, the new territory was named Rhodesia. In 1898, the area south of the Zambezi River was officially renamed Southern Rhodesia; the rest was called Northern Rhodesia. (In the twentieth century, Southern Rhodesia became Zimbabwe and Northern Rhodesia became Zambia.) Rhodes was the quintessential **imperialist**, believing that Africans could not govern themselves and that it was Britain's destiny to rule the world. He expressed this point of view in his will, saying, "I contend that we are the first race in the world and that the more of the world we inhabit the better it is for the human race."

In ill health for his entire life, Rhodes was barely fifty when he died in 1902, just at the end of the Boer War. At the time of his passing, he was one of the wealthiest men in the world. In his will, Rhodes created the Rhodes Scholarship, which allows students from around the world to study at the University of Oxford.

---

eventual self-rule, the British opened universities and developed programs to improve transportation, health care, and agriculture. The British did not, however, prepare future African politicians to lead because they did not believe that independence would come as soon as it did. The first British colony to gain independence was Ghana (the former Gold Coast) in 1957. Nigeria and Somaliland were granted independence in 1960, Sierra Leone and Tanganyika in 1961, followed by Uganda (1962), Kenya and Zanzibar (1963), The Gambia (1965), Lesotho (1966), Botswana (1967), and Swaziland (1967). The British did not oppose independence for its colonies by force of arms, so all of the transitions to sovereignty were peaceful. South Africa left the British Commonwealth in

1961. (The Commonwealth is a voluntary association of independent nations that were once British colonies and that today includes many former African colonies, including South Africa, which rejoined in 1994.) Southern Rhodesia, which had been self-governing since 1923, became the nation of Zimbabwe in 1979.

***See also:*** Aswan Dam; Boer War; Colonization; Egypt; German Colonies; Nigeria; Somalia; South Africa; Sudan; Suez Canal; Uganda.

## FURTHER READING

Meredith, Martin. *The Fate of Africa. From the Hopes of Freedom to the Heart of Despair: A History of 50 Years of Independence.* New York: Public Affairs, 2005.

Mitchell, Peter, ed. *Peoples and Cultures of North Africa.* New York: Chelsea House, 2006.

# C

# Civil Wars

Since gaining independence in the mid-twentieth century, at least twenty African nations have fought bloody civil wars with devastating consequences. Among the worst conflicts were:

- the civil war in the Democratic Republic of the Congo (DRC), 1998–2004, which has been called the deadliest war since World War II; more than 4 million people died, mostly from disease and famine;
- the Angolan civil war (1975–2001), at 26 years Africa's longest civil conflict;
- the war in Sierra Leone, which was financed by what have come to be called "blood diamonds," as rebels stole diamonds and sold them to finance the carnage;
- the Rwandan civil war (1990–1993) in which Hutu peoples murdered hundreds of thousands of Tutsis;
- the conflict in Sudan, beginning in 2003, in which government-sponsored militias known as the Janjaweed have killed 200,000 people and displaced 2 million in Darfur in eastern Sudan.

Other conflicts have occurred in Uganda, Algeria, Ethiopia, Mozambique, Somalia, Central African Republic, Guinea-Bissau, Namibia, Zimbabwe, Nigeria, Cote d'Ivoire, Congo, Liberia, Burundi, and Senegal.

## WHY AFRICA?

Historians and scholars have long asked the question, Why Africa? What is it about this continent that seems to breed civil conflict? The answer most often cited is ethnic hatred made worse by the legacy of colonization. This theory suggests that European colonial powers drew the national boundaries of their colonies arbitrarily, grouping together historic enemies under the governance of a single state. When the colonial powers left Africa in the 1960s and 1970s, these ancient hatreds made national unity impossible. Indeed, in some of Africa's civil wars, such as that between the Hutus and the Tutsis in Rwanda, the combatants were divided along ethnic lines. Many of those alignments, however, were the result of other factors, which were themselves the root causes of the conflicts.

In "Why Are There So Many Civil Wars in Africa?" an article published in the *Journal of African Economics*, Ibrahim Elbadawi and Nicholas Sambanis of the World Bank argue that there are three crucial factors that have led to so much civil war on the continent: poverty, an economy dependent on raw natural resources (as opposed to manufactured goods), and a poorly functioning political system. Even among developing regions worldwide, Africa has the lowest **gross domestic product (GDP)**—less than half of Asia's. Many young African men, the group most likely to be recruited to fight in civil wars, are poor, uneducated, and hopeless about the future. They have essentially nothing to lose and everything to gain by rebelling against the status quo.

Many African nations are rich—in some cases extraordinarily so—in natural resources such as uranium, gold, and diamonds. This wealth carries with it tremendous potential for economic growth as well as tremendous potential for abuse and misuse. African dictators, such as Uganda's Idi Amin (r. 1971–1979) and DRC's Mobutu Sese Seko (r. 1965–1997), amassed huge personal fortunes by looting national resources. On the other hand, anti-government rebel troops have taken over mines by force and sold the raw materials

## INTO THE 21ST CENTURY

### Blood Diamonds

Also called "conflict diamonds." This term refers to African diamonds mined during civil wars by rebel groups and sold to finance their rebellions. In many cases, the ability of insurgents to sell diamonds for arms prolonged wars and caused more bloodshed and death. In the late 1990s and early 2000s, wars in Angola, Sierra Leone, Cote d'Ivoire, Democratic Republic of the Congo, and Republic of Congo all have been paid for partly in illegally obtained diamonds.

On December 1, 2000, the United Nations unanimously adopted a resolution stating that conflict diamonds are "a crucial factor in prolonging brutal wars in parts of Africa," yet underscored that "legitimate diamonds contribute to prosperity and development elsewhere on the continent." In 2001, members of the international diamond industry formed the World Diamond Council, which created the Kimberly Process Certification Scheme (KPCS), a method by which diamonds could be certified as coming from a legitimate, nonconflict source. In 2003, the United States passed the Clean Diamond Trade Act, which implemented the KPCS in the United States, a crucial piece of legislation because the United States is the world's largest consumer of diamonds.

In the 1990s, the United Nations estimated that as much as 15 percent of the world's diamond production was being sold to finance conflicts in Africa. By 2004, however, this figure had fallen to 1 percent.

---

to finance their rebellions or have forced mining companies to pay protection to keep takeovers from occurring.

Natural resource dependence itself has contributed to the third factor in African civil conflicts: unstable political institutions. Many African nations are so rich in natural resources that governments have no need to impose taxes on the people. Without the need to tax, rulers can distance themselves from the people who elect them, which, in turn, leads to corruption and other abuses. In countries in which people are taxed, the people tend to pay attention to what the government is doing to be sure their tax dollars are properly used. In Africa, however, as a result of despotic rulers, the resources of many nations have not been used for the public good—to build schools, roads, and hospitals—but instead to either line the pockets of politicians or finance rebellions. This, in turn, damages the economy, leading to poverty among the vast majority of people, which in turn leads to disaffected youth with nothing to lose.

Oxford professor of economics Paul Collier, in an article entitled "Natural Resources and Conflict in Africa," notes that natural resources tend not to be dispersed evenly across a nation, but are located in pockets here and there. When the people of a mineral-rich region become tired of national officials getting rich by raiding "their" treasure, they often attempt to **secede**—to set up their own independent nation—leading to civil war. This happened in Biafra in 1967, an oil-rich region in Nigeria, and in the DRC's Katanga Province in 1960, with its stores of cobalt, copper, tin, radium, uranium, and diamonds.

Once a rebel group begins a civil war, people often take sides based on ethnic

## CIVIL WARS

**MAJOR CIVIL WARS, BORDER DISPUTES, AND GUERRILLA ACTIVITIES IN MODERN AFRICA, 1960–PRESENT**

Civil wars, border disputes, and guerrilla activities have torn Africa apart since 1960. Millions have died across the continent. In recent years, the African Union (AU) and the United Nations (UN) have increased efforts to stem the violence and bloodshed.

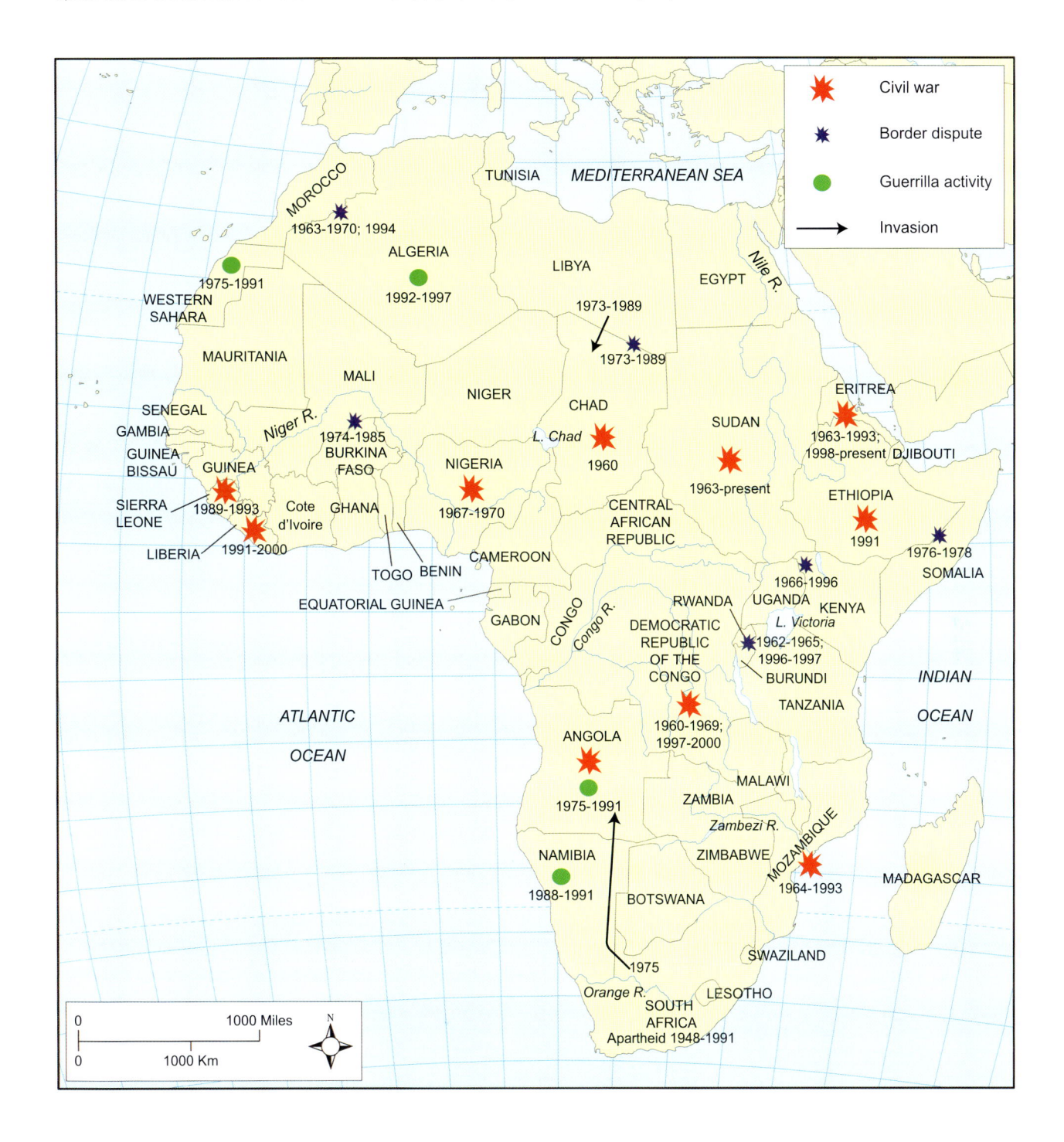

loyalties, experts say, but ethnic hatred is often not the root cause of civil war in Africa. In fact, ethnic diversity can actually be a factor in preventing civil wars as long as parties negotiate and compromise and work to prevent gross inequalities. That is, if the political system embraces democratic institutions, diversity can be an asset. This has been the case in South Africa since free elections were held in 1994. Different ethnic groups have found productive ways to live and work together. The major exceptions to this are nations with one large ethnic majority and one or two small disenfranchised minorities, such as happened in Rwanda between the majority Hutus and the minority Tutsis.

### ENDING CIVIL WAR

Clearly, economic growth based on factors beyond natural resources—such as manufacturing, agriculture, retail, and financial institutions—will be important in reducing the chance of civil war on the African continent. The African Union, an African organization modeled in part on the European Union, was designed to help nations across the continent develop industrialized economies and work cooperatively together for the good of all. An even more significant deterrent to civil war will be increased political freedom and the dialogue among different ethnic groups that it will bring.

*See also:* Algeria; Colonization; Congo; Democratic Movements; Economic Development and Trade; Ethiopia; Liberia; Nigeria; Rwanda; Somalia; Sudan; Tutsis and Hutus.

### FURTHER READING

Arnold, Guy. *Historical Dictionary of Civil Wars in Africa.* Lanham, MD: Scarecrow Press, 1999.

Habeeb, William Mark. *Civil Wars in Africa.* Broomall, PA: Mason Crest, 2006.

# Colonization

The European nations of Great Britain, France, the Netherlands, Portugal, and Spain, began colonizing Africa in the fifteenth century. Italy, Germany, and Belgium were also colonial powers in Africa, but they did not begin to establish colonies there until the nineteenth century. By 1875, only about 10 percent of the continent was dominated by Europe; by the early twentieth century, almost the entire continent was under European control.

### MOTIVES

The primary motive for colonizing Africa was economic. By the 1880s, Britain and many other European economies suffered from an unfavorable balance of trade, which means that they were importing more than they were exporting. By colonizing Africa, the European powers could import relatively inexpensive raw materials such as palm oil, groundnuts (the edible tubers of an African climbing plant), cotton, and uncut diamonds and sell profitable manufactured goods to captive markets in the colonies. Colonists could also be sure of a ready supply of cheap labor to work in colonial plantations and mines. Another motive for the colonization of Africa was rivalry for power, influence, and security among European powers. While the earliest European explorers contented themselves with building forts and trading posts along the African coast, explorations that began in the 1830s and continued through the 1860s revealed the previously unknown riches in the interior of the continent. In the early 1880s, the British explorer Henry Morton Stanley negotiated treaties with the Kongo Kingdom on behalf of King Leopold II of Belgium. The new Congo Free State became Leopold's personal possession, and he amassed a huge personal fortune by exploiting his colony's mineral wealth and natural resources.

Great Britain's earliest inroads into Africa were more strategic than economic. After outlawing the slave trade throughout the empire in 1807, the British built forts along the west coast of Africa to prevent other nations from taking and transporting slaves. Britain settled Cape Town at the southern tip of Africa to protect British ships as they rounded Africa on the way to India. In 1882, after the construction of the Suez Canal reduced the strategic importance of the Cape of Good Hope (since ships now no longer had to sail around the continent on the way to India), the British took formal control of Egypt. The government there was unstable and the British feared that its trade routes would be disrupted if they did not occupy and directly administer the government of Egypt and later that of Sudan to the south.

The French occupied Algeria in 1830, in response to an assault on the French consul by the governor of Algiers. While this colony was founded as an act of vengeance, France proceeded to expand its colonial holdings partly because of rivalry with Germany. After losing the region of Alsace-Lorraine to the Germans following the Franco-Prussian War of 1870–1871, the French searched for ways to make up for both the lost territory and the lost prestige. The French also came to believe that they had a duty to "civilize" Africa, a goal they called their *mission civilisatrice.*

Germany, which had not been a unified nation until the 1870s, also sought the riches and prestige that could result from holding territory in Africa. At the request of Portugal, German chancellor Otto von Bismarck convened the Berlin Conference of 1884–1885 to help regulate what had come to be called the Scramble for Africa. During the conference, fourteen nations negotiated the rules by which Africa was to be carved into European colonies. The rules had little to do with what was best for Africa and Africans and everything to do with preventing bloodshed among European powers as they staked out their territory.

## KINDS OF COLONIES AND COLONIAL ADMINISTRATIONS

In general, Europeans created two different kinds of colonies in Africa—exploitation colonies and settlement colonies. The most common kind of colony in Africa was the colony of exploitation, which usually did not have a large numbers of settlers. Those who came to these colonies—administrators, merchants, plantation owners, and military personnel—were interested only in removing as much wealth as possible. One of the worst examples of a colony of exploitation was the Belgian Congo. There King Leopold II, who originally held the colony as a personal domain, committed atrocities on the native people, killing almost half the population in his efforts to enrich himself. The British colonies of Nigeria and Ghana were also colonies of exploitation.

In colonies of settlement, Europeans came by the thousands to live, bringing their own culture, animals, and crops and displacing native peoples, their cultures, and **indigenous** animal and plant species. As settlers and native people came into conflict, many of the latter were forcibly displaced or killed. Between 1904 and 1907, for example, German colonists virtually exterminated the Herero people, killing 80 percent of the population. Others succumbed to diseases brought by European settlers. Eventually, the settlers developed their own unique cultures and forms of government and became independent of

## COLONIZATION

**AFRICA ON THE EVE OF THE BERLIN CONFERENCE, 1884–1885**

Before the Berlin Conference of 1885, only a tiny portion of Africa had been colonized by Europeans, mainly along the coasts. After the Conference, however, European powers raced to control as much of Africa as possible. By 1914, only Liberia and Ethiopia were not under foreign control.

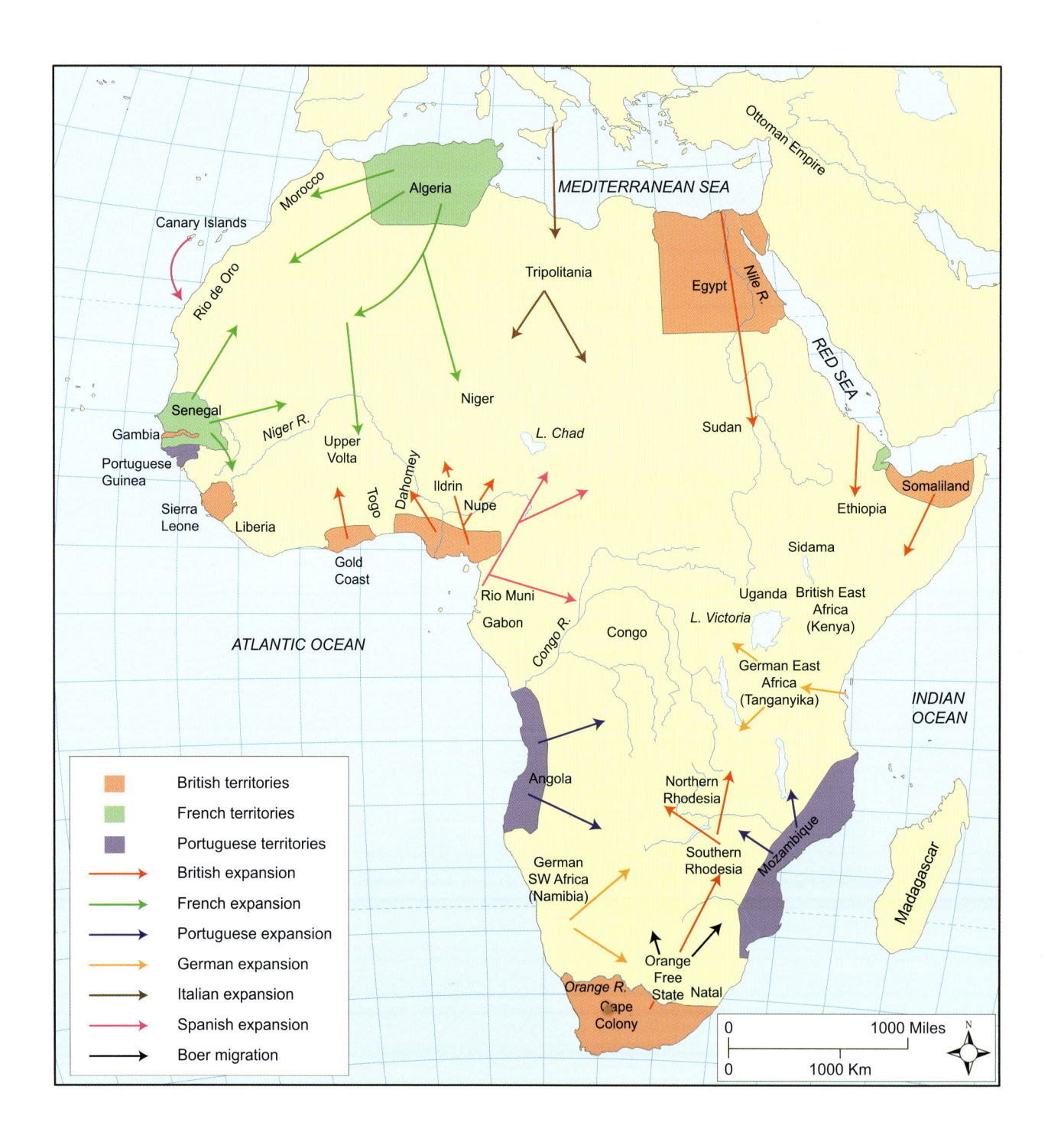

## TURNING POINT

### Berlin Conference of 1884-1885

Chancellor Otto Von Bismarck of Germany called thirteen European nations and the United States together in 1884 to decide the rules for carving up the African continent into European colonies. Bismarck's goal was to allow European powers to divide Africa by a set of agreed-upon policies rather than by warfare. The thirteen European nations that attended the conference were Austria-Hungary, Belgium, Denmark, France, Great Britain, Germany, Italy, the Netherlands, Portugal, Russia, Spain, Sweden-Norway, and the Ottoman Empire.

A major focus of the conference was to control the slave trade and promote humanitarianism in Africa, but the conferees did little except pass resolutions on these issues, which were never enforced. The conference did, however, confirm the Congo as the private property of King Leopold II of Belgium and allowed for free trade throughout the Congo basin for those who attended the conference. The conferees also endorsed the Principle of Effectivity, which stated that nations could own colonies only if they actually had established a colonial administration, signed treaties with local chiefs, and created a force to maintain order. This principle was created to prevent countries from establishing colonies in name only. The conferees also agreed that anyone of the fourteen nations present had to inform the others of plans to claim territory.

At the time, European leaders believed they had behaved rationally in preventing war. They also believed that the African people were not capable of governing themselves and therefore justified their actions by taking over native lands.

---

the parent country. Algeria, considered a department, or administrative district, of France itself, is a good example of a settlement colony, as is South Africa; in both cases, many Europeans settled in the colonies permanently.

The two main types of colonies—exploitation and settlement—were both ruled by the parent country, either by a direct or an indirect form of government. Indirect rule was used primarily by the British, who tended to have very few administrators and often ruled through traditional tribal leaders. In some cases, however, they appointed leaders at their convenience, disrupting traditional tribal hierarchies. In Nigeria, for example, the British ruled through those willing to work with them, whether or not they were actual leaders in their communities. Other colonial powers, including France, Germany, Portugal, and Belgium, used a direct form of government, placing all power in the hands of their own colonial administrators. The British method tended to create a ruling **elite**, fracturing the native culture, while the French method tended to be more unifying—as long as the native peoples accepted French culture and were willing to be assimilated. Like the French, the Germans, Belgians, and Portuguese tended to use a form of direct rule in their colonies, although they did not assimilate native peoples as the French did.

### LEGACIES

The legacy of colonialism in Africa has been almost entirely negative for the peoples and nations of Africa. Although some colonial powers made substantial contributions to infrastructure—building roads, hospitals, and schools—most simply exported raw materials and left nothing behind that could help the former colonies become independent, well-functioning states. These nations came into an industrialized world with little or no industry and with a population ill prepared to develop industrialized solutions to problems. When the French left Guinea in 1958, for example, they took literally everything with them, including telephones from the walls, leaving the new nation to start the process of modernization almost from scratch. In most cases, colonial administrations did not help prepare African people for nationhood, so when independence came, military dictators often seized power and democratic processes never took hold.

In addition, many Africans, after years of subjugation and second-class citizenship, had lost a sense of their own cultures and traditions and were left adrift, unable to accept the culture of their subjugators. In his acclaimed novel *Things Fall Apart* (1958) and other works, Nigerian author Chinua Achebe creates characters who are adrift in this sense, caught between two cultures, unable to fully accept either.

Among the worst legacies of colonialism was the drawing of more than fifty entirely artificial national boundaries that had little or nothing to do with intertribal alliances and hatreds. Without a colonial administration to keep the peace, independence often cast ethnic groups with ancient rivalries into armed conflict. At least twenty African nations have fought long and bloody civil wars, prompted at least in part by ethnic differences and artificially imposed borders.

Because of years of domination by colonial powers, Africa still struggles with issues of national identity, economics, and governance—even more than fifty years after most nations achieved independence.

***See also:*** Algeria; British Colonies; Civil Wars; Congo; Democratic Movements; Egypt; French West Africa; German Colonies; Italian Colonies; Portuguese Colonies; South Africa.

### FURTHER READING

Bowden, Rob. *Kenya.* New York, Chelsea House, 2003.

Lovejoy, Paul E., and Toyin Falola, eds. *Pawnship, Slavery, and Colonialism in Africa.* Trenton, NJ: Africa World Press, 2003.

Mwaura, Mdirangu. *Kenya Today: Breaking the Yoke of Colonialism.* New York: Algora, 2005.

Reader, John. *Africa: A Biography of the Continent.* New York: Vintage, 1999.

# Communist Movements

Movements in African nations that attempted to install and maintain communist governments. Although there were communist parties in Egypt and South Africa as early as the 1920s, **communism** did not take hold in most of Africa until after World War II. Even then, only four nations—Angola, Mozambique, the Republic of the Congo, and Ethiopia—experimented seriously with communism. Some nations, however, advocated an economic system that African leaders, including Kwame Nkrumah of Ghana, called "African socialism."

According to this view, the fact that precolonial African societies were classless and communal meant that a sophisticated modern society could be created based on communal, rather than state, ownership of property.

## COMMUNIST MOVEMENTS, 1920–1992

**1920s** Communist parties founded in Egypt and South Africa

**1964** Republic of the Congo's President Alphonse Massamba-Débat founds the National Movement for the Revolution along Marxist-Leninist lines, outlawing all other parties

**1974** Emperor Haile Selassie of Ethiopia overthrown by the Communist Provisional Military Administrative Council led by Mengistu Haile Mariam

**1975** Angola institutes a one-party socialist government

**1984** Mengistu renames Ethiopia the People's Democratic Republic of Ethiopia

**1991** Mengistu overthrown; Angolan Civil War ends

**1992** Republic of the Congo allows first democratic elections; Angola allows first multiparty elections

After World War II, the Soviet Union (USSR) offered support to many African nationalists who were trying to escape the bonds of colonialism. In 1958, for example, the Soviets paid about one-third of the cost for constructing the Aswan High Dam in Egypt. In 1969, Ghana signed a $45 million contract with the Soviets for the development of mineral rights (that is, the Soviets were granted the right to mine certain areas even though they would not actually own the land). Over the years, the Soviet Union and Cuba sent arms, soldiers, and money to support communist rebels in several civil wars, notably in Angola and Ethiopia.

The **Cold War** between the United States and the Soviet Union led to American fears of the "domino effect." Many people believed that if the Soviets gained control of one nation, other nearby nations would "fall" to communism. The United States had similar concerns about Africa and used both military and financial aid to support noncommunist governments, even when some of the leaders of these governments were corrupt military dictators, such as Mobutu Sese Seko of Zaire (now the Democratic Republic of the Congo).

The first African nation to form a Soviet-style government was the Republic of the Congo, a small country that had been a French colony. In 1964, President Alphonse Massamba-Débat founded the National Movement for the Revolution along **Marxist-Leninist** lines and outlawed all other political parties. Various other leftist presidents and parties followed, until 1992, when President Denis Sassou-Nguesso allowed multiparty elections. Part of his reason for this action was the collapse of the Soviet Union. Since he needed Western support, he made a decision to initiate Western-style democracy.

Emperor Haile Selassie of Ethiopia was overthrown in 1974 by an organization called the Provisional Military Administrative Council led by Mengistu Haile Mariam, who declared Ethiopia a one-party **socialist** state. In 1984, Mengistu renamed the country the People's Democratic Republic of Ethiopia. Because Mengistu was largely dependent on the Soviet Union for his power, his government was overthrown and replaced by a **coalition** government after the fall of the Soviet Union in 1991.

The country of Angola, a former Portuguese colony, was granted independence in 1975, at which time the Popular Movement for the Liberation of Angola, with help from the USSR and Cuba, instituted a socialist, one-party government. Civil war broke out almost immediately, with the resistance party, the National Union for the Total Independence of Angola, receiving support from South Africa and the United States. The war continued until 1991, when both sides agreed to the Bicesse Accords, which allowed for multi-party elections.

Mozambique was also a former Portuguese colony that followed virtually the same path as Angola from one-party communism beginning at liberation in 1975 to multiparty elections in 1992. A group of four mediators worked with the opposing parties to negotiate the Rome General Peace Accords, signed later that year.

*See also:* Civil Wars; Colonization; Congo; Ethiopia; Imperialism; Independence Movements; Portuguese Colonies; South Africa; Suez Canal.

### FURTHER READING

Albright, David E. *Africa and International Communism.* New York: Macmillan Education, 1980.

Reader, John. *Africa: A Biography of the Continent.* New York: Vintage, 1999.

# Congo

One of the largest nations in Africa, also called the Democratic Republic of the Congo (DRC) and, between 1971 and 1997, known as Zaire. This nation in south-central Africa is bordered by the Republic of Congo, the Central African Republic, Sudan, Uganda, Rwanda, Burundi, Tanzania, Zambia, Angola, and the Atlantic Ocean. It is home to more than 250 ethnic groups who speak hundreds of different languages. DRC is about one-fourth the size of the United States and is home to more than 60 million people.

The first Europeans to come to Congo were the Portuguese, who arrived in 1482. They stayed in coastal areas, however, and did not penetrate into the interior.

In 1877 English journalist Henry Stanley navigated the Congo River, which opened the interior of the region for further exploration. Thanks in part to treaties Stanley negotiated with the European colonial powers at the Berlin Conference of 1885, Congo became the personal possession of Belgium's King Leopold II, who used Congolese slave labor to amass a huge fortune in ivory and rubber. An estimated 10 million people died at the hands of Leopold's brutal administrators between 1885 and 1907, when the Belgian government took over and named the colony the Belgian Congo. Joseph Conrad's novel *The Heart of Darkness* (1902) is in part based on his outrage at the horrors perpetrated in Leopold's name.

After years of internal unrest, including a series of violent riots in Kinshasa in 1959, Belgium granted Congo independence in 1960. The first president was Joseph Kasavubu; the first prime minister was Patrice Lumumba, head of the leftist Mouvement National Congolais. The country was named the Democratic Republic of the Congo.

During the first year that Congo was an independent nation, the mineral-rich Katanga Province seceded from the

**republic**, followed by South Kasai Province. The United Nations (UN) sent in a peacekeeping force to try to prevent all-out civil war between secessionist groups and the central government. Lumumba's chief of staff, General Joseph-Désiré Mobutu, staged a military **coup**, took Prime Minister Lumumba into custody, and handed him over to Moise Tshombe, the president of Katanga Province. Tshombe had Lumumba killed, and some historians believe that the United States and Belgium had a hand in the assassination. After the coup and Lumumba's execution, Mobutu restored Kasavubu to power.

Despite several attempts to bring peace to the region, Tshombe continued to fight for independence until 1963, when he surrendered to government forces. In order to stem further rebellion, Kasavubu named Tshombe premier. In 1965, however, Kasavubu forced Tshombe to step down and then was deposed himself in a second coup headed by Mobutu. Upon seizing power, Mobutu suppressed all political parties other than his own, nationalized many foreign companies, including the Union Minière, a Belgian mining operation, and declared that all Congolese had to adopt African names. To lead the way, he renamed the country the Republic of Zaire and himself Mobutu Sese Seko.

The **Cold War** between the United States and the Soviet Union played an important role in sustaining Mobutu's regime. Western powers feared that the Congo might fall to **communism** and so continued to support Mobutu, despite his history of suppressing opposition and looting the national treasure for personal gain. As the Cold War ended in the late 1980s, the West lost interest in supporting

**Mobutu Sese Seko seized power and declared himself president of Zaire (now the Democratic Republic of the Congo) in 1965. After 32 years as dictator, he fled the country during a 1997 coup and died in exile in Morocco in 1997.** (Pascal Guyot/AFP/Getty Images)

## GREAT LIVES

### Mobutu Sese Seko

Joseph-Désiré Mobutu was born in Lisala in what was then the Belgian Congo in 1930. He was educated in missionary schools and joined the Belgian army when he was nineteen years old. In the late 1950s, he joined the leftist Congolese National Movement headed by Patrice Lumumba. When the nation gained independence in 1960, Joseph Kasavubu was appointed president and Lumumba his prime minister. Lumumba, in turn, appointed Mobutu his chief of staff.

Lumumba appealed to the Soviet Union for aid, which earned him the hostility of the United States and other Western nations. Three months after Lumumba came to power, Mobutu staged a coup; Lumumba was arrested and eventually executed. Some believe that the U.S. Central Intelligence Agency (CIA) was involved in Lumumba's death because it feared he would allow the Congo to fall to Soviet influence. Mobutu handed the reins of government back to Kasavubu, but in 1965 staged a second coup, overthrew Kasavubu, and declared himself president.

One of Mobutu's early programs was to return the country to "African authenticity." In 1971, he renamed the nation Zaire, which he claimed was the ancient name for the Congo River. He also changed his name to Mobutu Sese Seko Kuku Ngbendu wa za Banga (officially translated as "the all-powerful warrior who, because of his endurance and inflexible will to win, will go from conquest to conquest leaving fire in his wake.") He also banned Western names and clothing, and encouraged the use of African languages in addition to French, the official language.

Mobutu ruled Zaire for more than thirty years (1965–1997). He and his administration were so corrupt that the word "kleptocracy" (from the Greek word for "to steal") was coined to describe his administration. His position was secure, however, because Western nations such as the United States continued to support him; they assumed he prevented the Congo from falling under Soviet influence. As the Cold War came to an end, the West withdrew its support, leaving Mobutu vulnerable. The challenge finally came from Laurent Kabila, who overthrew the Mobutu government in May 1997. Mobutu fled to Rabat, Morocco, where he died of prostate cancer only four months later.

---

Mobutu's government because they no longer feared a Soviet takeover. Mobutu was further weakened by civil unrest, international criticism of his human rights abuses, and a worsening economy. Although Mobutu agreed to multiparty elections in 1994, he never allowed them to occur.

In 1996, Hutu militia forces, known as the Interhamwe, escaped into Zaire from neighboring Rwanda. The Interhamwe had been part of a plan to exterminate the minority Tutsi people, but the Tutsi fought back and were able to take control of the Rwandan government. Despite an end to this civil war, the Interhamwe continued to attack Rwanda from bases in Zaire. In response, Rwandan troops assisted Congolese rebel Laurent-Desiré Kabila and his forces in his campaign to overthrow the Mobutu government.

In May 1997, Mobutu fled the country.

Kabila declared himself president and renamed Zaire the Democratic Republic of the Congo. Rwandan and Ugandan troops that had assisted Kabila in his rebellion remained in the country to help ensure stability. Rwanda was particularly concerned about protecting its borders from Hutu militia still in DRC. Within a year, however, Kabila demanded that Ugandan and Rwandan forces leave the country. They refused and, instead, brought in more troops, ushering in a war that lasted through 2003. This conflict is often referred to as Africa's "World War," because it eventually involved six African nations and killed more than 3.8 million people.

In 1999, a peace agreement known as the Lusaka Accord was signed by representatives from DRC, Rwanda, Uganda, Angola, Namibia, and Zimbabwe, as well as several rebel groups that had participated in the conflict. The provisions of the accord were not fully implemented, however, and fighting continued. In 2001, Kabila was assassinated and succeeded by his son Joseph, who at age thirty became the world's youngest head of state. Joseph moved quickly to end the war, allowing United Nations peacekeeping forces into the country and promoting dialogue among the various parties to the conflict.

In April 2003, a series of talks culminated in a power-sharing agreement among government representatives, rebel groups, various political parties, and Mai Mai (Congolese local defense militias.) Still, the fighting continued. In April 2003, hundreds were killed in an ethnic conflict in the eastern province of Ituri, and Rwanda has continued to support rebel groups.

In May 2005, DRC adopted a new constitution and, in 2006, held its first elections since 1970. Joseph Kabila won 44.8 percent of the vote, which was not enough to declare him the winner. In a runoff election in October, Kabila won 58 percent of the vote to become the country's first elected head of state since 1970. Despite the great mineral wealth of DRC, decades of corruption and civil war have left the country one of the poorest in the world and much of its infrastructure has been destroyed and must be rebuilt if the economy is to be restored.

**See also:** Civil Wars; Colonization; Rwanda; Tutsis and Hutus; Uganda.

### FURTHER READING

Edgerton, Robert. *The Troubled Heart of Africa: A History of the Congo.* NY: St Martin's, 2002.

Hochschild, Adam. *King Leopold's Ghost: A Story of Greed, Terror and Heroism.* NY: Mariner Books, 1999.

Oppong, Joseph R. *Africa South of the Sahara.* New York: Chelsea House, 2005.

Tayler, Jeffrey. *Facing the Congo: A Modern-Day Journey into the Heart of Darkness.* New York: Three Rivers Press, 2002.

# Culture and Traditions

Throughout its long history, Africa has been home to a number of peoples, each with its own traditions, customs, and spiritual practices, transmitted from generation to generation. Beginning with European exploration of the continent in the late 1400s, African cultures have changed in response to European rule and forms of government, as well as European languages, cultures, and religions. Modern Africans face the challenge of reclaiming and maintaining their native cultures and traditions in the twenty-first century.

## FAMILY LIFE

Although there are many large and populous cities in Africa, most Africans still live somewhat traditional lives in rural areas. Unlike the typical nuclear family of Western nations, which includes only parents and their children, most Africans live in extended families that include grandparents, aunts and uncles, and cousins. Life is largely communal, with all members of the extended family pitching in to help with meals, farming, child rearing, and choosing marriage partners.

### Marriage

Marriage is an extremely important institution in Africa, partly because children represent wealth and status. In rural communities, children are needed to help with agricultural work, so large families are the norm; childless couples are pitied. In Africa, children also represent a kind of life after death, because children honor and keep alive the memory of departed ancestors. Ancestors are a very important part of African culture, and every parent hopes his or her spirit will be honored by children after death. Children are charged with keeping their parents' memories alive.

Although child marriage is illegal in many parts of Africa and discouraged by the United Nations (UN) and other international aid agencies, in many areas, very young girls—some as young as ten—are offered in marriage. Often child marriage is motivated by a belief in the importance of virginity, and families want their daughters safely married as soon as possible. Many parents fear that their daughters will lose their virginity if they are not married off before the surge of hormones and interest in sex that come with puberty. More often, however, child marriage is motivated by poverty. Girls become financial contributors to their families, which barter with suitors for the highest bride price.

In general, marriage in Africa is a communal affair. African men and women do not marry because they fall in love, as most people in the West do. This is certainly true in rural Africa, if not in the big cities. Relatives and elders often arrange marriages, based on hoped-for alliances with certain other clans or ethnic groups. Because entire families are involved and because of the institution of the bride price, traditional African marriages are generally stable; divorce is rare. If the husband and wife experience difficulties, relatives do whatever they can to help the couple solve problems. The wife's relatives work especially hard to keep the marriage together because if it dissolves, they must return the bride price. In some families, when a daughter marries, the wealth the family gains is given to her brother so that he may pay the price for his intended bride. Thus, if a family has already "spent" the bride price, it may be impossible for the bride's family to return the bride price in the event of a divorce. If the bride's family cannot keep the marriage together under these circumstances, the entire family may suffer.

**Polygamy**—having more than one spouse, in this case more than one wife—is prevalent in many parts of Africa. While this institution seems odd to many Westerners, it serves a distinct purpose in many African ethnic groups. The work of women is hard; they must raise the crops as well as rear the children, and even build the family home. Having several women in the family to help with these tasks eases the burden of each one. In addition, since women who do not bear children are often returned to their families, several wives take the pressure off those who may not be able to have children.

In many ethnic groups, such as the Tiv of Nigeria, men are obligated to marry their brother's widow; sometimes when a father dies, his son will marry the father's youngest wife. This system offers significant protection to widows and their children. In general, unmarried women are adrift in traditional African culture, often unable to provide for themselves.

### Children

Children are of primary importance in Africa and are treasured not only by their parents but also by a large, extended family. The phrase "It takes a village to raise a child" is of African origin and is a good description of how children are cared for in traditional African towns. Mothers carry their infants with them when they are working and often sleep with babies, creating a deep bond. Children begin to help their parents as soon as they are able, boys working with their fathers, girls with their mothers, learning the jobs they will do as adults. Many rural children do not receive formal education but rather learn from parents and from the stories and songs of elders in the village.

To foster a sense of community, the Igbo of Nigeria practice fostering, in which children are raised in the homes of relatives other than parents, often aunts and uncles. This practice literally "extends" the family beyond the bounds of the nuclear family.

A study conducted among the Ogu of Nigeria in 2006 suggested that the ideal of the extended family in this ethnic group is weakening and that there is a definite movement toward a more Westernized nuclear family. Some of this change is motivated by poverty, as people are increasingly expected to bear the costs of raising their own children while relatives show themselves less and less willing to take in children to foster. Nevertheless, the authors concluded that most Ogu still consider the extended family the ideal.

### Elders

As in many traditional societies, older people in towns and villages in Africa are revered for their wisdom and life experience. Rather than formal judicial systems, many African villages rely on older leaders to judge what would be both civil and criminal cases in Western cultures. Although divorce is rare in rural Africa, village elders rather than judges determine whether or not a couple should be allowed to divorce.

In African cities, however, the traditional system of laws and elders has given way to more Western-style legal codes, court systems, and judges. Inevitably, elders do not have the same status in cities as they do in rural areas.

## RITES AND RITUALS

Much of daily life in rural areas of the continent is governed by rites and rituals with both spiritual and cultural significance. Relatives and neighbors come together to celebrate births, the transition to adulthood, and weddings, as well as to mourn the passing of the dead.

### Birth

Most African cultures believe that the newborn child comes to earth from the world of spirits and that each child comes with a unique mission or gift. In order to determine what that gift is, many African parents commission a birth chart, similar to an astrological chart, which helps parents understand the child's temperament and predict his or her fate. Because most African names have a meaning that relates directly to the child's personality or destiny, African parents often wait for several days to name the child to be sure that he or she has the most appropriate name. The Akamba of West Africa, for example, wait three days before naming newborn children.

### Adulthood

Many traditional African ethnic groups have specialized initiation rites that are celebrated

Young Xhosa boys in South Africa, their faces covered in mud, prepare to go into the bush for ritual ceremonies to become men. Formal ceremonies initiating the end of childhood and the beginning of adulthood are common throughout Africa. (Per-Anders Pettersson/Getty Images)

to mark the transition of children to adulthood, rites that are generally conducted when the child reaches puberty. Some groups perform initiation rites for girls, but the vast majority are reserved for boys. These rites are often combined with circumcision, which marks the children as ready for marriage.

Typically, African initiation rites begin with the removal of the boys from the village, symbolizing their transformation and changing responsibilities. A group of boys is taken to a remote area, accompanied by elders whose job it is to teach them what they need to know to be men in the culture—how to behave, how to hunt, how to court women, how to participate in religious rituals, how to conduct themselves in general. In some instances, the boys must undergo an ordeal—in many cases, they are circumcised. They may also have their faces scarred in particular patterns or have teeth knocked out. These become outward signs of the inner changes the boys have undergone. Often, when the boys return to their villages, their mothers pretend not to know them because they have undergone such a profound change.

Some African cultures, such as the Nandi of Kenya, practice female circumcision, which has also been called female genital mutilation, since, unlike male circumcision, the female version often leaves women unable to experience sexual pleasure. Many Western groups have launched campaigns to stop this practice, but many traditional cultures still embrace it, feeling that it helps to keep girls pure for their husbands. They believe that the inability to experience sexual pleasure will make women less likely to have a reason to engage in sex outside of marriage.

### Marriage

Marriage, because it is so important in African society, is often the occasion of long and joyous celebrations, especially in rural areas. The couple may have met only briefly before the ceremony, because family members conduct the negotiations. The ceremony is an opportunity for the two families to come together and celebrate their new unity through the union of their children. The two families, formerly separate, are now allied. The family unit is extended to include what Westerners call "in-laws." Brightly colored clothing, music, and dancing are part of most African wedding ceremonies, and the couple's wrists are often bound together with grasses to symbolize their union.

Most African marriages, even those that are not polygamous, are patriarchal; that is, the husband is considered the head of the household and his word is law. Wives must obey their husbands, and women, in general, have few rights in most of Africa. In many places, they cannot even own land, despite the fact that most farming is done by women.

### Death

Many rural Africans believe that, just as children come from the spirit world, the dead return to it. The sprits of ancestors are believed to be present in the village and to take an active role in guiding the destinies of descendents.

Funeral customs also reflect the idea that the spirits of the dead live on. Some ethnic groups, fearful of what spirits may do to the living, try to bury the dead at a distance from the village. They may even remove the bodies, feet first, from their homes through holes in walls that are then sealed up. Once the hole is sealed, it is believed, the dead will not be able to find their way back into the house. Other ethnic groups bury the dead beneath houses to keep the sprits nearby.

To assist in the journey to the afterlife, conceived as very much like this life, Africans often bury their dead with household objects. While family members mourn the loss of a relative, the rest of the town may celebrate life with singing, dancing, and feasting.

## URBAN LIFE

Much has been written about the loss of traditional culture in Africa, as people move away from villages and extended families into the loneliness and poverty of city life. Without extended families to help raise children, and with poverty forcing women to work long hours, children must often be left by themselves. Many parents cannot afford to send their children to school, and there are few elders to teach the children the traditions of the tribe.

In areas of Africa that have been plagued with civil conflict, women have had to take over the role of head of the household while their husbands are away fighting. When the men return, **domestic** disputes often arise. Men may have difficulty finding work, forcing women to continue working to support the family.

Urban life in Africa creates many challenges for people who have been raised in traditional, village cultures. As more and more people become used to city life, however, the urban scene may change and improve.

*See also:* Agriculture; Economic Development and Trade; Religion; Society.

## FURTHER READING

Asante, Molefi Kete, ed. *African Culture: The Rhythms of Unity.* Lawrenceville, NJ: Africa World Press, 1989.

Reader, John. *Africa: A Biography of the Continent.* New York: Vintage, 1999.

# D-E

## Darfur  *See* Refugees; Sudan.

## Democratic Movements

Movements in various African nations that have attempted to bring about democratic reforms to the political systems. Among these are freedom of the press, **rule of law,** and fair and free elections.

The great push for freedom and independence by African leaders in the 1960s and 1970s did not lead to democratic political systems. In many nations, the first free elections after the end of colonialism were also the last free elections. Some presidents, such as Robert Mugabe of Zimbabwe, became virtual presidents for life. Having won a free election, they used their power to ensure that they were "reelected" time after time by suppressing opposition and intimidating voters. In other nations, military coups, often in the name of democratic reform, toppled elected leaders with the promise of a return to democratic elections sometime in the future. In some of these nations, such as the Democratic Republic of the Congo under Mobutu Sese Seko, those free elections never materialized.

Only the nations of Botswana and Mauritius have managed to maintain functioning democracies since independence. Since 1994, with the accession of the African National Congress (ANC) to power, South Africa, too, has maintained a true democracy. However, some historians and scholars have recently begun to worry about the fate of democracy in Botswana. In 2007, for example, the government of Botswana exiled Kenneth Good, a lecturer at the University of Botswana, for critical comments about government actions. In 2000, Senegal and The Gambia succeeded in holding what appeared to be free and fair elections.

More recently, under pressure from Western donors concerned about the lack of democracy in Africa and enhanced by new technology such as cell phones and the Internet, a number of democratic reform movements have arisen. Among the most prominent are Cameroon's Social Democratic Front, Egypt's Kifaya, and the Conférence National Souveraine (CNS) in the Democratic Republic of the Congo. Other groups have been around longer and have worked for years to ensure democratic processes in Africa, including the ANC in South Africa and several groups in Nigeria.

### SOUTH AFRICA

By 1910, South Africa was no longer a colony but a dominion of Great Britain with the same status as Canada. However, its native population was completely **disenfranchised**. In 1912, the African National Congress (ANC) was formed in order to defend the rights of the African people. The ANC was founded on the principle of nonviolent protest against discriminatory government policies.

In 1952, the ANC and other groups opposed to apartheid—the legal system of racial discrimination in South Africa—organized the Defiance Campaign, in which members were encouraged to violate oppressive laws. The campaign ended when the white government enacted laws prohibiting protest meetings.

## DEMOCRACY IN MODERN AFRICA

**1912** African National Congress (ANC) founded to promote racial equality in South Africa

**1952** ANC organizes the Defiance Campaign, a campaign of peaceful civil disobedience to win black rights in South Africa

**1960** South African police shoot unarmed protestors at Sharpeville

**1961** ANC forms military wing, Umkhonto we Sizwe; Nelson Mandela imprisoned

**1990** South African president F.W. de Klerk legalizes ANC; Social Democratic Front (SDC), pro-democracy movement in Cameroon founded; Mobutu Sese Seko of Democratic Republic of Congo announces and then retracts permission for three-party system; 100 student demonstrators killed in Congo

**1992** SDF candidate Ni John Fru Ndi denied election victory in Cameroon, held under house arrest

**1993** Chief Moshood Abiola wins election in Nigeria but President Ibrahim Babangida refuses to accept results; Babangida resigns; Congolese opposition groups appoint rival Prime Minister Faustin Birindwa

**1994** Democratic elections in South Africa; Chief Abiola of Nigeria imprisoned when he declares himself winner of the Nigerian elections

**1998** Nigerian president Sani Abacha and Chief Abiola both die under mysterious circumstances on same day

**1999** Nigeria's first free elections in sixteen years

**2000** Senegal and The Gambia hold free elections

**2004** Egyptian opposition movement Kifaya founded to oppose Hosni Mubarak's continued rule

**2005** Hosni Mubarak asks Parliament to allow multiparty election; Ayuman Nour, Egyptian opposition candidate, sentenced to prison

---

In 1960, the ANC again planned a campaign of nonviolent protest, this time against the so-called "pass laws," which required blacks to carry identification at all times or be subject to arrest. A rival anti-apartheid organization, the Pan-Africanist Congress (PAC), conducted a similar protest before the scheduled ANC event. As unarmed PAC protesters showed up without passes at a police station in the township of Sharpeville, South African police fired into the crowd, killing 69 and wounding 186. This incident became known as the Sharpeville massacre. Afterward, the government banned both the ANC and the PAC.

Driven underground, the ANC leadership decided that it had to renounce its code of nonviolence and use military tactics against the government. In 1961, the ANC formed a military unit known as Umkhonto we Sizwe ("Spear of the Nation") with Nelson Mandela as its first leader. Within a year, however, Mandela was arrested, charged with treason, and sentenced to life in prison.

International pressure on South Africa and the collapse of the Soviet Union, which had long funded ANC activities, brought the two sides to the negotiating table. President F.W. de Klerk legalized the ANC and PAC in 1990. In 1994, the first democratic elections were held in South Africa, and ANC leader Nelson Mandela was elected president.

## NIGERIA

From the time Nigeria gained independence from Great Britain in 1960 until 1999, it had been ruled largely by military dictators, including Ibrahim Babangida (1985–1993) and Sani Abacha (1993–1998). During these years, many individuals and movements rose to challenge the government and to demand a democratic political system. Many of these organizations were moved to action by the elections of 1993. That year, business leader Chief Moshood Abiola won the presidency, but Babangida refused to accept his victory. Vehement protests both in the streets and in the media caused Babangida to resign in August 1993. He appointed his own successor, Ernest Shonekan, who was deposed in November by General Sani Abacha. Under Abacha, human rights abuses by the government escalated but so did pro-democratic protests. When Abiola proclaimed himself president in 1994, Abacha had him thrown in prison.

As these events were unfolding, the National Democratic Coalition (NADECO) was formed to coordinate the activities the pro-democracy movements in Nigeria. Other **coalitions** included the Campaign for Democracy and the United Democratic Front for Nigeria. These groups lobbied with various international organizations, such as Amnesty International and Human Rights Watch, to bring the crimes of the Nigerian government to the attention of the world.

In July 1998, Abacha died under mysterious circumstances. On the same day, Chief Abiola died in prison. Although many suspected that Abiola had been poisoned, an international team of pathologists determined that he had died of natural causes. In 1999, after sixteen years of military rule, Nigeria held its first free elections and chose Olusegun Obsanjo as its president. Obsanjo was reelected in 2003 and attempted unsuccessfully to change the constitution to allow him to run for a third term in 2007. Presidential elections were held in April 2007, with more than twenty-five candidates competing. The elections were won by Umaru Yar'Adua, the candidate from Obsanjo's own People's Democratic Party (PDP). Many observers, including former U.S. secretary of state Madeleine Albright, felt the election was not conducted fairly. "In a number of places and in a number of ways," said Albright, "the election process failed the Nigerian people." The work of the democracy movements in Nigeria is not finished.

## EGYPT

The first president of an independent Egypt was Gamal Abdel Nasser, a member of the group of young military officers who deposed Egypt's King Farouk in 1952. Nasser served as Egypt's president from 1954 to 1970 and was succeeded by Anwar Sadat, who allowed much greater political freedom than had Nasser. Sadat was assassinated by Islamic extremists in 1981 because of his policies toward Israel, and was himself succeeded by Hosni Mubarak, who has been reelected four times. In September 2005, under pressure from pro-democratic movements, Mubarak asked the parliament, which was largely under his personal control, to amend the constitution to allow for multiparty elections. Although that appeared to be a step toward democratic reform, the entire process and most of the news media were under the direct control of President Mubarak. The election, held in September 2005, was transparently unfair; votes were bought, ballot boxes stuffed, and people transported to and from the polls in government vehicles. In addition, the primary opposition candidate, Ayuman Nour, was arrested in January 2005 on trumped-up charges and jailed. In March, under pressure from the United States and other nations, Mubarak freed Nour and allowed him to continue his campaign. Nour's trial, however, was postponed until after the election, forcing him to campaign under a cloud of suspicion. Mubarak was reelected and Nour sentenced to five years in prison in December 2005. Many supporters feared that Nour, who is diabetic, would die in prison.

The major pro-democracy movement is Egypt is called Kifaya, which means "Enough!" Kifaya was born out of committees that formed in Egypt to support the second Palestinian intifada, or "uprising," a violent attack on Israel by the Palestinians, which began in 2000. These groups took to the streets in 2003 to protest the U.S. invasion of Iraq—demonstrations that eventually evolved into anti-Mubarak protests. In 2004, the fear that Mubarak was planning to pass the presidency to his son, Gamal, led to the birth of Kifaya from the original committees. Thanks to a series of effective protests, the organization was successful in forcing Mubarak to hold multiparty elections in 2005. It soon became apparent, however, that the elections were a sham. Although Mubarak did not ban Kifaya, plain-clothed police frequently attacked demonstrators. On September 27, 2005, the day of Mubarak's swearing in as president, Kifaya held a demonstration that attracted more than 5,000 people. A movement called Youth for Change, allied to Kifaya, was formed in 2005 and many college students were active in anti-government protests.

In 2006, Kifaya changed its focus to relations between Egypt and Israel, demanding that Egypt annul its 1979 peace treaty. The change in direction resulted from the United States's support of Israel against the radical Islamic Hezbollah **guerrillas** in Lebanon in July and August 2006.

## CAMEROON

Paul Biya, Cameroon's president since 1982, has been reelected many times, but international observers have questioned the fairness of the elections. Biya, in fact, has been labeled among the world's worst dictators. Not only did he rig elections, but he also paid international observers to assert that they were fair. The major pro-democracy movement opposing Biya is the Social Democratic Front (SDF), founded in 1990. On May 26, 1990, the founders held a rally to formally launch the party. During the rally, which attracted tens of thousands of supporters, troops opened fire and killed seven unarmed civilians; the government claimed that those killed were not shot but trampled by the crowd.

In February 1990, the government arrested several of the party's founders. They were tried on charges of subversion, and three were jailed. When members of the Cameroon Bar Association protested the sentencing, some received death threats; one, Pierre Mbobda, was killed by police under mysterious circumstances.

In 1992, Ni John Fru Ndi was the Social Democratic Front's candidate for the presidency. Many believe that Fru Ndi actually won the presidential election in that year, but Biya is thought to have manipulated the results. He also placed Fru Ndi under house arrest for two months. Opposition parties boycotted elections in 1997 because the government refused to establish an independent election commission. In

2000, the National Assembly created the National Elections Observatory (NEO), which supervised the 2004 election and found it to be generally fair. Biya was reelected. Since 2004, however, there has been considerable censorship of the press by the government.

## CONGO

Mobutu Sese Seko, ruler of the Democratic Republic of the Congo from 1965 until 1997, announced in 1990 that he would allow a three-party system. In response, the banned Union for Social and Democratic Process (UDPS), a reformist party, demonstrated in favor of its leader, Étienne Tshisekedi, but was brutally suppressed by government forces. Tshisekedi himself was hospitalized after an attack by members of the government security service. Two other parties, the Democratic and Social Christian Party (PDSC) and the Congolese National Movement-Lumumba (MNC-Lumumba) were founded. Then, a month after his original announcement, Mobutu rescinded his statement.

Over the next several years, Mobutu alternated between moves toward greater democracy and crackdowns on any form of dissent. In May 1990, government security forces killed as many as 100 protesting students at the University of Lubumbashi. The international outcry prompted Mobutu in December to permit the registration of opposition parties and allow them access to the media. He also convened a constitutional convention in August 1991. The convention, known as the Sovereign National Conference (CNS), hosted more than 2,800 individuals representing 225 organizations. Almost as soon as the conference began, however, Mobutu suspended its activities. Repeatedly, he allowed the group to convene, then prohibited its activities. In 1993, opposition parties, tired of Mobutu's tactics, appointed Faustin Birindwa as the prime minister of a rival organization known as the "government of national salvation." Mobutu did not suppress this rival government and eventually agreed to multiparty elections. The elections never took place, however, and he was overthrown in 1997.

The lack of success of Western-style democracy in Africa has led some scholars to ask if a genuine African democracy may emerge that is different from the Western multiparty system. Yet no one has stepped forward to propose such a system in explicit terms, let alone implement one, and one-party systems continued to predominate across the African continent.

*See also:* Congo; Egypt; Independence Movements; Nigeria; South Africa.

### FURTHER READING

Berman, Bruce. *Ethnicity and Democracy in Africa.* Columbus: Ohio University Press, 2004.

Diamond, Larry, ed. *Democratization in Africa.* Baltimore, MD: Johns Hopkins University Press, 1999.

Reader, John. *Africa: A Biography of the Continent.* New York: Vintage, 1999.

# Drought

An extended period during which there is not enough rainfall to support the needs of a population for drinking water and agricultural production. Southern Africa is particularly susceptible to drought, and countries such as Zimbabwe and Mozambique have often been affected. The Sahel, a band that stretches across the upper third of the continent from Senegal to Ethiopia, has also experienced increasingly severe droughts in recent years. Major droughts in the region occurred in 1972, 1975, 1984, and 1985, with declines in annual rainfall ranging from 20 to 50 percent.

While periods of diminished rainfall occur in many parts of the world, some African nations are particularly hard hit because of poverty and the lack of resources and **infrastructure** needed to cope with disaster. Because of poor soil and poor agricultural methods in many parts of the continent, even in years with enough rain, farmers are not able to produce surplus crops; so when drought does occur, nations quickly run out of food. Even when food arrives, either purchased or donated by international aid agencies, many countries lack efficient methods to transport food to the people who need it most. Warfare also interferes with the delivery of food to a starving population. Corrupt leaders, too, might sell donated food for a profit, lining their own pockets while the people starve.

Even when droughts end, recovery can be slow for African countries. During droughts, oxen and other animals used to plow the fields die, leaving farmers without the means to sow a new crop when the rains finally come. Sometimes people are so close to starvation by the end of the drought that they are too weak to do the heavy work of farming. After years of planting the same crops in the same fields, the soil can become so depleted of minerals that, despite sufficient rainfall, crops still do poorly. In addition, heavy rainfall may simply run off soil that has become hardened after several dry years.

Scientists are still trying to understand the causes of recent droughts in Africa. A 2002 study conducted by Australia's Commonwealth Scientific and Research Organization (CSIRO) suggests that sulphur dioxide from factories in Europe and North America caused cooling in the Northern Hemisphere in the 1970s and 1980s. This cooling, in turn, drove Africa's tropical rain belt south, away from the Sahel. A study published in the journal *Science* in 2003 has tied African droughts to global warming. As the oceans warm, the currents that propel monsoons weaken, causing rain to fall over the ocean instead of over the land where it is needed. El Niño, a warm ocean current that flows southward off the coast of Peru, has also been associated with lower-than-normal rainfall amounts in Africa. As El Niño heats up the water, it causes thunderstorms over the ocean; rain that might have fallen on land now falls into the ocean instead.

Although they have increased in severity in the last decades, droughts in Africa are nothing new. In fact, scientists have discovered evidence of an extensive drought about 70,000 years ago, at about the same time that humans began to migrate out of Africa. It could be that a drought was the cause of the migration of humans that led to the population of the entire globe.

*See also:* Agriculture; Environmental Issues; Famine.

### FURTHER READING

Reader, John. *Africa: A Biography of the Continent.* New York: Vintage, 1999.

# Economic Development and Trade

Despite having been blessed with oil, gold, diamonds, and other valuable natural resources, many parts of Africa today lag behind the rest of the world—and even the rest of the so-called developing world—in economic development. The failure to develop strong economies is partly due to the legacy of colonialism and partly due to the failure of many African nations to develop political systems in which free markets can flourish.

## FACTORS INFLUENCING ECONOMIC DEVELOPMENT

Africa's economic woes stretch as far back as the beginnings of the slave trade in the late 1500s. Although the trade was profitable for some African middlemen, large portions of West Africa lost generations of young, healthy people, leaving families and whole ethnic groups devastated. Some West African economies that were based on the slave trade collapsed when the trade was outlawed by the British in 1807.

In large measure, the Industrial Revolution bypassed Africa. European nations colonized Africa in the nineteenth century to take raw materials to turn into finished products at home, but those nations did not bring the benefits of new technology to Africa. In places like South Africa, colonists built roads and railroads, hospitals, and schools. However, in many other parts of the continent, Europeans left little in the way of **infrastructure** when their colonies became independent. Even in places where there were railroads, roads, and other modern amenities, the abrupt departure of Europeans often meant that there was neither the expertise nor the money to maintain what had been built; much fell into disrepair.

An additional factor in Africa's failure to develop thriving economies has been civil unrest, another legacy of colonialism. European nations, when they drew boundaries for their African colonies in the nineteenth century, ignored ancient hatreds and alliances. When the colonies became independent, there was little sense of nationhood to hold all the various ethnic groups together, leading, in many cases, to sustained warfare. Constant fighting made it impossible to develop functioning economies and resulted in the destruction of what infrastructure there was.

The newfound power that came with independence led to many corrupt dictatorships. In the late twentieth century, leaders such as Idi Amin of Uganda and Mobutu Sese Seko of Zaire (now Democratic Republic of Congo) became rich at the expense of the population. Sustainable economic development—the growth of manufacturing and financial sectors—was ignored while leaders plundered the natural resources for their own ends. Moreover, African nations such as Ghana developed **socialist** economies in which the state owned the vast majority of banks, utilities, and industries. As a direct result, economies in these nations saw slow growth. Beginning in the 1980s, some African countries began to move toward private ownership of businesses and industries, but many have not made the change, including numerous countries in sub-Saharan Africa. Zambia and Nigeria both embarked on experiments with privatization, with some success.

## AFTER INDEPENDENCE

The end of colonialism came at a time of economic prosperity for most of Africa. Rebuilding after World War II required all the raw materials (such as wood, rubber, copper, and other metals) that Africa could provide, and the economy boomed until the early 1970s. At the same time that African nations provided raw materials for Europe and the United States, they also borrowed heavily in order to develop the infrastructure to sustain economic growth. Over time, however, the foreign debt of these nations became a serious financial burden that hurt their economies.

The 1970s, however, saw a tremendous decline in the economies of many African

ECONOMIC DEVELOPMENT AND TRADE | 51

## GROSS DOMESTIC PRODUCT OF AFRICAN COUNTRIES

Africa is the world's poorest continent, with few of its nations having a gross domestic product (GDP) near the world average. South Africa, the most industrialized nation in Africa, is also the wealthiest nation on the continent. The nations of North Africa draw wealth from oil, with Libya being the wealthiest nation in that region. The poorest country on the continent is São Tomé and Príncipe.

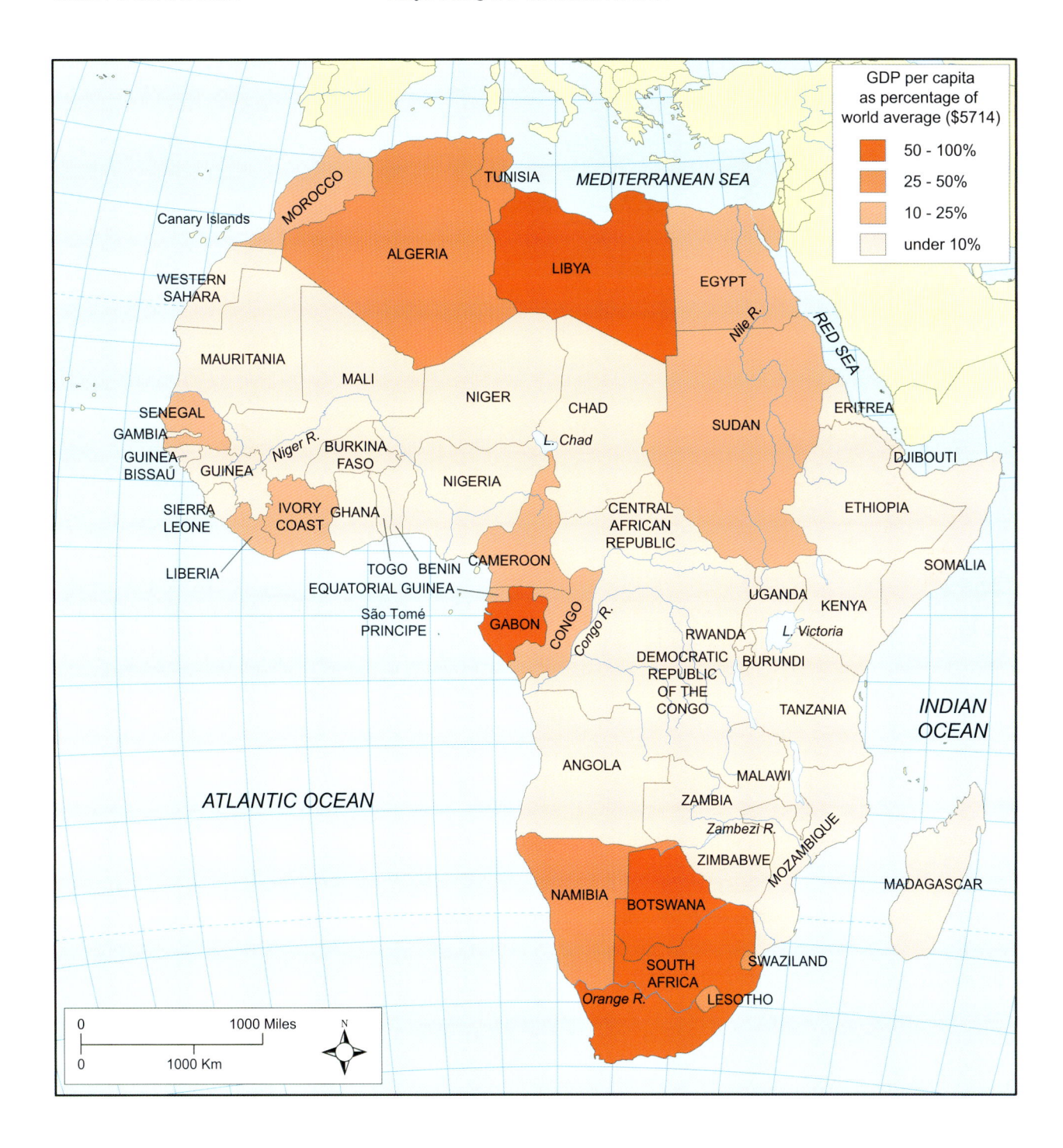

GDP per capita as percentage of world average ($5714)
- 50 - 100%
- 25 - 50%
- 10 - 25%
- under 10%

The township of Soweto was once a symbol of South Africa's apartheid past. It is now a bustling neighborhood and home to Maponya Mall, one of South Africa's largest shopping malls. (Alexander Joe/AFP/Getty Images)

countries because of a worldwide economic decline and rising oil prices. These developments, coupled with corruption and political instability in many nations, created serious economic problems. Debts incurred in the 1960s became a heavy burden in the 1970s as the economy slowed down. The World Economic Forum reported in 1970 that 10 percent of all the world's poor people lived in Africa; by 2000, the same organization reported that fully half of all poor people lived in Africa.

There are sharp regional variations in the African economy. South Africa has long enjoyed Africa's strongest economy with the highest **gross domestic product (GDP)** of any nation on the continent. Zimbabwe has the worst performing economy, with a GDP less than one-tenth of South Africa's. North Africa, particularly those nations on the Mediterranean, tends to be richer and have more stable economies than Africa south of the Sahara, which is among the poorest regions in the world.

## MAJOR ECONOMIC SECTORS

Three major economic sectors influence the economy of Africa: agriculture, mining and drilling, and manufacturing.

### Agriculture

More than half of all workers in Africa are farmers, and more than half of those are subsistence farmers, who grow just enough to feed themselves and their families. Most of the rest of Africa's farmers work on huge mechanized farms—operated by corporations and covering thousands of acres. These farms produce cash crops—such as coffee, cotton, cocoa, and rubber—that are exported to Europe, Asia, and America. Thus, much of Africa's land that is suitable for farming is not used to grow foodstuffs for **domestic** consumption, leaving many African nations without safe surpluses. When there are droughts or other difficulties that interfere with food production or transportation, many Africans starve. In a 2007 drought in Malawi, for example, nearly 4 million people were at risk of starvation.

## Mining and Drilling

Much of Africa's wealth is in minerals—including precious materials such as gold and diamonds—and oil. These commodities, however, are not equally distributed across the continent. Much of Africa's mineral wealth is located in the south, while Nigeria and Libya have large oil reserves. The mining and oil industries employ only a small proportion of Africa's population and tend to profit either large corporations or governments. Individual Africans seldom see any benefit from this wealth, and many regard it as a curse, since wars have been fought over nothing more than who owns the rights to certain minerals.

## Manufacturing

The economies of most prosperous nations depend on manufacturing. Industries bring employment, and the export of manufactured goods brings wealth. Africa, as the world's least industrialized continent, must depend on the export of nonmanufactured commodities such as coffee and gold for its wealth. Unfortunately, this dependence on commodities leaves Africa's markets vulnerable to price fluctuations, which can lead to huge losses and all the problems that accompany market downturns, such as mounting debt and widespread poverty. Despite the fact that Africa has plenty of inexpensive labor, only about 15 percent of all its workers are employed in industrial jobs. According to the 2003 United Nations Conference on Trade and Development, Africa's only important manufactured export items are undergarments, and those account for only about 1.7 percent of the continent's total exports. Moreover, two countries alone, Mauritius and Swaziland, account for about 85 percent of the total export of this product.

## ROADBLOCKS TO DEVELOPMENT

There are several major reasons for the failure of African nations to develop a profitable manufacturing sector. Many African governments limit foreign investment, causing large international companies to look to Asia, rather than Africa, to build manufacturing plants. African governments also tend to maintain strict control over industries, further discouraging investment. Political stability, reliable sources of electrical power, and an educated workforce are also lacking in large parts of Africa.

From ancient times to the present, strong economies have also been built on trade—the ability to move goods from one part of a continent to another. Africa's ability to trade is limited by its geography. Several barriers make it difficult to transport goods easily from one part of the continent to another, including a nearly impenetrable rainforest that covers much of the center of the continent, and Africa's two deserts—the Kalahari in the south and the Sahara in the north. Although there are great river systems in Africa—including the Nile, the Niger, the Congo, and the Zambezi—they do not link the entire continent as do rivers in Europe or Asia, and many are not easily navigable. Moreover, Africa is home to more landlocked nations—those with no access to the sea—than any other continent, making trade with the rest of the world difficult.

Another factor inhibiting economic growth in Africa is disease—tropical diseases like malaria as well as the modern scourge of AIDS. AIDS has reached epidemic proportions in parts of Africa, and it often kills young people, the very population that constitutes the labor force in most countries. Money spent to treat AIDS patients, as well as the victims of other diseases, creates an economic burden for governments that are already struggling.

## RECENT DEVELOPMENTS AND FUTURE DIRECTIONS

In 2007, the United Nations Economic Commission for Africa reported that the continent's overall GDP grew by 5.7 percent, an increase of 0.4 percent over 2006. Over the previous seven years, real GDP growth averaged 4.5 percent per year. While the GDP is slowly inching upward, this rate of progress is much too slow to reduce poverty or to reach the United Nation's Millennium Development Goals, a set of eight targets established to help end poverty and its attendant ills by the year 2015. The goals are to:

- eradicate extreme poverty and hunger
- achieve universal primary education
- promote gender equality and empower women
- reduce child mortality
- improve maternal health
- combat HIV/AIDS, malaria, and other diseases
- ensure environmental sustainability
- develop a global partnership for development

Most economists believe that conditions in Africa will improve only if two major shifts occur. The first is diversification. Africa must develop a manufacturing sector and begin to export manufactured products, as opposed to raw materials. Only by adopting this fundamental strategy can Africa expect the kind of growth that many Asian markets have seen in recent years. To encourage manufacturing, African nations must have political stability to encourage foreign investment, must invest in research and development, and must build or rebuild infrastructure to support a manufacturing sector.

The African Union (AU), successor to the Organization of African Unity (OAU), currently has economic growth at the center of its agenda. Its goals, which are modeled after those of the European Union (EU), include developing a common currency for all of Africa, as well as a common market and a central bank.

Africa today is poised for economic growth and development. There is a great deal of work to be done, but Africa is a continent with tremendous potential for the future.

*See also:* African Union; Agriculture; Colonization; Drought; Famine; South Africa; Slavery and Slave Trade.

### FURTHER READING

Arnold, James R., and Roberta Weiner. *Robert Mugabe's Zimbabwe*. Minneapolis: Lerner Books, 2007.

Lawrence, Peter, and Colin Thirtle, eds. *Africa and Asia in Comparative Economic Perspective*. New York: Palgrave Macmillan, 2001.

Panford, Martin Kwamina, ed. *Africa's Development in the Twenty-first Century: Pertinent Socioeconomic and Development Issues*. London: Ashgate, 2006.

Shah, Anup. *Helping Africa Help Itself: A Global Effort*. Broomall, PA: Mason Crest, 2006.

Underwood, Deborah. *Exploring Africa*. Portsmouth, NH: Heinemann, 2006.

# Egypt

Located on the Mediterranean coast of northeastern Africa, the second most populous country on the continent and the most populous country in the Arab world. The vast majority of Egypt's people live in Cairo and Alexandria and along the Nile Delta, making this region among the most densely populated in the world.

**A modern resort hotel, complete with swimming pool, and other contemporary buildings offer a vivid contrast to the ancient pyramids at Giza, Egypt.** (Will & Deni McIntyre/Stone/Getty Images)

In 1798, the French general Napoleon Bonaparte invaded Egypt and defeated the ruling Ottoman Turks at the Battle of the Pyramids. The British, fearing that Bonaparte would use his foothold in Egypt to interfere with their trade with India, helped the Turks defeat the French in 1801. In 1805, an Albanian commander of Turkish troops, Muhammad Ali, proclaimed himself pasha, or governor, of Egypt, and in 1807 he drove the British from Egypt. He ruled Egypt until 1848 and founded the dynasty that ended with King Farouk I (1936–1952).

Muhammad Ali Pasha is credited with beginning the modernization and, to some extent, the Westernization of Egypt. During the reign of one of his successors, Ismail (r. 1863–1879), the Suez Canal was built. So expensive was the construction, however, that in 1875 Ismail was forced to sell his shares in the Suez Canal Company to Great Britain, giving that nation controlling interest in the canal. Britain's growing influence in Egypt led to a nationalist revolt, which the British put down at the Battle of Tel-El-Kebir in 1882. From this point, Britain essentially ruled Egypt. It was never officially made a colony and Egyptian kings continued to rule, but as puppets of the British government. Even after Egypt gained full independence in 1922, Britain continued to play an important role in its political life.

In 1952, army Lieutenant Colonel Gamal Abdel Nasser and a group of military men who called themselves the "free officers" overthrew Egypt's King Farouk. Egypt was declared a **republic** in 1953; Nasser became prime minister in 1954 and president in 1956. Nasser **nationalized** the Egyptian economy and took steps to distribute land more equitably to peasants.

In 1956, Nasser precipitated what came to be known as the "Suez Crisis" when he nationalized the canal. Israel, France, and Great Britain began military operations on October 29 to retake the canal, which they accomplished in a matter of days. At the outbreak of hostilities, Lester Pearson (who would later become prime minister of Canada) appealed to the United Nations (UN) to send a force to keep the peace while a solution could be worked out. Israeli,

## GREAT LIVES

### Muhammad Ali Pasha

Muhammad Ali Pasha is often cited as the founder of modern Egypt. Beginning in 1805, he and his descendants ruled that nation for almost 150 years and oversaw many aspects of Egypt's modernization.

Muhammad Ali was born in 1769 in Kavala, a seaport on the Aegean Sea, in what is now Greece, but which at the time was part of the Ottoman Empire. As a young man Ali worked as a tobacco merchant before joining the Ottoman Army. It was as a member of this army that Ali first came to Egypt, in 1801, as part of the British and Turkish force that drove the last of Napoleon's occupying force from their stronghold in Cairo.

Ali stayed in Egypt and in 1805 proclaimed himself pasha, or governor. He knew that to consolidate his power, he would have to take on the Mamluks, the ruthless ruling **elite** who owned most of Egypt's land. In 1807, the British, supporters of the Mamluks, launched an attack on Ali, whose 5,000 well-trained Albanian soldiers defeated the British soundly. In 1808, Ali seized all of Egypt. The Mamluks, though weakened, were not yet defeated. In 1811, Ali invited 500 Mamluk leaders to join a military procession at his citadel in Cairo. As the procession ended, Ali had the gates of the citadel closed, trapping the Mamluks inside. His army began firing and killed all but one of the Mamluk leaders.

One of Ali's great legacies is Egypt's cotton crop. Today, Egyptian cotton is regarded as among the best grades of cotton in the world. It was Ali who ordered the Egyptian peasantry to grow the crop, which made a vital contribution to the growth of the economy. He also created an efficient government **bureaucracy** and encouraged European visitors to come to Egypt.

In addition, Ali established a modern military force of well-trained and disciplined fighters. With this force and the help of his son Ibrahim, in 1839 Ali set out to conquer the Ottoman Empire. Eventually the British intervened on behalf of the Turks and Ali's army was defeated in Beirut. In the Treaty of London of 1841, Ali agreed to limit the size of his army and to give up his navy entirely; in return, he and his descendants were granted hereditary rule over Egypt.

Ali grew senile and was deposed by his son in 1848. He died the next year.

---

French, and British forces eventually withdrew, leaving Egypt in possession of the canal.

Nasser opposed the existence of Israel, and in the late 1960s, he formed an alliance of Arab states surrounding Israel and began to prepare for war. Israel did not wait to be attacked but instead invaded and captured the Sinai Peninsula and the Gaza Strip from Egypt, as well as additional territory in Syria and Jordan during the 1967 Six-Day War. This defeat of several Arab armies by the tiny state of Israel was a tremendous blow to Nasser personally and to the Arab world in general.

Nasser headed Egypt until his death in 1970. He was succeeded by his vice president and fellow "free officer" Anwar Sadat. Sadat began what is known as the Yom Kippur War when Egypt attacked Israel on Yom Kippur in 1973, the holiest day of the Jewish year. Sadat eventually

## GREAT LIVES

### Gamal Abdel Nasser

Gamal Abdel Nasser, Egypt's president from 1956 to 1970, was born in Alexandria, Egypt, in 1918, the son of a postal clerk. He was educated at the Royal Military Academy in Sandhurst, England, graduating in 1939. When Egypt joined several other Arab nations in the Arab-Israeli war of 1948, Nasser served as a major in the Egyptian army. In 1949, he joined the "free officers," a revolutionary group that was planning to overthrow the Egyptian royal family.

In 1952, Nasser and the "free officers" staged a coup that deposed King Farouk. Nasser played a behind-the-scenes role as an adviser to the new government until he was officially elected president in 1956.

As president, Nasser introduced an economic system he called "Arab socialism." He took over the holdings of wealthy landowners and redistributed the land to poor farmers, limiting how much any individual could own. Nasser also nationalized banks and industries. In 1956, when the United States and Britain refused to finance the construction of the Aswan High Dam to harness the power of the Nile River, Nasser nationalized the Suez Canal with the intention of using the tolls to finance construction of the dam. This action led to an invasion by Israeli, French, and British forces, who wanted to protect their interests in the region and their access via the canal to India and China. Worried about the consequences of a wider war, the United Nations intervened and forced the foreign troops to withdraw. Not only did Egypt keep the canal, but Nasser managed to get money from the Soviet Union to build the dam.

Nasser became a powerful force the Arab world. In 1958, Egypt and Syria formed the United Arab Republic (UAR) with Nasser as president. He hoped that all Arab nations would eventually join the UAR, but that wish was never fulfilled. In fact, in 1961, Syria itself withdrew.

After the humiliating defeat of Arab forces by the Israeli military during the Six-Day War in 1967, Nasser publicly offered to resign as president, but the Egyptian people made it clear in a number of large demonstrations that they wanted him to stay in office. He did so, until his death of a heart attack in 1970.

changed his policies from confrontation to negotiation, partly in order to ensure a "peace dividend" for Egypt—the economic growth that can come from political stability. He made a historic visit to the Israeli capital of Jerusalem in 1977, and while he was there addressed the Israeli parliament, known as the Knesset. Sadat also accepted U.S. president Jimmy Carter's invitation to join him and Israeli prime minister Menachem Begin in peace talks. The three leaders negotiated the Camp David Accords, which were signed in 1978. These accords led to the Egypt-Israeli peace treaty, which allowed Egypt to regain control of the Sinai Peninsula in 1982. Although Sadat made peace with Israel and gained the United States as an important ally, he made many enemies in the Arab world. His diplomatic efforts were opposed by other Arab states, who felt he was betraying them.

Sadat instituted many reforms during his time as president, including the *infitah* or "open door" policy, which allowed private investment in the Egyptian economy. He restored due process to the legal system and banned torture. In the late 1970s, Egypt was wracked by sectarian violence, which resulted in Sadat's assassination by Islamic extremists on October 6, 1981.

Sadat was succeeded by Hosni Mubarak, an air force commander who had been vice president since 1975. Mubarak has been continually reelected since 1975. The political process in Egypt, said to be democratic, is marred by repression and strict limitations on political parties. Although Mubarak was reelected in 2005, for example, he was the only candidate. During Mubarak's tenure, Egypt has maintained peaceful relations with Israel while emerging as a leading force in the Arab world. Mubarak has continued Sadat's process of economic reform and has succeeded in expanding the private-sector economy by promoting foreign investment.

***See also:*** British Colonies; Civil Wars; Colonization; Economic Development and Trade; Independence Movements.

### FURTHER READING

Asante, Molefi Kete. *Culture and Customs of Egypt.* Westport, CT: Greenwood Press, 2002.

Goldschmidt, Arthur. *Modern Egypt: The Formation of a Nation State.* Boulder, CO: Westview Press, 2004.

Hobbs, Joseph J. *Egypt.* New York: Chelsea House, 2007.

Perry, Glenn E. *The History of Egypt.* Westport, CT: Greenwood Press, 2004.

# Environmental Issues

Problems with water quantity and quality, pollutants and pesticides, land use, and diseases that plague the African continent. While northern and sub-Saharan Africa share many of the same environmental issues, there are significant differences as well.

### SUB-SAHARAN AFRICA

The forty-seven nations of sub-Saharan Africa face a variety of serious environmental issues, including air and water pollution, deforestation, soil erosion and diminished soil fertility, disease brought on by environmental factors, and decline in biodiversity. Diseases caused by environmental factors include respiratory illnesses due to pollution, pesticide poisoning, and malaria, whose increase is caused by a warming climate. Rapid population growth makes many of these problems worse, and extreme poverty leaves governments unable to deal with them effectively. As nations attempt to improve economic production, they often do so at the expense of the environment.

Although sub-Saharan Africa does not have major industries, the manufacturing that does exist is centered in urban areas where the population is growing rapidly. Because industrial emissions are not regulated by the government in most African nations, large numbers of people are increasingly exposed to toxic wastes. Moreover, many industrialized countries such as the United States send their own toxic wastes to Africa for disposal, making the problem even more severe. African countries accept this waste because there is money to be made—even at the expense of a healthy populace.

In crowded cities, such as Cairo, Lagos, and Kinshasa, air pollution results not just from industrial emissions but also from

ENVIRONMENTAL ISSUES | 59

## CLIMATE MAP OF AFRICA

Africa is a continent of contrasts. It has the largest desert in the world, as well as the largest tropical area, including rain forests. Most areas have either too much or too little rainfall, which means that only a very small part of the continent is suitable for agriculture.

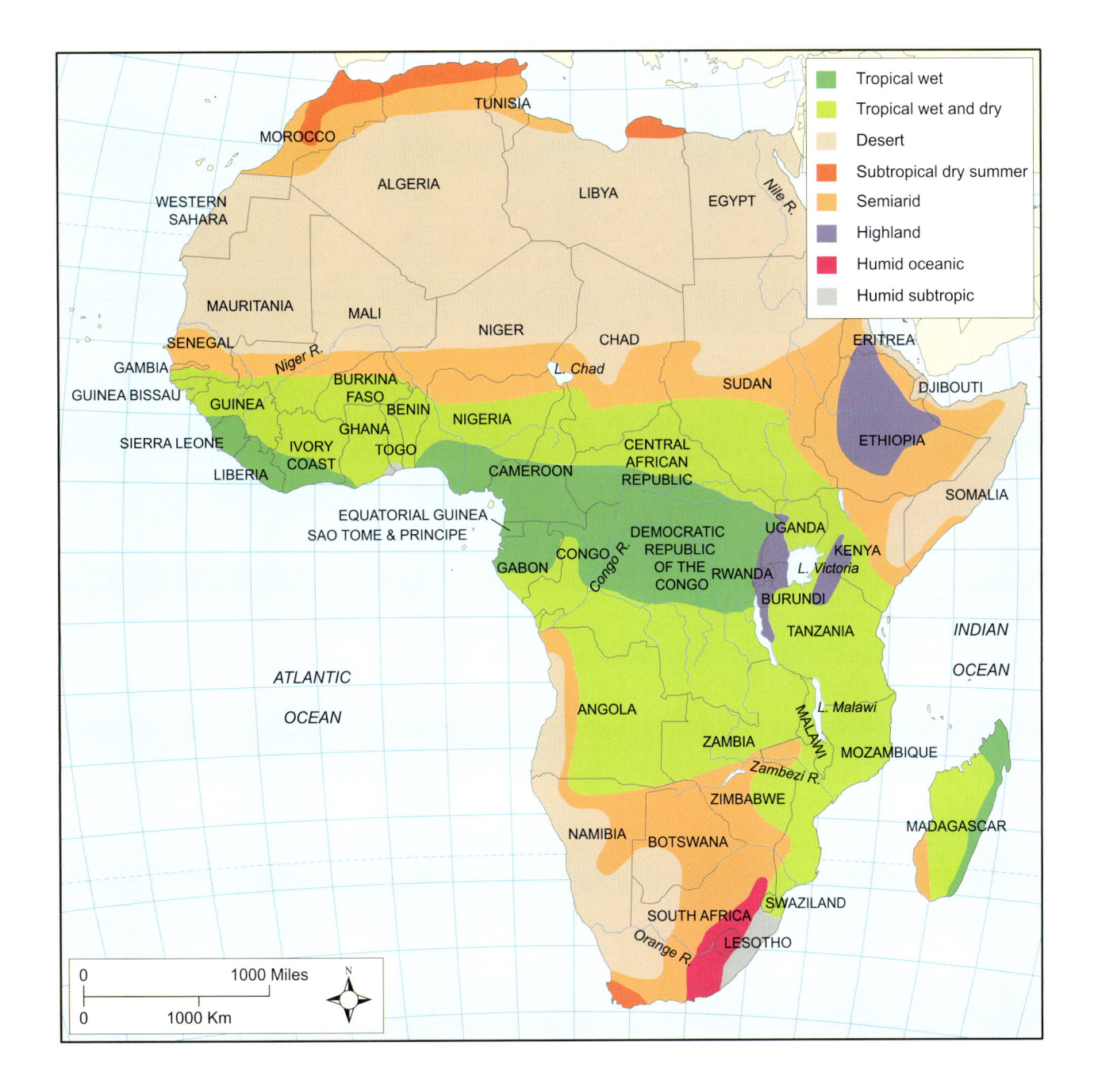

Legend:
- Tropical wet
- Tropical wet and dry
- Desert
- Subtropical dry summer
- Semiarid
- Highland
- Humid oceanic
- Humid subtropic

automobile exhaust. Cars are seldom inspected and use leaded gasoline, leading to heavy concentrations of toxic lead in the air.

Much of Africa's air pollution derives not from industrial sources but from the burning of fossil fuels. As many as 95 percent of households in sub-Saharan Africa burn

**Poaching is a major environmental threat in many African nations. Tanzanian park rangers confiscate the ivory tusks, worth thousands of dollars, from the remains of an elephant killed by poachers.** (Tom Stoddart Collection/Hulton Archive/Getty Images)

wood, charcoal, dung, grass, or crop residues to cook and provide heat and light. Breathing in smoke—which contains carbon monoxide, nitrogen oxides, formaldehyde, benzine, and hydrocarbons—in enclosed spaces causes severe respiratory illnesses, especially in children. Pneumonia is a frequent cause of death among the very young. As trees are cut for fuel, Africa's woodlands disappear, leaving deserts where once there were lush forests. The Sahara is getting larger every year while rivers and lakes such as the Nile River, Lake Victoria, and Lake Chad are gradually drying up.

Mining and oil production are also major sources of pollution in sub-Saharan Africa. Oil spills in seaports and from pipelines pollute surrounding sources of water, compromising water quality and leading to loss of natural habitats for plants and animals. Failure to regulate mining has also led to toxic wastes, such as arsenic, lead, and sulphuric acid, leaching into water and soil. As ore is removed from the rock in which it is embedded, the dust that results often contains multiple toxins. If the dust and debris are not properly managed, they can get into the water supply.

Most people in sub-Saharan Africa earn their subsistence through agriculture. In some areas, modern farming practices have improved production but at the same time have caused a number of environmental problems as farmers use increasing amounts of chemical fertilizers and pesticides. Lack of careful handling of pesticides has led to large-scale poisoning, affecting as many as 11 million people a year. As recently as 2005, empty pesticide cans were used to store water in Nigeria, leading to a number of deaths. In some areas, pesticides have been kept in nylon bags, which leak when wet, contaminating both soil and water.

As more land is cleared to feed a growing population, valuable forests, wetlands, and woodlands are disappearing at an alarming rate. As Africa's population grows, further demands are placed on the land, and overfarming and overgrazing damage topsoil. These factors have led to the rapid **desertification** of much of Africa's farmland. Whole populations of animals, many of which exist nowhere else in the world, are increasingly threatened by the destruction of natural habitats. Even traditional farming methods create problems. Since traditional farmers do not rotate crops, the soil may become rapidly depleted of nutrients and no longer usable for agriculture.

Throughout sub-Saharan Africa, water supplies are undrinkable, contaminated by sewage, pesticides, heavy metals, and industrial wastes. In some nations, less than 20 percent of the population has access to safe drinking water. Though Africa is home to many great rivers, getting water to the people who need it is often difficult. Water projects, such as dams and irrigation systems, if not properly planned and managed, sometimes create more problems than they solve. Dams actually diminish total water supply because silt builds up in reservoirs and water evaporates more rapidly from reservoirs than from freely flowing bodies of water. Standing water becomes a breeding ground for malaria-carrying mosquitoes.

In cities, garbage and human waste are not properly disposed of. Many public spaces are clogged with solid wastes, which attract disease-carrying insects and rodents. Waste is often dumped along waterways. Toxins leach into the water supply, causing diseases such as cholera and dysentery. Children often play in precisely the locations where waste accumulates.

## NORTH AFRICA

The environmental issues facing northern Africa are similar to those of the Middle East. Land suitable for agriculture is rapidly diminishing, especially in southern regions. Less than 6 percent of the region's total land area can now be used for farming. Drought and wind, as well as poor land management, including deforestation and failure to rotate crops, are the root causes of the problem.

Water is also scarce in many parts of North Africa. Countries such as Morocco, Egypt, and Algeria use 80 percent of all the rainwater that falls on their lands, in contrast with South America, sub-Saharan Africa, and the Caribbean, which use only 2 percent. This means that as populations grow, water scarcity will reach crisis levels. More than 85 percent of all water in the north is used for agricultural purposes, with only 7 percent reserved for **domestic** use. Water quality is also an issue in the north for many of the same reasons as in the south, including pesticide and fertilizer runoff. The Aswan High Dam, built to allow for more efficient irrigation of land along the Nile River and to harness **hydroelectric power**, has brought many benefits to the area, but it has also created problems of water quality and scarcity. Standing water breeds mosquitoes and also leads to increased evaporation and accumulation of silt at the bottom of Lake Nasser (an artificial lake created when the dam was built), diminishing the water supply.

There are also serious problems with pollution and coastal erosion along the Mediterranean Coast. As much as 38 percent of Africa's northern coast is under a high degree of threat from development. Coastal populations are growing rapidly and industrial and human wastes are polluting coastal waters. The effects on the marine fishing industry have been profound, leading to significant decreases in the number of fish caught each year. Fishery experts, for example, predict that it may already be too late to save the Mediterranean bluefin tuna from extinction.

Africa's environmental problems remain overwhelming. They will be very difficult to solve without international intervention and substantial infusions of money.

*See also:* Agriculture; Algeria; Aswan High Dam; Drought; Egypt.

### FURTHER READING

Hillstrom, Kevin. *Africa and the Middle East: A Continental Overview of Environmental Issues.* Oxford, UK: ABC-CLIO, 2003.

Reader, John. *Africa: A Biography of the Continent.* New York: Vintage, 1999.

# Eritrea

A country situated in the northern part of the Horn of Africa, bordered by Sudan on the west, Djibouti on the southeast, Ethiopia on the South, and the Red Sea on the east. Once a province of Ethiopia, Eritrea became a colony under Italian rule beginning in 1890 and an independent nation on 1993. Thus, Eritrea is the first African state to successfully split off from an independent African country.

In the Scramble for Africa—the desperate efforts of European countries between 1880 and the beginning of World War I to colonize and exploit Africa's natural resources—Italy had its eye on the northern portion of Ethiopia because of its strategic access to the Red Sea. In 1885, the Italian government bought the holdings of a shipping company at the port of Asseb. In 1889, the Treaty of Wuchale (also known as the Treaty of Uccaile) gave Italy **sovereignty** over parts of Eritrea, after which Italy consolidated and expanded its control over the area. In 1896, Italian forces launched their disastrous invasion of Ethiopia from Eritrea. The Ethiopian army won a stunning victory over the Italian troops.

In 1941, during World War II, the British seized control of Eritrea and then administered it as a United Nations (UN) Trust Territory until 1952. After the war, the UN ignored the Eritrean people's wish for independence and created a **federation**, joining Eritrea to Ethiopia in 1952. Under the UN plan, Eritrea was to have its own parliament, representation in the Ethiopian legislature, and a measure of independence. Nevertheless, Ethiopian emperor Haile Selassie almost immediately set about to undermine the spirit of the agreement by putting his own relatives into positions of leadership in Eritrea, banning political parties and limiting freedom of the press. In 1961, Selassie closed the Eritrean Parliament, ending any pretense of adhering to the UN plan. On November 14, 1962, Salassie declared Eritrea the fourteenth province of Ethiopia.

Selassie's actions led to the formation of the Eritrean Liberation Front (ELF), a grassroots opposition movement that began to harass Ethiopian troops in a **guerrilla**-style war. In 1970, the ELF split into two factions—the Eritrean Liberation Front and the Eritrean People's Liberation Front (EPLF). Both groups claimed to advocate Marxist policies and were dedicated to liberating Eritrea from Ethiopia. After a bitter civil war between the ELF and the EPLF in the early 1980s, the latter became the dominant force in the resistance. After nearly thirty years of warfare, Eritrea expelled Ethiopian forces from the region in 1991. Casualties of the war were very high. By some estimates, 60,000 people were killed, another 60,000 were badly injured, and 50,000 children were left without parents. In a UN-supervised **referendum** in 1993, more than 99 percent of the people of Eritrea voted for independence, which was declared on May 24, 1993.

Isaias Afwewerki, former secretary general of the EPLF, was elected Eritrea's first president. Eritrea's proposed constitution has never been implemented, however, because of the continued unrest in the country. No other elections have been held since 1993, and the EPLF remains the only legal political party.

Peace for Eritrea was short-lived. A bloody border war with Ethiopia broke out in 1998 and continued for two years, until the United Nations brokered a peace agreement. The disputed border is still patrolled by UN peacekeeping troops today.

Eritrea's economy is primarily agricultural and its people are poor. The country has frequently been afflicted by drought, as have other countries on the so-called Horn of Africa. Eritrea is home to people of many ethnic backgrounds and languages, including Afar, Arabic, Tigre, Kunama, and Tigrinya; most are from the Semitic and Cushitic language families. About half the population is Muslim, and the other half is Christian. Most of the Muslim population belongs to the Sunni sect. Eritrea recognizes four official religions: the Eritrean Orthodox Tewahdo Church, Sunni Islam, Catholicism, and Lutheranism. Members of other religions are not free to practice their faith. In fact, the U.S. State Department has labeled Eritrea as one of the worst violators of religions freedom in the world.

Eritrea's greatest challenges are rebuilding the **infrastructure** destroyed by the years of war and educating its largely illiterate population. Although there is still much to be done, major projects have been completed since the war, including a 500-mile (800-km) coastal highway. The Eritrean Railway has also been rebuilt, an important step in connecting Eritrea's cities for trade and transportation.

***See also:*** Ethiopia; Italian Colonies.

### FURTHER READING

Mengisteab, Kidane. *Anatomy of an African Tragedy: Political, Economic and Foreign Policy Crisis in Post-Independence Eritrea.* Trenton, NJ: Red Sea Press, 2005.

Wrong, Michael. *I Didn't Do It for You: How the World Betrayed a Small African Nation.* New York: Harper, 2000.

# Ethiopia

On the east coast of Africa, country bordered by Eritrea to the north, Sudan to the west, Kenya to the south, and Djibouti and Somalia to the east. Except for a brief occupation by Italy during World War II, Ethiopia is the only East African nation to have escaped foreign rule during the Scramble for Africa—the efforts of European countries between 1880 and the beginning of World War I to colonize and exploit Africa's natural resources. Ethiopia may also be the place where humans first evolved from their humanoid ancestors; bones found in eastern Ethiopia date back more than 3 million years. Historically, Ethiopia was also known as Abyssinia.

The first Europeans to visit Ethiopia were the Portuguese in 1493. At the time, Ethiopia was a Christian nation with a large Muslim population. The Portuguese sent missionaries to convert the people to Roman Catholicism, which led to a hundred years of conflict between pro- and anti-Catholic factions. In 1630, Ethiopia expelled all foreign missionaries, beginning a period of isolation that persisted into the nineteenth century.

From the early eighteenth to the middle of the nineteenth century, Ethiopia had no centralized government, and local rulers battled one another for control. Beginning in 1859, the kingdom was consolidated under Emperors Theodore II (r. 1855–1868), Johannes IV (r. 1872–1889), and Menelik II (r. 1889–1913). It was Menelik who resisted Italy's 1896 attempt to conquer Ethiopia and make it a colony. At the Battle of Andow on March 1, 1896, Ethiopia defeated the Italians.

Menelik was succeeded by his grandson Lij Iyassu, who was deposed by the Christian

Haile Selassie, the last emperor of Ethiopia, ruled from 1930 until a 1974 coup. His many titles included "King of Kings," "Conquering Lion of the Tribe of Judah," and "Elect of God." He died in Ethiopia in 1975. (Hulton Archive/Stringer/Getty Images)

majority because of his ties to Islam. The Christian nobility made Menelik's daughter, Zewditu, empress and appointed her cousin, Ras Tafari Makonnen, as regent. When Zewditu died in 1930, her cousin succeeded to the throne as Emperor Haile Selassie, who ruled Ethiopia from 1930 to 1974.

In 1936, Selassie was forced into exile in England when Fascist Italy under Benito Mussolini again invaded Ethiopia. In 1941, British and Ethiopian forces defeated the Italians and Selassie was restored to power.

In 1974, Selassie was deposed by a council of soldiers known as the Derg ("committee"). The new government executed many members of the imperial family along with government ministers. Selassie himself was arrested and died during his captivity, probably murdered by members of the Derg.

Lieutenant Colonel Mengistu Haile Mariam, a leader of the Derg, took over the government in 1977. He was an avowed communist who instituted a **totalitarian** rule and built a huge military force with aid from the Soviet Union and Cuba. He also murdered thousands of suspected enemies of the state in a purge known as the Red Terror.

Throughout the 1980s, Ethiopia was plagued by droughts, famine, rebellion, and attacks by neighboring Somalia. Then, in 1989, rebel forces from the northern regions of Eritrea and Tigray formed the Ethiopian Peoples' Revolutionary Democratic Front

## GREAT LIVES

### Haile Selassie

Haile Selassie was born Tafari Makonnen in 1892 in Harer Province, Ethiopia (then known as Abyssinia). He was a cousin of Emperor Menelik II. Educated by a private European tutor, Tafari proved to be such an adept student that Menelik appointed him governor of the Sidamo province at the age of fourteen.

When Menelik died in 1913, Ras (Prince) Tafari, who was a Coptic Christian, led a movement to depose Menelik's son, who had converted to Islam. Tafari was appointed regent and heir to Menelik's daughter, Zewditu, who ruled as Ethiopia's first empress since the ancient Queen of Sheba. Zewditu died under mysterious circumstances in 1930, and Ras Tafari became emperor, calling himself Haile Selassie, "Power of the Trinity."

Selassie worked hard to modernize Ethiopia, but his efforts were cut short when Italy, led by Fascist dictator Benito Mussolini, invaded of the country in 1935. Selassie fled Ethiopia, which lost its independence for the first time in its history. Taking refuge in Great Britain, Selassie went before the League of Nations in 1936 to plead for help for his country. His charismatic presence and eloquence made him an international celebrity. So powerful did he seem that many Jamaicans began to worship him as the future king of blacks, thus founding a new religion called Rastafarianism. The League of Nations, however, did not come to Selassie's aid.

A joint force of British and Ethiopian soldiers retook Ethiopia in 1941 and restored Selassie to power. During the 1940s and 1950s, Selassie improved the nation's health care, transportation, and education, while also expanding and consolidating his power. In 1960, after the failure of an attempted coup, Selassie took a more conservative view of reform and began to direct his attention to foreign affairs. He was the first African head of state to visit many counties, and he was a leader in the Pan-Africanism movement, which called for African unity. He also helped found the Organization of African Unity (now the African Union), headquartered in the Ethiopian capital of Addis Ababa.

Eritrean rebels began a civil war in 1963 in an attempt to gain independence. In 1977, Somalia attacked Ethiopia in hopes of regaining the Ogaden region in southeastern Ethiopia, formerly Somalian territory. In 1973, a drought led to widespread starvation. All of these factors led to a decline in Selassie's power, and in 1974 the Derg, a committee of military officers, forced him to resign. He was arrested and held in Addis Ababa until his death—widely attributed to murder—in 1975.

(EPRDF) and in May 1991 forced Mengistu to flee to Zimbabwe. In 1993, after nearly thirty years of fighting, Eritrea declared its independence from Ethiopia, leaving Ethiopia country completely landlocked, with Eritrea in control of the entire coastline on the Red Sea.

Under Prime Minister Meles Zenawi, elected in 1995, Ethiopia has developed a federal system of government in which re-

## GREAT LIVES

### Menelik II

Menelik II, emperor of Ethiopia (then known as Abyssinia) from 1889 to 1913, reigned during the Scramble for Africa and was the only African leader to successfully resist a European attempt at colonization.

Menelik was born in 1844 in the city of Ankober in the Shewa Province and served as governor of Shewa before becoming emperor. As emperor, Menelik doubled the territory under his rule and made substantial strides in modernizing Ethiopia. He built bridges, telegraph lines, hotels, hospitals, and schools. He also established Addis Ababa as the nation's capital and created a postal system and a national newspaper.

Italy, which had already colonized Eritrea to the north of Ethiopia, attempted to expand its influence and, in 1889, occupied the town of Adwa in northern Ethiopia. It was there that on March 1, 1896, Menelik and his army defeated the Italians. This was the first time in 2,000 years that an African army had defeated a European one. The last time was in 218 B.C.E. when the Carthaginian general Hannibal crossed the Alps and attacked Rome. Menelik died in 1913 after a long illness.

---

gions and tribal areas have significant power and autonomy.

In 2005, Ethiopia held what appeared to be a free and fair election campaign. Irregularities in the election process, however, resulted in violent protests in June of that year. When the election results were announced, opposition parties called for a boycott of Parliament and civil disobedience. In November, the Ethiopian government arrested many opposition leaders and journalists, and held tens of thousands of civilians in detention camps for months. During protests in June and November, it is estimated that police killed as many as 200 protesters including 40 teenagers.

*See also:* Colonization; Communist Movements; Eritrea; Famine; Italian Colonies.

### FURTHER READING

Gillespie, Carol Ann. *Ethiopia.* New York: Chelsea House, 2002.

Haile, Rebecca G. *Held at a Distance: My Rediscovery of Ethiopia.* Chicago: Academy Chicago, 2007.

Paulos, Milkias. *Haile Selassie, Western Education, and Political Revolution in Ethiopia.* Youngstown, NY: Cambria Press, 2006.

# F-1

## Family Structure  *See* Culture and Traditions.

## Famine

In Africa, famines have occurred throughout history and into modern times. They are especially prevalent in the Horn of Africa, which includes Ethiopia, Somalia, and parts of Sudan. According to a 2007 report by the United Nations Food and Agriculture Organization (FAO), every year nearly half the population of sub-Saharan Africa goes hungry. The report also notes that the region is "worse off nutritionally than it was 30 years ago." In fact, Africa's people are the worst nourished in the world, according to the United Nations.

Although parts of Africa have long fought the effects of famine, during the later quarter of the twentieth century the continent has endured repeated devastating famines, including one that affected Ethiopia in 1984–1985 in which more than a million people died. Other famines and the countries most affected include: 1988, Ethiopia; 1992, Somalia; 1994, Sudan and Ethiopia; 1997, Kenya; 2002–2003, Ethiopia, Eritrea, Somalia, Zimbabwe, and Mozambique, among others. Since the 1980s, millions of people have died in Africa from starvation and associated illnesses.

The causes of famine in Africa are complex. Drought is a major problem in parts of the continent and is a primary culprit in food shortages. Many Africans are **subsistence** farmers, growing barely enough to feed their own families. When a crop fails because of low rainfall, there is no extra food stored away to help the family get through the bad times.

When a food shortage occurs, for whatever reason, African nations may be more devastated than other parts of the world because much donated food never reaches the people who need it most. In some cases, this occurs because of a lack of transportation—keeping food from reaching those who are hungry. In other cases, the reason is political: corrupt leaders may line their own pockets or see to it that people from their own political party get food while the opposition does not. In some instances—notably in Ethiopia in 1984—the government may even sell the donated food in order to buy weapons.

Another problem is mismanagement of land. Many African governments have pressed their people into growing cash crops (such as coffee) instead of food crops, leaving fewer workers and less land dedicated to growing food. The money from cash crops is often used by governments to buy weapons, not to help improve the lives of the people. Most African farmers know little about modern agricultural methods that can lead to greater yields per acre, such as crop rotation. Thus, African farmers suffer from low yields and soils that are depleted of essential nutrients.

AIDS has also contributed to famine in Africa. Most agricultural workers in Africa are women, and women are disproportionately affected by AIDS. About 75 percent of all HIV positive people in Africa are women, leaving fewer people to till the soil.

Famine is an issue of dire importance in Africa in the twenty-first century. There are

Refugees from the Sudanese famine await medical treatment at an emergency health care center. The famine is one result of a long civil war between Sudan's Muslim north and Christian south.
(Eric Feferberg/AFP/Getty Images)

no easy solutions to the problem, and many experts believe that it will only worsen in the coming years.

*See also:* Drought; Eritrea; Ethiopia; Somalia; Sudan.

### FURTHER READING

Reader, John. *Africa: A Biography of the Continent.* New York: Vintage, 1999.

Von Braun, Joachim. *Famine in Africa: Causes, Responses, and Prevention.* Washington, DC: International Food Policy Research Institute, 2000.

# French West Africa

A confederation of eight French colonies in West Africa. French West Africa was originally created in 1895 as an administrative entity and included the colonies of Senegal, Sudan, Guinea, and the Cote d'Ivoire. Later Benin, Mali, Niger, and Burkina Faso were added to the **federation**.

# FRENCH WEST AFRICA

**FRENCH COLONIES IN AFRICA IN THE EARLY 1900S**

France's African colonies were centered in West Africa. Algeria became a French colony in 1830. Tunisia became a French protectorate in 1881, as did Morocco in 1912. French West Africa was a federation of eight French colonies administered from Dakar, Senegal. Similarly, French Equatorial Africa was comprised of a federation of four French colonies governed from Brazzaville in the French Congo.

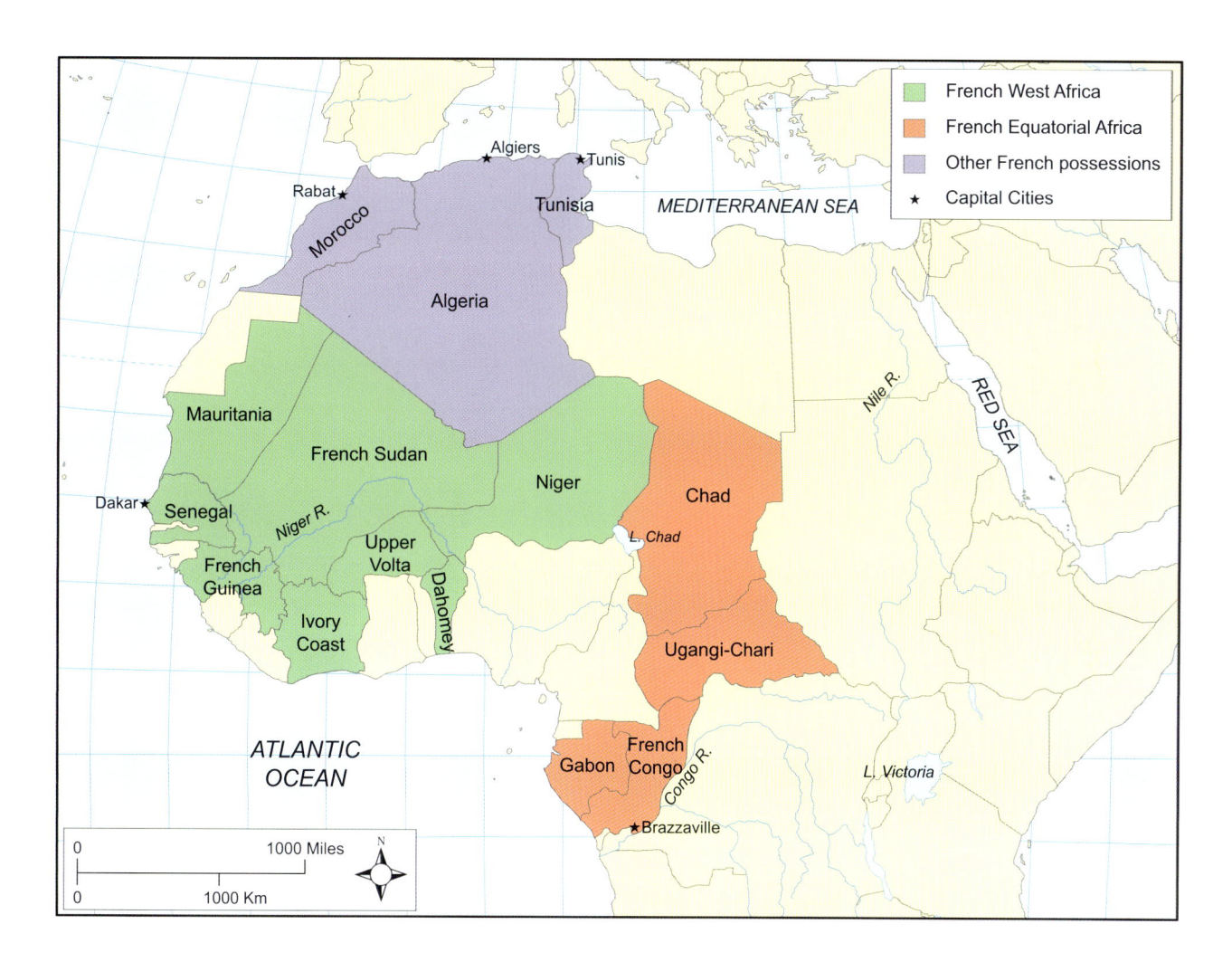

## COLONIZATION

French influence in West Africa began with the founding of the city of Saint Louis in Senegal in 1659. French interest in the area was motivated primarily by economics. Although the French participated in the Atlantic slave trade, they did so to a lesser extent than the British, Dutch, and Portuguese. The French were more interested in agricultural products, such as gum arabic (a sticky substance that had a number of uses including controlling the thickness of ink), groundnuts, and other raw materials.

French attitudes toward native inhabitants differed from those of the British and other European powers, who tended to regard Africans as racially inferior. The French felt strongly that as long as Africans learned the French language and accepted

## GREAT LIVES

### Ahmed Sékou Touré

Ahmed Sékou Touré was born in Faranah, Guinea, in 1922, the son of poor Muslim parents. His education began in the local Koranic school and he attended a technical school in the Guinean capital of Conakry. In 1937, he was expelled after organizing a food riot.

In 1941, Sékou Touré took a position with the French post and telecommunications department and rose to head the Postal Union in 1945. In 1953, Sékou Touré led a successful general strike against the government and was elected to the Territorial Assembly. He continued to seek political office and was elected vice president of the national assembly in 1957. The next year, under Sékou Touré's leadership, Guinea became the only territory in French West Africa to vote for complete independence from France.

Sékou Touré, now the president of Guinea and an avowed Marxist, negotiated aid from the Soviet Union and convinced Kwame Nkrumah of Ghana to lend him £10 million (equivalent to about $35 million.) Sékou Touré's attempt at a socialist economy was a complete failure, however, and in 1978, he abandoned his socialist policies and began to trade with the West. As Guinea's president, Touré restricted political activity and perpetrated a series of human rights abuses.

Touré died in Cleveland, Ohio, in 1984, during heart surgery. At the time of his death, he was still the president of Guinea.

---

French values and culture, they could become French themselves. This was particularly true in the French colony of Algeria, which had representatives in the French government, and to a lesser extent in Senegal. In the early years of the twentieth century, however, the French abandoned this goal in much of the rest of West Africa and made little effort to help the population assimilate. It had become clear that many Africans did not want to abandon their own cultures, languages, and worldviews.

### COLONIAL ADMINISTRATION

Unlike the British, the French used a system of direct rule to administer their colonies. While the British ruled through traditional tribal chiefs, the French brought in their own administrators to safeguard their interests. French West Africa, with a population of more than 15 million by the 1940s, was run by a mere 385 colonial administrators. The governor general, stationed first in Saint Louis and eventually in Dakar, reported to a minister of colonies in Paris. Reporting to the governor were a number of territorial lieutenant governors. These individuals were, in a sense, absolute rulers who had little respect for traditional chiefs, values, or customs. Thus, African culture was weakened more by the French method of direct rule than by the British method of indirect rule, which in many cases preserved traditions and customs.

The French were harsh rulers in West Africa, using a system of forced labor and imprisonment to attain their economic goals. They forcibly moved people to places where their work would best benefit the French economy, regardless of family or tribal ties. In the British colonies, the African "middle class" (those favored and employed by the British to help them rule) benefited to some extent from economic prosperity, but this was not the case in French West Africa. The French did little in West Africa to improve the lives of the native peoples, though they did make some efforts to improve heath care and education.

### INDEPENDENCE

The native people of French West Africa had fought on the side of the French in World War I and World War II, both in Africa and on the European front. After World War II, many Africans began to realize that they did not share in the democracy they had fought so hard to preserve, and many nationalist movements arose. In French West Africa, three major leaders influenced the course of events. In 1946, Félix Houphouët-Boigny of Cote d'Ivoire founded the African Democratic Rally (Rassemblement Démocratique Africain, or RDA), an organization dedicated to helping all African nations achieve independence. In 1960, when Cote d'Ivoire attained independence, Houphouët-Boigny became its first president. He continued lead the nation until his death in 1993.

Léopold Senghor, a French citizen born in Senegal and a poet who taught for many years in France, founded the Bloc Démocratique Sénégalais (Senegalese Democratic Bloc) and was elected Senegal's first president in 1960, serving until 1980. Senghor was one of the originators of the concept of *négritude*, which refers to the consciousness of belonging to the black race. The concept had a major impact on African and African American literary expression.

A third leader to emerge in this era of independence was Ahmed Sékou Touré of Guinea, who had helped Houphouët-Boigny found the RDA. In 1958, the French under Charles de Gaulle sponsored a referendum in which the territories of French West Africa could choose to become to become autonomous **republics** within the French community. Seven of the eight territories voted for the referendum, but Guinea, under Sékou Touré's leadership, did not. A poet like Senghor, Sékou Touré famously told French president de Gaulle, "We prefer poverty in liberty to riches in slavery." Within two years, all of the nations of French West Africa had followed Sékou Touré's lead and gained their independence from France.

*See also:* British Colonies; Colonization; Independence Movements; Sudan.

### FURTHER READING

Bohannon, Paul. *Africa and Africans.* Long Grove, IL: Waveland Press, 1995.

Meredith, Martin. *The Fate of Africa. From the Hopes of Freedom to the Heart of Despair: A History of 50 Years of Independence.* New York: Public Affairs, 2005.

Mitchell, Peter, ed. *Peoples and Cultures of West Africa.* Chelsea House, 2006.

# German Colonies

The territories ruled by the Germans from the 1880s through World War I. After the war, the colonies were granted to the Allied Powers as **protectorates** by the League of Nations. The colonies included German Southwest Africa, now Namibia; German East Africa, now Tanzania, Burundi, and Rwanda; Togo; Kamerun, now Cameroon; and a tiny colony, Wituland, now part of Kenya.

## GERMAN SOUTHWEST AFRICA

Because Germany was not a united nation until the 1870s, it was relatively late in coming to Africa, and its occupation was the shortest of any of the European colonizers. A German merchant, Adolf Lüderitz, founded German Southwest Africa in 1883 when he bought some land along the coast from a native chief. To prevent the British from encroaching on his territory, Lüderitz in 1884 asked the German government for protection. The German flag was raised on the territory that same year. In 1890, the Heligoland-Zanzibar Treaty between Britain and Germany allowed for the growth of the colony through the acquisition of an area called Caprivi (named after a German chancellor who served from 1890 to 1894), which allowed access to the Zambezi River. In the same treaty, the Germans gained Heligoland, an island in the North Sea, and gave up Zanzibar and the tiny colony of Wituland to Great Britain. Ironically, the people of Wituland protested violently when the Germans left. The sultan of Witu had invited the Germans to help him fend off his traditional rival, the sultan of Zanzibar, and the protectorate was established in 1885. Thus, when the Germans left, the people of Wituland felt betrayed.

German West Africa was the only German colony in which large numbers of Germans settled. Many came because of the riches in diamond and copper mining; others came as farmers. By 1914, there were about 12,000 Germans in the colony, along with 80,000 Herero natives, 60,000 Ovambo, and 10,000 Nama—all referred to by the Germans as "Hottentots."

Many of the native groups rose up and tried to drive the Germans from their lands. The largest of these attempts was later referred to as the Herero Wars of 1904. At first, the Herero were successful, destroying German farms and driving settlers away, but the Germans brought in reinforcements and defeated the Herero at the Battle of Waterberg on August 11, 1904. The defeated Herero were herded into the Kalahari Desert, where thousands died of thirst. German troops later found skeletons in holes as deep as 50 feet (15 m), which the Herero had dug in an attempt to find water.

During World War I, South African and German troops fought each other in South West Africa, as the territory was called, and many German settlers were transported to concentration camps in South Africa for the duration of the war. After the war, the League of Nations placed the territory under the protection of the British. The former German colony remained as a British protectorate until it became the independent nation of Namibia in 1990.

## GERMAN EAST AFRICA

In 1885, Germany granted an imperial charter to the Society for German Colonization, an organization founded with the sole purpose of establishing German colonies in East Africa. The sultan of Zanzibar, believing that the territory in question was his, protested. In response, German chancellor Otto von Bismarck sent ships, which arrived in the waters around Zanzibar and directed their cannons at the sultan's palace. As a result, the sultan backed down and in 1886, the British (who already had a consulate in Zanzibar) and the Germans divided the territory in question between them.

Few Germans settled in East Africa. The small number of administrators and soldiers relied on native chiefs to maintain order, collect taxes, and force their people to grow cotton for export. Beginning in about 1905, a spirit medium called Bokero created a "war medicine" of water, castor oil, and millet seeds and told his followers that this medicine would turn German bullets into water. The Swahili word for water is *maji*, and when Bokero and his followers began to attack Germans, their uprising became known as the Maji Maji Rebellion. By the time the rebellion ended in 1907, several hundred Germans and more than 75,000 natives had died.

During World War I a young German general, Paul Emil von Lettow-Vorbeck, with a small force of Germans and 11,000 native forces known as Askaris, successfully fought the 330,000-strong British imperial forces under South African commander Jan Smuts. At the 1914 Battle of Tanga, von Lettow-Vorbeck defeated a British unit that was eight times larger than his own force. Overall, von Lettow-Vorbeck was responsible for more than 60,000 causalities. After hearing that Germany surrendered, von Lettow-Vorbeck agreed to a cease-fire.

The 1919 Treaty of Versailles that ended World War I divided the German colony of East Africa, giving Ruanda-Urundi to Belgium, a small area known as the Kionga Triangle to the Portuguese, and the rest to the British, who called their new colony Tanganyika.

### TOGO AND CAMEROON

In 1884, Germany established a colony on the coast of east-central Africa that they called Kamerun. The German colonialists built railways, roads, bridges, and hospitals in the colony, but they used native forced labor to do the work, creating lasting resentment among the native people.

During World War I, the British invaded the German colony and forced the surrender of the last German fort there in 1916. After the war, Cameroon (now known by its English spelling) was partitioned between Britain and France, and the two resulting areas were referred to as British and French Cameroon, respectively.

In 1884, German chancellor Otto von Bismarck sent Gustav Nachigal to Togo to persuade the local chiefs to accept the protection of the German empire. The chiefs agreed, and by the next year, Togoland was recognized by the European powers as a German colony. Using forced labor as they had in Kamerun, the Germans established rubber, palm oil, cotton, and cocoa plantations. After World War I, Togoland, like Cameroon, was divided between the French and the British. By 1919, Germany had no colonies in Africa.

*See also:* British Colonies; Colonization; French West Africa; Rwanda; South Africa.

### FURTHER READING

Farwell, Byron. *The Great War in Africa, 1914–1918*. New York: Norton, 1989.

Reader, John. *Africa: A Biography of the Continent*. New York: Vintage, 1999.

# Global Warming *See* Environmental Issues.

# Imperialism

The policy of expanding national power by acquiring and controlling territory. In the late nineteenth and early twentieth centuries, the continent of Africa became the main target of European imperialism. Europeans had set up trading posts and small settlements along Africa's coast in the 1400s. European interest in Africa grew, however, after the Europeans discovered the vast resources of the continent's interior.

## MOTIVATIONS

From 1815 until the 1870s, Great Britain was the undisputed economic leader of the world, the only modern industrial power. After 1870, however, Britain found itself confronted by competition from France, Germany, and the United States, as these nations began to build more factories and manufacture more goods. Britain and other European powers began to see captive overseas markets as the solution to their economic challenges. Africa, as the least developed region of the world, became a particular target, though Asia also saw massive colonization efforts.

The economic theory behind imperialism held that developed nations needed to import cheap raw materials to convert into manufactured products. They also needed captive markets to export their manufactured goods to. In addition, wealthy bankers and businesspeople in Europe needed ways to invest their excess capital, or money, and underdeveloped nations in Africa provided the perfect arena.

Imperialism was also politically motivated. Small European countries competed to see who could "own" the largest overseas territory. Britain was the clear winner. By 1921, Britain ruled over 458 million people, about a quarter of the world's population, and a quarter of the total land area of the earth, about 14.2 million square miles (36.8 million sq km). Britain also held more territory in Africa than any other nation.

A belief in the cultural and racial superiority of Europeans over Africans and Asians also motivated imperial expansion. Rudyard Kipling expressed this view in his poem "The White Man's Burden" (1899), telling his readers that they must "take up the White Man's burden," ruling over "new-caught sullen peoples/half-devil and half-child." Many Europeans believed that Africans were, in fact, like children, unable to rule themselves. They also believed that it was imperative that Africans be converted from their **pagan** religions to Christianity. Most Europeans of the late nineteenth and early twentieth century did not see their imperial policies as exploitation; rather, they believed they were "called" to "save" the poor, benighted African people.

Yet another motivation for imperialism was strategic. Britain, in particular, saw its presence in Africa as essential to protecting its interests elsewhere. Britain **annexed** both the Suez Canal in Egypt (1882) and Cape Town in South Africa (1795) in order to protect its ships on their way to its territories in India. Other nations sought access to crucial waterways and seaports. For example, one of the agreements at the Berlin Conference of 1884–1885 was to keep the Congo and Niger river basins neutral and open for river traffic by all interested parties.

## THE SCRAMBLE FOR AFRICA

The Berlin Conference of 1884–1885 began what has been called the Scramble for Africa. At the request of the Portuguese, Otto von Bismarck, chancellor of a newly united Germany, called European powers together to determine how to divide Africa among them without warfare. Attending the conference were Austria-Hungary, Belgium, Denmark, France, the United Kingdom, Italy, the Netherlands, Portugal, Russia, Spain, Sweden-Norway, the Ottoman Empire, and the United States. The conference was a success in that it did outline a plan that saved Europeans from deadly warfare. However, the conference did not protect Africans from being murdered by colonial powers, most notably by Leopold II of Belgium, who held the Belgium Free State as a personal possession and had nearly half the population killed in order to pursue his economic interests. Before the Berlin Conference, Europeans occupied about 10 percent of the continent.

By 1914, virtually the entire continent was ruled by European powers, including Britain, France, Belgium, Portugal, Italy, Spain, and Germany.

### EFFECTS

The effects of imperialism on the people of Africa were devastating. In particular, colonial powers forced Africans to abandon food crops, such as yams and grain, and grow cash crops, such as peanuts, coffee, tea, rubber, cotton, and cocoa, for export. The family farm became a thing of the past, and African laborers, mostly men, left home to work on large plantations. Those who could not or did not farm also left home to find jobs in the brutal and backbreaking mining industries. Ultimately, women were left to grow food crops on their own, and they were often unable to grow enough.

The fact that many men left their homes had a devastating impact on African families and traditional culture. Wealth generated in Africa was exported to Europe and little money was spent to build the **infrastructure** African societies needed to become modern nations themselves. Although some Africans were educated by their **imperialist** rulers in government or missionary schools, many people were left without the needed skills and knowledge to build industrial nations after the colonial powers left. Since Westerners ran the schools, many of those who were educated learned only Western ideas. These young people were taught that their traditional ideas and beliefs were inferior to Western ideas, and this led to further loss of traditional culture.

*See also:* Agriculture; British Colonies; Colonization; Culture and Traditions; French West Africa; German Colonies; Italian Colonies; Portuguese Colonies; Suez Canal.

### FURTHER READING

Mackenzie, John. *The Partition of Africa and European Imperialism, 1800–1900.* New York: Routledge, 2007.

Reader, John. *Africa: A Biography of the Continent.* New York: Vintage, 1999.

Said, Edward. *Culture and Imperialism.* New York: Vintage, reprint, 1994.

# Independence Movements

At the end of World War II, there were only three independent nations in Africa: Liberia, which had been settled by former slaves from the United States and declared its independence in 1847; Ethiopia, which had never been colonized except for a brief occupation by Italy; and Egypt, which had achieved independence from Great Britain in 1922. By 1970, however, Africa had thirty-seven additional independent nations. Namibia, the last nation to gain independence, did so in 1990.

### FACTORS INFLUENCING THE DESIRE FOR INDEPENDENCE

A major influence on African independence movements was Mahatma Gandhi, who led India to freedom from its British colonizers in 1947. Gandhi, who lived in South Africa from 1893 to 1914 and started his method of nonviolent protest there, served as a model for many African nationalists in the 1950s and the 1960s.

Another important influence was the Pan-African Movement, an organization founded toward the end of the nineteenth century with the goal of uniting and uplifting all Africans—no matter where in the world they lived. Many of the delegates to

## INDEPENDENCE MOVEMENTS, 1912–1994

**1912** African National Congress (ANC) founded to fight for equality for Africans in South Africa

**1946** Founding of the African Democratic Rally (Rassemblement Démocratique Africain, or RDA), an independence movement in French West Africa, by Félix Houphouët-Boigny

**1949** Kwame Nkrumah founds the independence-minded Convention People's Party in Gold Coast, later Ghana

**1952** ANC organizes Defiance Campaign to nonviolently protest apartheid laws

**1954** The National Liberation Front (FLN) of Algeria begins attacks on French colonial targets

**1956** Popular Movement for the Liberation of Angola (MPLA) is founded; African Party for the Independence of Guinea and Cape Verde (PAIGC) is founded

**1957** Gold Coast gains independence as the nation of Ghana under the leadership of Nkrumah

**1962** Algeria becomes independent of France; rebel groups seeking independence are founded in Angola (National Liberation Front of Angola, or FNLA), and in Mozambique (Mozambique Liberation Front, or FRELIMO)

**1975** Angola, Mozambique, and Guinea-Bissau win independence from Portugal

**1990** ANC is legalized in South Africa; Namibia granted independence

**1994** First democratic elections in South Africa

---

the 1945 Pan-African Congress were individuals who later led their nations to independence, including Hastings Banda of Malawi, Kwame Nkrumah of Ghana, Obfemi Awolowo of Nigeria, and Jomo Kenyatta of Kenya. The ideals of the Pan-African Movement, including a belief in the basic equality of all humans, led many to become involved in independence movements.

World War II had a major impact on many African soldiers who served in national armies and fought in Africa alongside their European colonizers. Having battled to save the world for democracy, returning soldiers began to wonder why they continued to live under colonial rule. Indeed, the 1941 Atlantic Charter, created by American president Franklin Roosevelt and British prime minister Winston Churchill, proclaimed that one of the principles for which World War II was fought was "respect [for] the right of all peoples to choose the form of government under which they lived."

### AFRICAN DEMOCRATIC RALLY (RDA)

Among the earliest independence movements in Africa, formed in French West Africa, was the African Democratic Rally (Rassemblement Démocratique Africain, or RDA), founded in 1946 by Félix Houphouët-Boigny, who would, in 1960, become the president of the Cote d'Ivoire.

Kwame Nkrumah, the prime minister of the Republic of Ghana, signed the African Charter that established the Organization of African Unity (OAU). The OAU's attempts at African unity were largely unsuccessful. In 2004, the OAU was replaced by the African Union (AU), an organization with greater authority to preserve peace on the continent. (Keystone/Stringer/Hulton Archive/Getty Images)

This organization represented all of French West Africa and was not associated with any particular colony. Although harshly suppressed by the French, the RDA eventually achieved its goal of helping African nations attain independence. The RDA is still an active political party in many West African nations.

## GHANA

The first sub-Saharan African nation to become independent was the Gold Coast, now Ghana, which won its independence from Great Britain under the leadership of Kwame Nkrumah. Nkrumah was educated in the United States and returned to Africa in 1947 to serve as the general secretary to the United Gold Coast Convention (UGCC) under politician Joseph Danquah. The UGCC's primary purpose was to advocate for independence from Great Britain. In early 1948, police shot at African service members who were protesting sharp increases in the cost of living. When the shootings led to rioting across the country, British leaders, believing the UGCC had incited the riots, had several of its leaders, including Nkrumah, arrested. The British soon realized that the UGCC was not involved and released the leaders. Upon his release, Nkrumah traveled around the country making speeches and demanding immediate self-rule. By 1949, he had organized his many followers into the Convention People's Party.

When the British proposed a new constitution that limited voting rights to those who owned property, Nkrumah and his followers responded with the Constitutional Proposals of October 1949, which demanded universal suffrage and self-government. Soon after the British rejected these proposals in 1950, Nkrumah began a campaign for "Positive Action" that included civil disobedience, boycotts, and strikes. Nkrumah was arrested and spent three years in prison. In 1951, Nkrumah's party won in free elections, and in 1952, because he was leader of the party that won the elections, Nkrumah became the prime minister of a new transitional government that would eventually lead to freedom. In 1957, following a series of strikes and protests, Gold Coast became the independent nation of Ghana, with Nkrumah still at the helm as prime minister. In 1960, Nkrumah was elected Ghana's first president. Nkrumah's path to freedom for Ghana inspired other African leaders to strive for independence.

## ALGERIA

Among the most violent of all the African struggles for independence was that of Algeria. In 1954, the **socialist** political party, National Liberation Front (FLN), began a series of attacks against military posts, police stations, and other state-owned facilities. The French, determined not to allow independence, brought additional troops into Algeria and fought back. The FLN used **guerrilla** tactics, striking quickly at French positions, then hiding among the civilian population. Both sides in the conflict engaged in acts of terrorism against noncombatants.

In 1958, General Charles de Gaulle, leader of the Free French Movement during World War II and former president of France, was called to form a new government. The previous administration, referred to as the "Fourth Republic," had lost the confidence of the public, partly because of its handling of the conflict in Algeria. Although de Gaulle at first pursued the war, by 1959 he had accepted the idea of Algerian independence. De Gaulle's stance, however, angered the French settlers in Algeria, who, with the support of French troops in Algeria, staged two revolts, which de Gaulle had to put down by force.

In March 1962, the parties to the conflict between the French settlers and the French government declared a cease-fire, and in July of the same year, Algerians voted to become independent of France. There are differing estimates of the number of deaths that occurred during the eight years of fighting. Algerians set the death toll at 1.5 million, while the French set it at about 350,000.

## PORTUGUESE COLONIES

Portugal, under the leadership of Fascist dictator António Salazar from the early 1930s to the late 1960s, was determined to hold onto its colonies in Africa. Long after other colonial powers had realized that their tenure in Africa was over, the Portuguese continued to battle independence movements in Angola, Mozambique, and Guinea-Bissau.

### Angola

In 1961, a brief rebellion by native Angolans against their Portuguese colonizers was put down, and many of the rebels fled to neighboring Congo. The next year a group of these refugees led by political activist Holden Roberto came together as the National Liberation Front of Angola (FNLA). From its base in the Congo, the FNLA fought a guerrilla war against the Portuguese. By the early 1970s, Portugal had more than 50,000 troops in Angola to ward off attacks by the various guerrilla groups. In 1972, Portugal declared Angola an "autonomous state," allowing self-determination in all areas except defense and foreign policy. In 1974, a group of left-wing military leaders overthrew the government of Portugal in a bloodless coup that came to be known as the Carnation Revolution. The new government granted Angola independence in 1975, and the socialist Popular Movement for the Liberation of Angola (MPLA) established a government in the capital of Luanda. The FNLA and National Union for the Total Independence of Angola (UNITA), however, were opposed to socialism and established a rival government in Huambo. The MPLA received financial and military aid from the Soviet Union and Cuba, while the United States supported the FNLA and UNITA. These groups fought a prolonged civil war that did not end until 2002.

### Mozambique

Another Portuguese colony, Mozambique, began its struggle for independence in 1962 with the founding of the Mozambique Liberation Front (FRELIMO). Based in Tanzania and led by U.S.-educated anthropologist Eduardo Mondlane, FRELIMO began to attack targets in northern Mozambique in 1964. After Mondlane's assassination in 1969, Samora Machel took over leadership of the movement and extended the warfare into central Mozambique. To defend its colony, Portugal stationed 70,000 troops in Mozambique, but they could not put down the insurgency. After the 1974 Carnation Revolution against the Portuguese government, Mozambique was granted independence. FRELIMO became the only legal political party.

### Guinea-Bissau

Marxist Amilcar Cabral established the African Party for the Independence of Guinea and Cape Verde (PAIGC) in 1956. PAIGC's original strategy was peaceful, and the party worked for independence. When in 1959 Portuguese soldiers fired on a crowd of protesters, many Africans who had not been in favor of independence began to advocate for self-determination.

PAIGC changed its tactics in 1962 and began to launch attacks against Portuguese targets. Like other leftist African independence movements, PAIGC looked to the Soviet Union and China for support and received both weapons and training from those nations. Embroiled in conflicts in Angola and Mozambique, Portugal found itself hard pressed to fight back against the guerrillas, and by 1967 PAIGC had control of most of the countryside. The tide turned, however, when Portuguese soldier and politician António Spínola took over as governor of the colony. He sought to influence public opinion by building schools, hospitals, and roads, but at the same time, the Portuguese Air Force began dropping napalm and defoliants in order to kill guerrillas and destroy their hiding places. Nevertheless, in 1973, PAIGC declared Guinea-Bissau to be an independent nation. It was recognized as such by the United Nations, which condemned the Portuguese occupation. Portugal formally declared Guinea-Bissau independent in 1975, along with all its other colonies in Africa.

## SOUTH AFRICA

By 1910, South Africa was no longer a colony but a dominion of Great Britain, with the same status as Canada. (Britain granted dominion status to former colonies that were essentially self-governing.) However, South Africa's native population was completely disenfranchised. In 1912, the African National Congress (ANC) was formed in order to defend the rights of the African people, whether living inside or outside the borders of South Africa. The ANC was founded on the principle of nonviolent protest against discriminatory government policies.

In 1952, the ANC and other groups opposed to apartheid—the legal system of racial discrimination in South Africa—organized the Defiance Campaign, in which members were encouraged to deliberately violate oppressive laws. The campaign ended when the white government enacted laws prohibiting protest meetings in 1953.

In 1960, the ANC planned a non-violent protest against the "pass laws," which required blacks to carry identification cards. Not to be outdone, the Pan-African Congress (PAC) planned a pass law protest of their own, to try to draw away ANC's supporters. The PAC protesters gathered at the Sharpeville police station in an attempt to turn themselves in for traveling without papers. The protest turned bloody when the police, on edge due to the massive crowd, began firing into the crowd, killing 69 and wounding 186. In the aftermath of the Sharpeville massacre, the South African government banned the ANC and PAC.

Because nonviolence had failed to achieve their goals, the ANC leaders altered their tactics. Umkhonto we Sizwe ("Spear of the Nation") was formed in 1961 to be the military arm of the African National Congress. Nelson Mandela led the newly formed unit, though he was arrested within a year and sentenced to life in prison for terrorism.

During the 1970s and 1980s, the ANC attacked a number of targets in South Africa from bases in Botswana, Mozambique, and Swaziland. Tactics included bombings, torture, and even murder. In return, the South African government routinely bombed ANC bases and may have been responsible for the 1988 assassination of ANC member Dulcie September.

Eventually, outside pressure from other world leaders brought both the South African leaders and the ANC to the negotiating table. International pressure and economic embargo were damaging the power of the government, while the fall of the Soviet Union in 1991 meant that the ANC was no longer receiving weapons and money. As a result of their meetings, President F.W. de Klerk legalized the ANC and PAC and released Nelson Mandela from prison in 1990. Four years later, South Africa held its first democratic elections, and Mandela was elected president.

It is one of the great ironies of history that, having fought so hard for independence, many African nations still do not have multiparty democracies and solid democratic institutions. Many nations were wracked by civil war, and many newly elected leaders refused to hold subsequent elections, instead staying in power for decades, robbing the national treasuries and outlawing dissent. South Africa, at least, hopes to escape this fate and sustain its democratic governments.

**See also:** Algeria; British Colonies; Civil Wars; Colonization; French West Africa; Pan-African Movement; Portuguese Colonies; South Africa.

### FURTHER READING

Enwezor, Okwui, and Chinua Achebe, eds. *The Short Century: Independence and Liberation Movements in Africa.* New York: Prestel, 2001.

Meredith, Martin. *The Fate of Africa. From the Hopes of Freedom to the Heart of Despair: A History of 50 Years of Independence.* New York: Public Affairs, 2005.

Reader, John. *Africa: A Biography of the Continent.* New York: Vintage, 1999.

# Italian Colonies

Italy's holdings in Africa, which by 1934 included the territories of Cyrenaica and Tripolitania (now Libya), Somaliland (now a part of Somalia), Eritrea, and Ethiopia. Like Germany, Italy was relatively late in becoming a unified nation, beginning the process in

## TURNING POINT

### The Treaty of Wuchale

The Treaty of Wuchale, also known as the Treaty of Uccaile, was signed by Emperor Menelik II of Ethiopia and Count Pietro Antonelli of Italy on May 2, 1889. The treaty, which was written in two versions, one Italian and one Amharic, the language of Ethiopia, ceded several provinces of Ethiopia to Italy. These provinces eventually became the Italian colony of Eritrea. Menelik signed the treaty because he viewed Italy as a threat to Ethiopian independence and hoped the ceded territories would satisfy Italy's colonial ambitions.

Shortly after the treaty was signed, however, the Italians began taking over provinces that were not part of the original agreement. Then, in October of the same year, Italy notified other colonial powers in Africa that it regarded Ethiopia as a protectorate. Italy justified its claim by referring to Article XVII of the Italian version of the Wuchale Treaty, which stated that Ethiopia was under the control of the Italian government. The Amharic version, however, did not clearly state that Italy was in control, only that the two nations were partners. In 1893, Menelik repudiated the treaty and declared it invalid. In response, Italian forces advanced upon Ethiopia, but were defeated at the Battle of Adwa in 1896. The Treaty of Addis Ababa, signed in 1896, ended the war and forced Italy to recognize Ethiopia's independence.

---

about 1815, after the defeat of Napoleon, and ending in about 1870. Also like Germany, Italy was a latecomer to Africa, beginning its colonization efforts with Somaliland and Eritrea in 1889.

### FIRST ITALIAN-ETHIOPIAN WAR

In 1889, Menelik II, the ruler of Ethiopia, signed the Treaty of Wuchale with Italy, which established Eritrea as an Italian colony. In 1893, Menelik, having consolidated his power over Ethiopia, declared the treaty void. In October 1895, Italy responded by attacking Ethiopia from Eritrea. The Italians expected that the Tigray and Amhara people, whom Menelik had conquered, would support them. The assumption proved incorrect, however, as they sided with Menelik. In the first battle of the war at Amba Alagi in December 1895, Ethiopian solders drove the Italian forces back into Eritrea.

Ethiopia's decisive victory over the Italians came at the Battle of Adwa on March 1, 1896. About 20,000 Italian troops planned an early morning attack on the Ethiopian forces, hoping to surprise the sleeping army. However, the Ethiopians had wakened early to attend church, learned of the Italian advance, and counterattacked. In defeating the Italians, Menelik and his army made history—becoming only the second African military force to defeat a European force since Hannibal's victory over the Roman army 2,000 years earlier. In October, Italy and Ethiopia signed the Treaty of Addis Ababa, which established the borders of the Italian colony of Eritrea and recognized the independence of Ethiopia.

## LIBYA

Italy gained control over the North African territories of Cyrenaica and Tripolitania as a result of its victory in a short war with the Ottoman Empire in 1911. Those in Italy who had dreams of a new Roman Empire based in modern Italy referred to Libya as Italy's "fourth shore." Despite this boast, the Italians encountered a determined resistance by the native people until 1914, by which time Italy controlled the vast majority of the territory. Italy consolidated Tripolitania, Cyrenaica, and a third territory—Fezzan—as the colony of Libya in 1934.

In the period between World War I and World War II, Idris I, **emir** of Cyrenaica, led a **guerrilla** war of resistance against Italy from a base in Egypt. During World War II, Libya was the site of many battles between Allied and Axis forces. Idris, fighting with the Allies, helped defeat the German forces in Libya under the command of Nazi general Erwin Rommel. After the war, Italy relinquished all claims to Libya, the once united colony was redivided, and Great Britain administered the territories of Cyrenaica and Tripolitania; the territory of Fezzan was transferred to French rule. When Libya gained its independence in 1951, Idris became the new nation's first king.

## SECOND ITALIAN-ETHIOPIAN WAR

Benito Mussolini, the **Fascist** dictator of Italy, was among those Italians who dreamed of a new Roman Empire and pictured modern Italy in control of the entire Mediterranean region. Mussolini had not forgotten Italy's defeat by Ethiopia at the Battle of Adwa in 1896, and he was determined to avenge the humiliation. Ethiopia was also an obvious choice for Italian expansion because it was one of the few African nations not already colonized by a European nation, and it bordered the Italian colonies of Eritrea and Somaliland.

The attempt to take over Ethiopia began in 1930 when the Italians built a fort in disputed territory on the border between Eritrea and Ethiopia at an oasis in the Ogaden Desert known as Walwal. In 1934, Ethiopian and Italian troops clashed, leaving 150 Ethiopian and 50 Italian troops dead. Soon afterward, the Italians began to mass forces on the Ethiopian border. Ethiopian emperor Haile Selassie mobilized his army to fight, but many of his forces were armed only with spears, bows, and arrows. In 1936, without a formal declaration of war, Italian forces crossed the border into Ethiopia and captured Adwa, the site of the 1896 Italian defeat.

In addition to conventional weapons, Italian forces used chemical weapons against the Ethiopians. It is now known that mustard gas was used both on the ground and in aerial bombardments, although the Italian government refused to acknowledge this fact until 1995. Civilians and Red Cross encampments were deliberately sprayed with the gas. In addition to using poison gas, the advancing Italian army forced Ethiopian civilians into labor camps, killed hostages, and mutilated the corpses of the dead. Captured rebels were thrown alive from airplanes, and Mussolini himself authorized his army to "systematically conduct a politics of terror and extermination." One of the worst incidents of the war occurred in 1937 in the capital of Addis Ababa when a bomb exploded next to an Italian general. In a rage, he ordered the Italian militia to "Avenge me! Kill them all!" The Black Shirts, as the militia was called, killed every Ethiopian civilian they could find, set fire to houses, and conducted mass executions. Nearly 30,000 people were killed.

Ethiopia fell on March 29, 1936, and Emperor Haile Selassie fled the country on May 2. On May 9, Italy declared Ethiopia, Somaliland, and Eritrea to be the state of Italian East Africa. Nevertheless, Ethiopians continued to resist Italian occupation until Allied forces liberated Ethiopia in 1941. Ethiopia regained its independence in

## INTO THE 21ST CENTURY

### Return of the Aksum Obelisk

For nearly 70 years, a 1,700-year-old Ethiopian stone monument stood in the Piazza di Porta Capina in Rome. Italian occupiers of Ethiopia had taken the 78-foot-tall (24 m) monument, known as the Aksum Obelisk, from Ethiopia in 1937. To transport the obelisk, which weighs more than 200 tons, the Italians had to break it into three pieces.

The obelisk, which was erected near the Ethiopian border with Eritrea in what was the ancient kingdom of Aksum to commemorate a royal death (date unknown), became a symbol of Ethiopian national pride, and the Ethiopian government tried for years to negotiate its return to its original site. On November 18, 2004, Italy and Ethiopia signed an agreement for the return of the monument. The structure, which had to be rebroken in order to be transported, arrived in Aksum in April 2005. A national holiday was declared in Ethiopia, and people danced in the streets.

When archeologists examined a site on which to place the obelisk, they found a number of underground tombs. Archeologists believe that only about 7 percent of all the artifacts in Aksum have been unearthed, and the prospect of uncovering so much ancient history is exciting to the nation. However, when people living nearby were asked to leave the area so that archeologists could explore the sites, they chose not to cooperate. The obelisk, meanwhile, was being held in two metal shacks, covered by blankets. Many in Ethiopia, one of the world's poorest countries, have begun to question the time, effort, and money expended to return the monument. The cost to remove and transport the obelisk was more than $50 million, paid for by the Italian government. Many Ethiopians wonder if that money would have been better spent on economic development.

---

1942, and in 1952 Eritrea was placed under Ethiopian control. Italian Somaliland became a part of Somalia in 1960.

### AFTERMATH

After World War II, many Italian political leaders, still influenced by fascist **ideology**, worked actively to regain their colonies. Even after signing a peace treaty in 1947 in which it renounced its control over its former colonies, the Italian government sent diplomats around the world to lobby the Allies in an attempt to regain their territory. The treaty also required the Italian government to return objects they had looted from Ethiopia after 1935. Little was ever returned, but the Aksum Obelisk, an ancient Ethiopian artifact taken in 1937, was finally returned in 2005.

*See also:* Art and Architecture; Colonization; Eritrea; Ethiopia; Somalia; Tools and Weapons.

### FURTHER READING

Andall, Jacqueline, and Duncan D. Andall, eds. *Italian Colonialism: Legacy and Memory.* Oxford: Peter Lang, 2005.

Gillespie, Carol Ann. *Ethiopia.* New York: Chelsea House, 2002.

Palumbo, Patrizia. *A Place in the Sun: Africa in Italian Colonial Culture from Post-Unification to the Present.* Berkeley: University of California Press, 2003.

# L-N

# Language

More than 2,000 different languages are spoken in Africa, including both native languages and languages brought into Africa by conquerors and colonizers. Africa is the most linguistically diverse continent on Earth.

In addition to **indigenous** African languages, Africans speak Arabic, French, English, Portuguese, German, and Afrikaans, a language derived from Dutch and spoken mainly in South Africa. The two most prevalent African languages, spoken by the greatest number of people, are Hausa, spoken by 39 million people, and Swahili, spoken by 35 million people.

## CLASSIFICATIONS

Several different systems have been devised for classifying Africa's languages, but the most widely accepted is that devised by American linguist Joseph Greenberg in 1963. Greenberg divided Africa's many languages into four broad families. A language family is a grouping of related languages that scholars believe derive from a common ancestor language. The four families Greenberg identified are Afro-Asiatic, Nilo-Saharan, Khoisan, and Niger-Congo. These language families differ from one another in many significant ways, and even languages in the same family may be as different as English and Hindi.

Many African languages do not have writing systems and have been handed down orally. In some cases, writing systems using the Roman alphabet were developed to allow missionaries to translate the New Testament into the native tongue of those Africans they were attempting to convert to Christianity. To date, the New Testament has been translated into 680 African languages, including Zulu and Swahili. In many African languages, even today, the only written text is a translation of a portion of the Bible. This is true of many languages in the Nilo-Saharan and the Niger-Congo groups.

### Afro-Asiatic Family

This language family comprises nearly 400 languages, many of which are spoken in northern Africa. Afro-Asiatic includes Arabic, varieties of which are spoken in Algeria, Chad, Djibouti, Egypt, Eritrea, Libya, Morocco, Somalia, Sudan, Tanzania, and Tunisia. Other branches of the Afro-Asiatic family includes the Berber branch, spoken in parts of Morocco, Algeria, and Tunisia, and the Chadic branch, which includes Hausa, a language spoken in many areas in sub-Saharan Africa. The name "Afro-Asiatic" refers to the fact that some of these languages are also spoken in Asia. It is estimated that some 300 million people speak one of the Afro-Asiatic languages.

### Nilo-Saharan Family

The languages in the Nilo-Saharan family are found from the area around the Niger River in West Africa across the continent to Ethiopia and are spoken by about 11 million people. Languages from this family are also spoken in the upper Nile Valley—hence "Nilo" as part of the name—and in parts of Uganda and Kenya. South of Egypt, another branch in this family, Nubian, is spoken by about a million people.

### Khoisan Family

Among the most inter-esting of all African language families is Khoisan, which is also spoken by the smallest number of individuals. Only about 200,000 people speak the thirty languages in this group. Among

LANGUAGE | 85

OFFICIAL LANGUAGES IN MODERN AFRICA

Very few African nations have designated native languages as official. Most nations use a European tongue as their official language, a legacy of the colonial era.

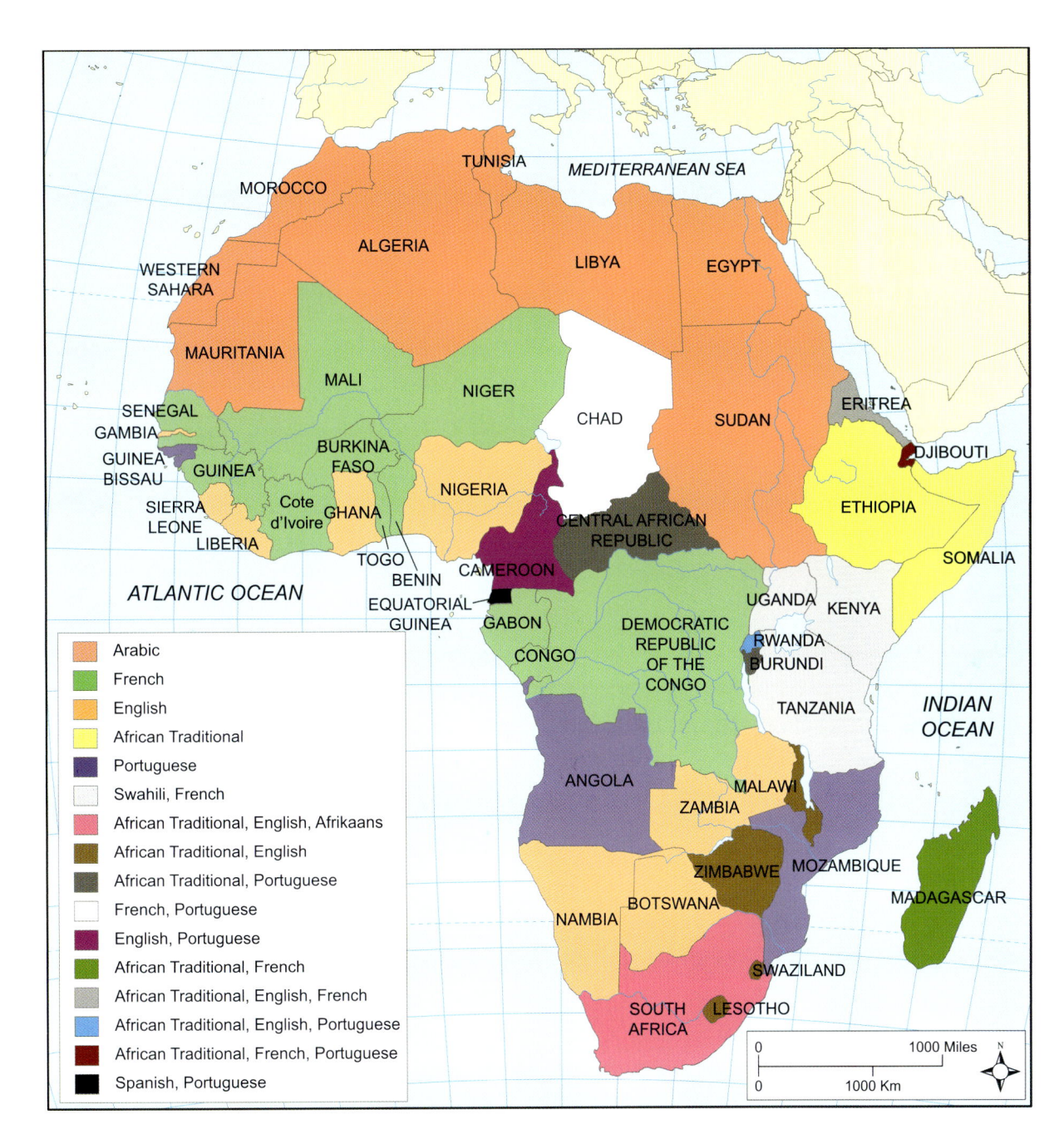

- Arabic
- French
- English
- African Traditional
- Portuguese
- Swahili, French
- African Traditional, English, Afrikaans
- African Traditional, English
- African Traditional, Portuguese
- French, Portuguese
- English, Portuguese
- African Traditional, French
- African Traditional, English, French
- African Traditional, English, Portuguese
- African Traditional, French, Portuguese
- Spanish, Portuguese

Khoisan languages are Nama, spoken in Namibia, and Sandawe, spoken in Tanzania. Khoisan are "click" languages, in which many consonants are pronounced with a clicking sound (the way English speakers might say "tsk, tsk"). In written versions of these languages, the click sound is often represented with a slash or exclamation mark.

In recent years, linguists who study the origins and development of languages, known as **glottochronologists**, have concluded that the very first human language may have been a click language similar to that still spoken today by the Khoi and the San of southwest Africa.

### Niger-Congo Family

This is the largest of all the African language families, comprising more than 1,400 languages. This family is divided into several subfamilies, some of which are found in only very small areas in Africa surrounded by other, nonrelated languages. The largest subfamily of the Niger-Congo family is the Atlantic-Congo, whose languages are found throughout almost all of sub-Saharan Africa. Within Atlantic-Congo, which is further divided into many subfamilies, are a group of languages known as Bantu, which is a word that means "the people" in many languages in the group. More than 100 million people in southern Africa speak Bantu languages. In studying the distribution of Bantu languages, linguists and historians have been able to trace the "Bantu migration." The original or root Bantu language was spoken in what is today Nigeria and Cameroon beginning in about 2000 B.C.E. Over the next 1,500 years, Bantu speakers moved across the continent, probably bringing iron-smelting technology with them, and absorbed or overcame many other cultures. Some Bantu languages spoken today include Zulu and Xhosa in South Africa, Shona in Zimbabwe, Bemba in Zambia, Swahili in Tanzania, Kikuyu in Kenya, Ganda in Uganda, and Fang in Cameroon. Part of the same subfamily as Bantu are other African languages with large numbers of speakers, including Yoruba with 22 million speakers and Igbo with 18 million speakers.

## CHARACTERISTICS

While there are great variations among African languages, many of the families share similarities, or common characteristics. In Niger-Congo languages, verbs are conjugated in a way that can emphasize the speaker's attitude toward an action rather than just the time of the action, or tense. English, on the other hand, emphasizes only tense in verb conjugation, using the present (I eat), past (I ate), and future (I will eat). In the Niger-Congo family, one can say such things as, "He eats all the time" or "She is likely to eat" by adding a prefix or suffix to the verb. Obviously, to translate these ideas into English would require many words.

Many of the Nilo-Saharan, Niger-Congo, and Khoisan families, and even some of the Afro-Asiatic families, are tonal languages, as is Chinese. This means that the pitch of the word conveys meaning. In Yoruba, which is spoken in Nigeria, the single word "ogun" has nine different meanings, depending on the pitch used. There are even some tonal languages that use whistle speech, in which each sound unit can be whistled according to the pitch with which it could be spoken such that native speakers can understand what is being whistled.

Tonality also makes possible the "talking drums" of the Yoruba. These drums are shaped like hourglasses. The drumheads are attached to both ends of the drum with a hoop, and a number of cords running the length of the drum are attached to the hoops. When the drummer applies pressure to the cords, he or she tightens or loosens the drumhead, which alters the tone when the head is struck. By changing the tone in a way that imitates the tonality of the language, the drummer can send messages over long distances.

## EUROPEAN LANGUAGES

Because Africa was colonized by Arab speakers and speakers of European languages, there are many non-African languages spoken in Africa today. Arabic, while among these languages, has been spoken for the longest period of time, primarily in northern Africa. Because of the continent's colonial legacy, the two primary European languages spoken in Africa are English and French, and scholars often refer to "Francophone" (French-speaking) and "Anglophone" (English-speaking) Africa. There are eighteen African nations in which English is an official language and twelve nations in which French is an official language. In many of these nations, there is more than one official language, including one or more African languages; in Nigeria, for example, official languages include English, Igbo, Hausa, and Yoruba. Other languages spoken in parts of Africa include Portuguese, German, and Afrikaans, which is derived from Dutch. Afrikaans is one of eleven official languages of South Africa today and is a widely accepted means of communication. In most nations with a European official language, individuals are bilingual, speaking both the official language, which is used for government, trade, and education, and a native language, which is used at home and among family members.

Many Africans, and especially African writers, perceive the prevalence of European languages in Africa as a problem. They feel that there is such a close relationship between language and culture that Africans who speak and write in English or French may lose their uniquely African way of thinking and seeing. To some, this domination of language is a continuation of colonialism, as if the European powers left their languages in their place to continue to make Africans subservient to them. The Kenyan writer Ngugi wa Thiong'o (who once wrote in English under the name James Ngugi), writes only in his native Kikuyu and has emphasized his belief that a truly African literature must be written in a native African language. The Nigerian writer Chinua Achebe, who writes in English, disagrees and believes that African writers can mold European languages to an African way of thinking.

Some politicians also advocate abandoning French and English and installing African languages as official. Others point out, however, that many African languages have no written form and thus could not serve as official languages. Moreover, no African leader wants to be responsible for choosing which of the many native languages in each nation to elevate to official status. Because the borders of African nations were drawn by Europeans with little regard for language or ethnicity, most nations today have speakers of hundreds of different languages within their borders (Cameroon, for example, has speakers of 248 different languages).

### PIDGINS AND CREOLES

Because of the great number of languages spoken in Africa, many pidgin and creole language variations have arisen. A pidgin language is a simplified form of speech that combines elements of two or more languages and facilitates communication between two groups who do not share a language. Pidgins are also sometimes referred to as "contact languages." Among the many pidgins in Africa are Nigerian Pidgin, which is a form of English, and Fanagolo, which combines Zulu, Afrikaans, and English and is used in the mines in South Africa.

A creole is a fully formed language that begins as a pidgin language and becomes the primary language of a people. While pidgins are spoken only during contact between two groups that do not share a language, a creole is spoken at home, just like a native language. Many African creoles are based on English, such as Kiro in Sierra Leone and Sheng in Kenya. Others, such as Cape Verde Creole and Guinea-Bissau Creole, which is spoken in both Guinea-Bissau and Senegal, are based on Portuguese. Some creoles, such as Juba Arabic, which is spoken in southern Sudan, are based on Arabic, and others are based on local languages, such as Sango, which is the main language of the Central African Republic.

More than 300 African languages are spoken by so few people that they are on the verge of dying out; some languages have already been lost. For example, a click language, Ku!khaasi, was last spoken sometime in the 1930s. The year 2006 was designated as the Year of African Languages by the African Union (AU) and the AU itself has declared all of Africa's languages "official." It also established the African Academy for Languages, situated in Bamako, Mali, in order to help preserve and promote the indigenous languages of Africa. The African Union also promotes the development of reading material in a number of African languages and publicizes the importance of preserving Africa's linguistic heritage.

*See also:* British Colonies; Colonization; Culture and Traditions; French West Africa; German Colonies; Imperialism; Literature and Writing; Portuguese Colonies; South Africa.

### FURTHER READING

Brock-Utne, Birgit. *Language, Democracy and Education in Africa.* Uppsala, Sweden: Nordic Africa Institute, 2002.

Heine, Bernd, and Derek Nurse, eds. *African Languages: An Introduction.* Cambridge, UK: Cambridge University Press, 2000.

Nurse, Derek. *The Bantu Languages.* New York: Routledge, 2000.

Webb, Vic, and Kembo-Sure, eds. *African Voices: An Introduction to the Languages and Linguistics of Africa.* Oxford: Oxford University Press, 2000.

# Liberia

A country in western Africa, bordering on the Atlantic Ocean and situated between Cote d'Ivoire and Sierra Leone, settled in 1821 by freed slaves from the United States. Liberia declared itself an independent nation in 1847. Its capital, Monrovia, was named after U.S. president James Monroe. The first Liberian settlers purchased a strip of land along the coast from the native leaders.

The early Liberian settlers modeled their new land on what they remembered from the United States. They continued to speak English and built churches and houses that resembled those of the American South. Also like white people in the South, the freed slaves tended to look down on the native people.

During the early years of independence, Liberians built schools and a university, managed a growing economy, and expanded the nation's borders. From the beginning, the country was ruled by and for the former slaves, who called themselves Americo-Liberians, with little attention paid to the needs of native populations.

In the early years of the twentieth century, Liberia's economy began to struggle, partly because the cost of what had to be imported far exceeded the value of exports. By 1909, the government was bankrupt and had to borrow extensively to stay afloat. In 1926, the government leased land to American rubber companies to increase revenues, but the rubber companies exploited the workers, leading to social unrest. In 1930, the League of Nations accused Firestone Rubber Company of employing "forced labour . . . hardly distinguishable from slavery." The scandal caused Liberian president Charles D.B. King to resign in order to avoid being impeached.

## INTO THE 21ST CENTURY

**Al-Qaeda in Africa**

Since the 1990s, al-Qaeda, the terrorist organization bent upon destroying the United States and its allies, has extended its network throughout Africa. Al-Qaeda first made inroads into African nations with large Muslim populations, such as Somalia, Sudan, and Algeria. In the early 2000s, the terrorist group has worked to expand its reach beyond heavily Muslim nations.

In western Africa, al-Qaeda took advantage of the lawlessness that accompanied the civil wars in Liberia, Sierra Leone, and Cote d'Ivoire. In Liberia in particular, al-Qaeda found that it could purchase weapons with impunity (often using so-called "blood diamonds"—diamonds mined in war zones), count on a supportive Muslim population for security, and set up training camps without interference. In 2004, the U.S. Federal Bureau of Investigation (FBI) confirmed that former Liberian president Charles Taylor had maintained strong ties to al-Qaeda and had allowed the organization to operate there for years.

---

In 1944, Liberian senator William Tubman was elected president, and he served in that capacity for seven terms until his death in 1971. Tubman traveled the world and was successful in promoting investment in Liberia. Profits from foreign investment and from newly discovered deposits of iron ore allowed his government to invest in crucial **infrastructure**, including schools, roads, and hospitals. However, Tubman did little to improve relations between the descendents of slaves, a mere 5 percent of the population, and native people. Most of the natives were impoverished and resentful of the ruling **elite**. In 1979, when Tubman's successor, William Tolbert, increased the price of rice, violent demonstrations resulted, and in 1980, a military coup led by Sergeant Samuel K. Doe overthrew the government. Tolbert and thirteen members of his cabinet were executed, and Doe and his party, the People's Redemption Council (PRC), formed a new government. In 1985, Doe claimed to have won an election despite the fact that the actual count of votes went against him, and then shut down newspapers and banned rival political parties. Civil war broke out in 1989, with rebel forces led by Charles Taylor, who had served as a commerce minister under Doe.

In 1995, after years of bloody fighting in which much of Liberia's infrastructure was destroyed and 250,000 people killed, Taylor agreed to a cease-fire. In 1997, he was elected president in what most observers regarded as a free election. His government proved brutal and repressive, too, leading to a new rebellion in 1999. International pressure, including a warrant issued by a United Nations justice tribunal for his arrest, forced Taylor to resign in 2003. He fled to Nigeria, where he stayed until 2006. Upon extradition, he was brought before the World Court at the Hague in the Netherlands and charged with war crimes.

In 2005, meanwhile, Liberia elected the continent's first female head of state, Ellen Johnson-Sirleaf. A former employee of Citibank and the World Bank, Sirleaf used her financial expertise to help reduce Liberia's $3.5 billion debt and worked to rebuild the devastated nation.

*See also:* Civil Wars.

**FURTHER READING**

Olukojo, Aodeji. *Culture and Customs of Liberia.* Westport, CT: Greenwood Press, 2006.

Pham, John-Peter. *Liberia: Portrait of a Failed State.* New York: Reed Press, 2004.

# Literature and Writing

Until the twentieth century, much African literature was oral. Most people, particularly south of the Sahara, were not literate, and many African languages did not even have a written form. Thus, stories and poems were passed down by word of mouth from generation to generation.

Only in the twentieth century did a written literary tradition develop. Until recently, most of the greatest works of African literature were written in English or French, not in **indigenous** African languages. Most well-educated Africans in the twentieth century were taught in European languages, and many considered those languages superior to their native tongues—or so they were told by their colonial masters. Since the 1970s and 1980s, there has been a movement among some African writers to produce literature in indigenous African languages. These writers, including Kenya's Ngugi wa Thiong'o and Uganda's Okot P'Bitek, believe that an African way of seeing and experiencing the world can only be expressed in an African language.

## ORAL TRADITIONS

The oral literature of Africa includes myths, epic poems, folktales, praise songs, riddles, and proverbs. This body of literature is closely associated with music, and much poetry was sung or chanted.

African mythology, like myths the world over, deals with many of the fundamental questions humankind has always asked. How was the world created and who created it? How did death and evil enter the world? How did the creatures of the earth come to be, and why do they behave as they do? There are literally thousands of myths, some bearing striking similarity to aspects of Western mythology, others uniquely and distinctively African. The Pangwa of Tanzania, for example, believe that the world was created from the excrement of ants. A Bantu creation story tells how the great god Bamba vomits up the sun, which begins the process of the creation of the universe. The Fulani of Mali, who are cattle herders, tell how the universe was created from a huge drop of milk.

The African poetic tradition includes praise names or praise songs, a form that is unique to Africa. The poet constructs the song from a series of pithy phrases that describe special qualities about the subject of the song—which can be a person, a god, an animal, or even a place. Following is a praise song about the Zulu chieftain, Shaka Zulu:

> He is Shaka the unshakeable,
> Thunderer-while-sitting, son of Menzi
> He is the bird that preys on other birds,
> The battle-axe that excels over other battle axes.

Another form of oral literature prevalent in Africa is the folktale, especially the animal-trickster tale. Although the nature of the trickster changes from culture to culture (taking the form of a hare, tortoise, or spider, for example), the stories themselves share a number of characteristics. Sometimes the trickster makes a fool of himself; sometimes he is a thorn in the sides of the gods, defeating their best-laid plans; sometimes he makes fun of the stupidity and pomposity of others. Often the trickster figure is a small creature that outwits larger and stronger creatures. Anansi the spider, of the Ashante culture of Ghana, is the subject of thousands of stories in which his cleverness is his greatest strength.

The African oral tradition also includes proverbs and riddles. Even today, the ability to use an apt proverb is considered a sign of learning among many ethnic groups. Proverbs reflect the values and the imagination of the culture. The Ibo teach proper behavior, for example, with "If a child washes his hands, he will eat with kings." African riddles, unlike Western ones, do not take the form of a question. For example, the answer to the riddle "People run away from her when she is pregnant, but they rejoice when she has delivered," is "a gun."

## LITERATURE IN AFRICAN LANGUAGES

The existing literature in African languages is not well known in the West, except perhaps for the work of Kenyan author Ngugi wa Thiong'o, who once wrote in English as James Ngugi but now writes in his native Kikuyu. His novel *Wizard of the Crow* (2006), written in Kikuyu, has been translated into English and widely read in the West as well as in Africa. This pointed satire of African political life tells the fantastic tale of a dictator who plans to climb to heaven up a modern tower of Babel, financed by the Global Bank.

Other literature in indigenous African languages includes works from West Africa in Yoruba and Hausa, from southern Africa in Sotho, Xhosa, and Zulu, and from East Africa in Amharic, Somali, and Swahili. The first full-length novel published in Yoruba is D.O. Fagunwa's *The Forest of a Thousand Daemons: A Hunter's Saga* (1968), the story of a hunter in a forest populated with strange, unnatural creatures. Fagunwa's work is influenced by Yoruba folklore.

Early literature in Hausa, spoken in the predominantly Muslim north of Nigeria, includes *Song of Mohammad* (1845), a poem about the prophet Mohammad by Asim Degel. Among the most popular **genres** in Hausa today is Kano literature, named for the Nigerian Kano State, the primary market where the books are sold. In Hausa, the genre is called *littattafan soyayya*, which means "books of love." Written primarily by women, these romances tell contemporary love stories. Although they are light fiction, these novels also reflect some of the most difficult issues for Hausa women, including **polygamy**, *purdah* (the practice of women being veiled in front of non–family members), coerced marriages, and lack of education.

The first South African work of fiction in an indigenous language was based on John Bunyan's allegorical work of the late seventeenth century, *The Pilgrim's Progress*. Like *Pilgrim's Progress*, Thomas Mofolo's *The Traveller of the East* (1906), written in the Sotho language, tells the tale of a spiritual journey of a newly converted Christian. Edward Krune Loliwe Mqhayi wrote both poetry and fiction in the Xhosa language, one of only very few writers to do so. His 1914 novel, *The Case of Two Brothers*, recounts cases tried in a traditional African court. The first book written and published in Zulu is a history of the Zulu people, *The Black People and Whence They Came* (1922) by Magema ka Magwaza Fuze.

In 2002, former South African president Nelson Mandela met with acclaimed Nigerian author Chinua Achebe in Cape Town, South Africa. After their meeting, Achebe received an honorary Doctor of Literature degree from the University of Cape Town.
(Anna Zieminski/Stringer/AFP/Getty Images)

In East Africa, Cismaan Yuusef Keenadiid developed a Latin-based alpahabet for the Somali language in the early years of the twentieth century. Most Somali literature is in verse, and one of greatest poets to write in that language is Sayyid Maxamed Cabdulle Xasan. His poetry, written toward the end of the nineteenth century, was highly critical of the European colonizers of Somaliland. Xasan was also a rebel leader who fought for years against colonizers (1899–1905) and was nicknamed the "mad mullah" by the British. (A mullah is an Islamic clergyman.) Religious works in Amharic, the language of Ethiopia, and in Swahili first appeared in the seventeenth century. The first modern writer to publish in Swahili was Shaaban Robert, who wrote both poetry and prose. His **utopian** novel, *Kusadikika* (1951) (the title means something like "Trustful Place") is a satire of colonialism and the abuse of power.

## AFRICAN LITERATURE IN ENGLISH

There are many great African works written in English, which is by far the most important literary language in Africa. While there is much fine African poetry in English—notably that of Nigerian poet Christopher Okigbo (*Labyrinths, with Path of Thunder*, 1971) and Ghana's Kifi Anyidoho (*A Harvest of Our Dreams*, 1984)—it is African fiction written in English that has caught the attention of the world.

### Nigerian Writers

The best-known contemporary **Anglophone** African writer is Nigerian Chinua Achebe, whose most acclaimed work, the novel *Things Fall Apart* (1958), tells the story of an Ibo village at the end of the nineteenth century and the destruction caused by the coming of Europeans. Achebe, like many African writers who followed him, deals with the theme of the end of traditional African life and the clash of African and European culture through the character of Okonkwo, a successful man who is destroyed by colonialism. *No Longer at Ease* (1960) continues the story of the Okonkwo family. Okonkwo's grandson lives in Lagos, the capital city of Nigeria, cut off from traditional life and values, adrift in a Westernized urban culture that is opposed to his deepest nature.

Amos Tutuola's novel *The Palm-Wine Drinkard* (1952) is based on Yoruba folktales. It is the story of a drinking man who follows his bartender into "Deads' Town," a place populated by demons and ghosts. Tutuola is among the many African writers

## LANDMARKS IN AFRICAN LITERATURE, 1845–2006

**1845** *Song of Mohammed*, a poem, published in the Hausa language

**1883** South African writer Olive Schreiner publishes the novel *The Story of an African Farm*

**1885** South African writer Rider Haggard's novel *King Solomon's Mines* published

**1906** First full-length South African fictional work written in the Sotho language published, Thomas Mofolo's novel *The Traveller of the East*

**1922** First published work in Zulu, Magema Fuze's history *The Black People and Whence They Came*

**1930s** *Négritude* movement begins, led by Léopold Senghor

**1948** Alan Paton's acclaimed novel, *Cry, the Beloved Country*, portraying black-white relations in South Africa, published

**1951** First modern novel published in Swahili, *Kusadikika* by Shaaban Robert

**1952** Amos Tutuola's novel *The Palm-Wine Drinkard*, based on Yoruba mythology, published

**1958** Chinua Achebe's novel *Things Fall Apart* published

**1964** Ngugi wa Thiong'o's first novel in English, *Weep Not Child*, published

**1968** First full-length novel in Yoruba, D.O. Fagunwa's *The Forest of a Thousand Daemons*

**1986** Nigeria's Wole Soyinka wins Nobel Prize for Literature—the first African to be so honored

**1988** Na Mahfouz wins Nobel Prize for Literature

**1991** South Africa's Nadine Gordimer wins Nobel Prize for Literature; Nigerian Ben Okri wins Booker Prize for his novel *The Famished Road*

**1995** Nigerian writer Ken Saro-Wiwa executed for "anti-government activity"

**2003** South African writer J.M. Coetzee wins Nobel Prize for Literature

**2006** Ngugi wa Thiong'o's novel, *Wizard of the Crow*, written in Kikuyu and translated into English, receives outstanding reviews worldwide

---

who weave traditional oral literature into the fabric of their modern tales.

Wole Soyinka, the most celebrated Nigerian who writes in English, is primarily a dramatist, although he has also written novels and poetry. The 1986 Nobel laureate in literature, Soyinka has written light drama and comedy, but his most serious plays are *The Strong Breed* (1963), *The Road* (1963), and *Death and the King's Horsemen* (1975), all of which are influenced by his Yoruba background and combine European and Yoruba culture into a poetic whole.

Ken Saro-Wiwa wrote plays and satirical novels, in addition to children's books. His first novel, *Sozaboy: A Novel in Rotten English* (1985), was written in pidgin English.

*Sozaboy* is pidgin for "soldier boy," and the novel deals with Saro-Wiwa's own experience as a soldier in the Biafran war. Saro-Wiwa's comic television series *Basi & Company* was canceled by the Nigerian government in 1990 after a five-year run because of its anti-government message. Several of its scripts, however, were turned into children's books. Saro-Wiwa was executed in 1995 for his participation in an anti-government group.

Ben Okri, born in Nigeria in 1959, won the Booker Prize (given each year for the best book in the British Commonwealth) for his magical novel *The Famished Road* (1991). The novel is the first in a trilogy about Azaro, a spirit child. Filled with horror and magic, it is ultimately a story of human survival in the face of harsh reality. As Azaro struggles to continue among the living, his family contends with hunger, disease, and violence. In combining the spirit world seamlessly with the real world, Okri pays tribute to the **animism** of African traditional religion—the belief that all things possess a spirit and that spirits are real and present in daily life.

## Kenyan Writers

Before deciding to write in his native language of Kikuyu, Ngugi wa Thiong'o wrote many novels and plays in English. His first novel, *Weep Not, Child* (1964) traces the effects of colonialism on two brothers. Like Achebe, Ngugi laments the loss of the traditional life as it comes into conflict with European ideas and values. His second novel, *The River Between* (1965), tells the tragic tale of two young lovers caught in the middle of a religious conflict brought about by Christian missionaries.

The Kenyan writer Grace Ogot has written both novels and short stories about traditional life among the Luo people, and she also writes about the conflict between traditional and modern culture. Two of her best short-story collections are *Land Without Thunder* (1968) and *The Other Woman* (1976). Her novel *The Promised Land* (1966) tells the story of Luo people who in the 1930s emigrate from Nyanza (a Kenyan province) to Tanzania in search of better land for farming.

## South African Writers

Although there is a large body of literature in Afrikaans, a language of South Africa based on Dutch, the best-known South African literature is in English. Five writers stand out: Rider Haggard, Olive Schreiner, J.M. Coetzee, Alan Paton, and Nadine Gordimer. Of the five, Haggard is the least literary, writing primarily adventure novels set in Africa. Among the best known is *King Solomon's Mines* (1885).

Olive Schreiner published the first great South African novel, *The Story of an African Farm* (1883), which tells the story of an independent woman running an isolated ostrich farm. Scheriner published two volumes of short stories, and two additional novels were published after her death.

Two South African authors have been awarded the Nobel Prize for literature—Nadine Gordimer in 1991 and J.M. Coetzee in 2003. Gordimer is a prolific writer, having penned fourteen novels, eighteen collections of short stories, a play, and several volumes of essays. Her work explores the impact of apartheid on the everyday lives of both whites and blacks. *The Conservationist* (1974), a highly symbolic and poetic novel, is told from three points of view: that of Mehring, a white farmer; his black overseer, Josephus; and an Indian shopkeeper. Mehring's farm is a symbol for the moribund nature of South African society under apartheid. *The Burger's Daughter* (1979), tells the story of Rosa Burger, the daughter of white anti-apartheid activists, and her growing understanding of her own place in South African culture.

The prolific J.M. Coetzee also writes in various ways about the effects of apartheid on his characters. *In the Heart of the Country* (1997) tells the story of a woman living with her father on an isolated farm and her frenzied reaction to his taking a black mistress. *Disgrace* (2000) follows a shamed professor to his daughter's remote farm where he and his daughter are brutally attacked by three black men.

Alan Paton's most famous novel, *Cry, the Beloved Country* (1948), tells the story of an aging Zulu minister and his son, Absalom, who has been corrupted by life in Johannesburg. Although condemned as revolutionary in South Africa, the novel was translated into a number of foreign languages and brought international attention to social conditions in South Africa.

## AFRICAN LITERATURE IN FRENCH

Among the best known of African poets who wrote in French is Léopold Senghor of Senegal, one of the founders of *négritude*, a literary and political movement that celebrates black identity. Beginning in the 1930s, Senghor and other poets, including the more combative David Diop, reversed all the European stereotypes about black and white, elevating African values and ideas above European. Senghor not only wrote his own poetry; he also compiled and edited the *Anthology of the New Black and Malagasy Poetry in the French Language*, published in 1948, the first work to bring African poetry to an international audience. Senghor went on to become president of Senegal, serving from 1960 to 1980.

Unlike the early African writers in English, many of the early African writers in French admired their colonizers and wrote fiction that showed colonizers and French ideas and values in a positive light. Both Ahmadou Mapaté Diagne's novel *Three Wishes* (1920) and Ousmane Socé's novel *Mirages of Paris* (1937) adopt this view. Later writers took an entirely different position, satirizing and criticizing the colonizers. These attitudes are reflected in two satirical novels, *Houseboy (*1966) by Ferdinand Oyono of Cameroon and *The Poor Christ of Bomba* (1971) by Mongo Beti of Cameroon.

African literature, in whatever language, reflects the great diversity of the continent and its peoples. It remains to be seen what direction its young writers will take and to what extent they will adopt Western forms or adapt African oral and folk traditions.

*See also:* Apartheid; British Colonies; Colonization; French West Africa; Language.

## FURTHER READING

Asihene, Emmanuel. *Traditional Folk Tales of Ghana.* Lewiston, NY: Edwin Mellen, 1997.

Griffiths, Gareth. *African Literatures in English: East and West.* Essex, UK: Longman, 2000.

Mathabane, Mark. *Kaffir Boy: The True Story of a Black Youth's Coming of Age in Apartheid South Africa.* Topeka, KS: Tandem Books, 1999.

Ogunjimi, Bayo, and Abdul-Rasheed Na'Allah. *Introduction to African Oral Literature and Performance.* Lawrenceville, NJ: Africa World Press, 2005.

Soyinka, Wole. *Myth, Literature and the African World.* Cambridge, UK: Cambridge University Press, 1990.

Tate, Eleanora E. *Retold African Myths.* Logan, IA: Perfection Learning, 1993.

# Migration

For a number of complex reasons, millions of Africans leave their homes every year and move to neighboring countries, Europe, or the United States. In the year 2000, there were an estimated total of 175 million immigrants worldwide. Of this number, about 16.3 million (9.3 percent) were African.

The primary cause for migration from Africa is economic. People leave their homes to be able to earn more money to support their families; many men, for example, leave home to work on large, industrial farms. Such migration can confer benefits to both the home and the host country. The host country gains a source of inexpensive labor for jobs that, in some cases, native people do not want to do.

In many situations, an individual who migrates leaves his or her family behind but sends money home, which can have a significant positive impact on the economies of the home countries. According to the United Nations Economic Commission for Africa, in 2004 Nigeria received more than $2.5 billion from migrants who sent money home to their families, constituting nearly 4 percent of the entire **gross domestic product (GDP)** of Nigeria. Lesotho, one of the poorest countries in Africa, depends on money sent home by migrants for fully 25 percent of its GDP.

On the other hand, many African countries have experienced a significant "brain drain," as well-educated young professionals leave in search of higher-paying jobs in more prosperous countries. The brain drain has reached crisis proportions in the medical field. Doctors and nurses who migrate from Africa leave behind an ever-growing population of people with AIDS—with fewer and fewer trained professionals to treat them.

Illegal migration is a growing problem in Africa and Europe. Many desperate young Africans take terrible risks to seek a better life and many die in the process. In 2006, for example, more than 20,000 African immigrants arrived in the Canary Islands, a Spanish possession located off the west coast of Africa, making the dangerous sea crossing in rickety boats. These young immigrants chose the Canary Islands because it is the closest European territory to the North African mainland. Experts estimate that more than 1,000 people a year die trying to make the journey. Behind much of this illegal immigration are unscrupulous people who traffic in human beings, taking what little money migrants have with the promise of a safe and successful passage. Sadly, the journey often ends in death or near-death for the migrants.

The 2006 Euro-African Ministerial Conference on Migration and Development, held in Rabat, Morocco, and including representatives from fifty-eight African and European countries, concluded with an agreement called the Rabat Plan. In it, African nations agreed to try to stem the flow of illegal immigrants to Europe in return for economic assistance from European countries. Many believed that the agreement would have little effect, however, because the aid promised was insufficient to solve the problems that cause African people to leave their homes.

Another major reason Africans migrate is civil unrest and warfare. Between 1989 and 2003, for example, four West African countries—Liberia, Sierra Leone, Guinea, and Cote d'Ivoire—were besieged by civil war and sectarian violence. In 2003 alone more than one million people from the region fled to neighboring countries. In the mid-1990s, millions fled ethnic cleansing in

Rwanda as members of the Tutsi ethnic group sought to exterminate the Hutu. Since 2003, in Darfur, a region of Sudan, violence has forced more than 1.8 million people to seek *asylum*. In many cases, they end up in poor countries that do not have the resources to feed or even provide water to the desperate migrants.

Clearly, migration in African is both a blessing and a curse. While it is beneficial for families to have relatives send money home, migrants are often separated from their families for years. While some who have been forced to flee violence in their homelands have found better lives, most have not and many spend years in dreadful conditions in refugee camps.

*See also:* Civil Wars; Economic Development and Trade; Liberia; Refugees; Rwanda; Sudan; Tutsis and Hutus.

**FURTHER READING**

Reader, John. *Africa: A Biography of the Continent.* New York: Vintage, 1999.

Reynolds, Jonathan T., and Erik Gilbert. *Africa in World History: From Prehistory to the Present.* Upper Saddle River, NJ: Pearson Education, 2004.

Veney, Cassandra R. *Forced Migration in Eastern Africa: Democratization, Structural Adjustment, and Refugees.* Hampshire, UK: Palgrave Macmillan, 2006.

# Mozambique *See Portuguese Colonies.*

# Nigeria

A sub-Saharan nation in West Africa, bordered by Niger on the north, Benin on the west, and Cameroon and Chad on the east. Nigeria's southern border is on the Atlantic Ocean. Today, Nigeria is the most populous nation in Africa, with about 126 million people, and is home to more than 250 different ethnic groups, including the Ibo, Hausa, Fulani, and Edo.

The first Europeans to visit Nigeria were the Portuguese, who arrived in 1481. From the seventeenth through the nineteenth centuries, European traders established ports along the coast to handle the growing traffic in slaves. Ibo middlemen, who grew rich by selling slaves to European traders, established several city states, including Bonny, Owome, and Okrika. In 1804, Usuman dan Fodio, a devout Muslim, and his followers launched a holy war during which they conquered most of the Hausa states of northern Nigeria.

In 1861, the British *annexed* the city of Lagos in an attempt to put an end to the slave trade there. With a foothold in Lagos, Britain laid claim to southern Nigeria during the Berlin Conference (1884–1885). The British gradually expanded their territory and, in 1914, unified the northern and southern parts of the country as the Colony and Protectorate of Nigeria. Despite unification, however, education and economic development progressed more rapidly in the south along the coast, leading to a split between the two regions that would have long-term effects on the future

Nigeria is one of the African continent's largest producers of petroleum. In recent years, conflict has arisen between the oil companies' owners and the local people, who are demanding higher wages and better working conditions. (STR/Stringer/AFP/Getty Images)

political life of Nigeria. Moreover, the colony was split along religious and tribal lines. Hausa and Fulani tribes in the north were Muslim and the Ibo in the southeast were Christian.

Great Britain granted Nigeria independence in 1960. Originally, Nigeria was established as a **federation** of three semi-autonomous regions—Western, Eastern, and Northern Nigeria—with the federal government in charge of defense, foreign relations, and the overall economy. As time passed, Nigeria continued to respond to ethnic, religious, and regional differences by creating more and more states. By 1996 Nigeria—with an area the size of California, Arizona, and Nevada combined—was divided into thirty-six separate states.

Since gaining its independence, Nigeria has undergone a number of coups and coup attempts, the first of which occurred just six years after it became a self-governing state. In 1966, Ibo army officers overthrew the government and assassinated both regional and federal leaders. The new government itself was overthrown just seven months later by Hausa soldiers, who placed Lieutenant Colonel Yakubu Gowon at the head of a military government. In retaliation for the original coup, Gowon's government soldiers massacred thousands of Ibo living in the north. Secessionist sentiments, already strong among the Ibo, were strengthened by these events, and many Ibo left the north and returned to their homelands in the southeast.

In 1967, Ibo leaders declared the independence of this region of Nigeria, and they named the new nation the Republic of Biafra. This began a civil war, which ended with the defeat of Biafra in 1970 and the reintegration of the region.

After the civil war, Nigeria was able to make rapid economic strides. In the early 1970s, the price of oil had risen dramatically, making Nigeria's massive petroleum reserves even more valuable. In 1975, however, Gowon's government was overthrown by General Murtala Muhammad, who accused Gowon of corruption and misuse of Nigeria's wealth and promised to return the nation to civilian rule. Only one year later, however, Muhammad was assassinated. He was succeeded by General Olusegun Obasanjo, who moved the nation toward civilian rule and used oil revenue to develop the nation's economy. He also supervised the drafting of a new constitution and a free multiparty election in 1979, in which Alhaji Shehu Shagari won

## TURNING POINT

### Biafran War, 1967–1970

Nigeria has long been home to ethnic and religious tensions and has been subdivided into regions along ethnic lines. After an abortive coup in 1966 by mostly Christian Ibo army officers, Muslim Hausa in the Northern Region retaliated by massacring tens of thousands of Ibo. Nearly a million Ibo fled the north and settled in the Eastern Region. Shortly afterward, the Ibo drove other ethnic groups out of the east.

On May 30, 1967, the head of the Eastern Region, Odumegwu Ojukwu, declared the region independent of Nigeria and gave the name Biafra to the new nation. Nigeria's president, Yakubu Gowon, rejected the secession and a civil war began.

Although Biafran troops made early military gains in their battle for freedom, Nigeria instituted an economic blockade and its troops captured Biafra's seaports, leaving the new nation landlocked and unable to receive shipments by sea. Starvation and disease resulted. No one is sure exactly how many people died in Biafra during the three-year conflict, but estimates range from 500,000 to 1 million.

On January 15, 1970, Ojukwu surrendered, fled to Cote d'Ivoire, and Biafra was made part of Nigeria again. The Nigerian government promised the Ibo that there would be no retaliation for the war and moved quickly to reintegrate them into the larger society. To this day, however, the Ibo continue to believe that they have been excluded from power since the war, a belief that could again create instability in the region.

---

the presidency. Reelected in August 1983 amid allegations of corruption, Shagari's government was overthrown by General Muhammadu Buhari in December of the same year. The new government, in turn, was overthrown in 1985 by Major General Ibrahim Babangida, who promised he would eventually return Nigeria to civilian rule.

In 1993, free elections were again held in Nigeria, but within a week Babangida declared the election void and handed the reins of government to Ernest Shonekan. Shonekan, however, was forced to resign almost immediately, ceding power to Defense Minister Sani Abacha, whose administration dealt severely with anyone who dared to protest government policies or lobby for change. Although Abacha promised free elections and civilian rule, he remained in power until his death in 1998. His successor, Abdulsalami Abubaker, released all political prisoners and appointed an independent commission to conduct elections.

The winner of the 1999 elections and Nigeria's new president was the former military head of state Olusegun Obasanjo. His presidency ended sixteen consecutive years of military rule. Almost immediately, Obasanjo forced many military officers from political positions, created a commission to investigate human rights abuses, ordered the release of political prisoners, and tried to recover millions of dollars that Nigeria's leaders had hidden away in overseas bank accounts.

Despite these improvements, Nigeria has suffered for many years from insurgencies and sectarian violence. Since 1999, more than 10,000 people in the northern portion of Nigeria have died in clashes between Muslims and Ibo Christians over the spread of Sharia, or Muslim law. As of 2004, twelve of Nigeria's thirty-six states were ruled by Sharia, which imposes punishments such as flogging or dismemberment for certain crimes. In 2004, a rebellion began in the Niger delta region, Nigeria's primary oil-producing area. The Ijew people of the region live in poverty, while the government takes the profits from the oil. Fueled by resentment about unequal distribution of the profits from oil, the rebels have disrupted production.

Although Obasanjo's government has taken forceful measures against corruption, he, his vice president, and many supporters themselves were accused of corruption, and the vice president was forced to resign in 2006. Corruption so dominates Nigeria's political culture that, despite being a major oil-producing nation, its people are among the poorest in Africa. Ethnic and religious conflicts continue, making any real economic stability difficult.

*See also:* British Colonies; Colonization; Democratic Movements; Economic Development and Trade; Religion; Slavery and the Slave Trade.

### FURTHER READING

Efiong, Philip. *Nigeria and Biafra: My Story.* New York: Seaburn Books, 2007.

Robson, Lorna. *Nigeria.* New York: Chelsea House, 2005.

Rosenberg, Anne. *Nigeria—The Culture.* New York: Crabtree, 2000.

Uzokwe, Alfred Obiora. *Surviving in Biafra: The Story of the Nigerian Civil War.* Media, PA: Writer's Advantage, 2003.

# P-R

# Pan-African Movement

The "all-African" movement based on the concept that all African people, whether living on the continent or not, share common goals and bonds. Chief among those goals are the idea of self-determination for African people and an end to racism in all forms.

The Pan-African Movement began in 1900, when an attorney from the Caribbean island of Trinidad, Henry Sylvester-Williams, held a conference in London in which black people from all over the world came to discuss common issues and concerns and to protest the treatment of blacks in Britain and in British colonies in Africa.

After this initial conference, the African American scholar and founder of the National Association for the Advancement of Colored People (NAACP), W.E.B. Du Bois, organized five Pan-African Congresses. The first, held in Paris in 1919 at the end of the World War I, brought together fifty-seven delegates from fifteen nations. The congress addressed issues stemming from the experience and aftermath of World War I. African and African American soldiers who had served in the war were angry at the discrimination they suffered both during and after the conflict, despite having fought—in the words of U.S. president Woodrow Wilson—to "make the world safe for democracy." Black leaders also hoped to persuade the League of Nations that the former German colonies in Africa should be allowed to become self-governing and independent as soon as possible. Despite the demands of the congressional delegates, however, the German colonies were divided up among European powers with little or no thought to their eventual independence.

Du Bois organized three other Pan-African Congresses, in 1921, 1923, and 1927. The 1921 conference, held over several months in London, Paris, and Brussels, issued a document known as the "London Manifesto" that criticized Britain for its treatment of African colonies. Britain, the Manifesto declared, "has . . . systematically fostered ignorance among the Natives, has enslaved them, and is still enslaving them, [and has] declined even to try to train black and brown men in real self-government." The 1923 and 1927 conferences (held in London and New York City, respectively) dealt with many of the same concerns as the earlier ones and also added a demand to stop lynching in the United States.

In the 1930s and early 1940s, a worldwide depression and another world war made it difficult for the Pan-African movement to make headway in achieving its goals. Thus, the next congress was not convened until 1945, in Manchester, England, after the war. Delegates passed a resolution demanding that discrimination be made a crime and condemned **capitalism** and **imperialism.**

The first sub-Saharan African nation to gain its independence was Ghana, in 1957. Its first president, Kwame Nkrumah, was a strong supporter of Pan-Africanism. He held that Ghana was not truly free until all of Africa was free. His dream of a united Africa proved elusive, however, because the leaders of newly independent nations resisted any limitations on their autonomy. Thus, they did not want a system of government like that of the United States, in which individual states give up some of their power to a central, federal government. In 1963, the

Organization of African Unity (now the African Union) was formed, with thirty-two nations agreeing to work cooperatively toward common goals while maintaining political independence.

The civil rights and black power movements in the United States in the 1960s and 1970s were influenced by the idea of Pan-Africanism, as many African American leaders identified their quest with the struggle against colonialism in Africa. In fact, Malcolm X, leader of the Black Muslim group known as the Nation of Islam, traveled through Africa in 1964 proclaiming that American blacks could never be free as long as Africa was not free.

A sixth Pan-African Congress was held in Dar es Salaam, Tanzania, in 1974, but conflicts between Marxist and non-Marxist delegates from all over the world, including 100 Americans, became the focus of the meeting and little was accomplished. Today, Pan-African ideas are still evident in regional cooperative groups such as the Economic Community of West African States and the Southern African Development Community, which work together to ensure favorable **tariff** and trade agreements with other nations.

*See also:* African Union; British Colonies; Colonization; Economic Development and Trade; Imperialism.

### FURTHER READING

Kunjufu, Jawanza. *Lessons from History: A Celebration of Blackness.* Chicago: African American Images, 1987.

Reynolds, Jonathan T., and Erik Gilbert. *Africa in World History: From Prehistory to the Present.* Upper Saddle River, NJ: Pearson Education, 2004.

Walters, Ronald W. *Pan-Africanism in the African Diaspora: An Analysis of Modern Afrocentric Political Movements.* Detroit: Wayne State University Press, 1997.

# Portuguese Colonies

Areas of Africa, including the modern countries of Cape Verde, São Tomé and Príncipe, Guinea-Bissau, Mozambique, and Angola, ruled by the Portuguese. The Portuguese were the first Europeans to reach Africa on August 21, 1415, when Henry the Navigator's fleet landed in and conquered Ceuta in what is now Morocco.

Not only were the Portuguese the first Europeans to colonize Africa, but they were also the last to leave. It was not until 1975 that Portugal ceded control of the colony of Angola to native peoples. With the exception of Mozambique, located on the east coast of Africa, all the Portuguese colonies were located along Africa's western shores.

Portugal's main exports from its African holdings were slaves. In fact, Portugal had a monopoly on the African slave trade for 200 years, from 1440 to 1640. It is estimated that the Portuguese transported more than 4.5 million Africans to the Americas, about 40 percent of the total. Even after the abolition of slavery in Europe and the Americas in the nineteenth century, Portuguese colonies continued to force African natives to work in farming, mining, and fishing enterprises that benefited only the colonizers.

In the late nineteenth century, Portugal sought to connect the colonies of Angola and Mozambique in order to have a territory that stretched the entire width of Africa. The British, however, planned to extend their African colonies from South

Africa north to Egypt and objected to the Portuguese plan. The British issued the Ultimatum of 1890, demanding that the Portuguese withdraw from all disputed territory in what was then Rhodesia. The Portuguese, no match for the British military, complied. Unlike many of the other nations that held colonies in Africa, Portugal was neither rich nor militarily powerful and depended on the wealth from its colonies for economic stability.

From 1932 to 1968, Portugal was ruled by Fascist dictator António Salazar, and his right-wing party, Estado Novo, continued in power until 1974. Beginning in 1961, Portugal was faced with the first of several independence movements in its colonies when Angolan rebel groups attacked the Luanda prison and killed seven police officers. In Guinea-Bissau, the Marxist African Party began a rebellion against the Portuguese in 1963, and the next year saw attacks against Portuguese targets in Mozambique. Although the Portuguese military was largely successful in holding back the rebel forces, in 1974 the costs of the ongoing war led to the collapse of the Portuguese government. The Carnation Revolution brought a democratic government into power, which immediately began negotiations to withdraw from Africa.

Almost as soon as Portugal withdrew, civil wars broke out in both Mozambique and Angola. The new communist governments of both nations found themselves battling insurgent groups supported by other African nations as well as by the United States. The civil war in Angola did not end until 2002, with the nation in ruins. In Mozambique, meanwhile, the civil war ended in 1992. Since that time, Mozambique has been politically stable, which has led to the return of hundreds of thousands of refugees who had fled the country during the war and to economic growth. Guinea-Bissau has not been politically or economically stable since the departure of the Portuguese and is among Africa's least developed nations today. Both São Tomé and Príncipe and Cape Verde instituted democratic reforms in the 1990s and have been relatively stable since then.

*See also:* Colonization; Communist Movements; Democratic Movements; Slavery and Slave Trade.

### FURTHER READING

Birmingham, David. *Portugal and Africa.* Hampshire, UK: Palgrave Macmillan, 2003.

# Refugees

According to the United Nations Convention on the Status of Refugees (1951), a refugee is someone who "owing to a well-founded fear of being persecuted ... is outside the country of his nationality, and is unable to, or, owing to such fear, is unwilling to avail himself of the protection of that country." Internally displaced persons (IDPs) are people who have been driven from their homes but have not moved to another country.

In 2006, the United Nations High Commission on Refugees (UHNCR) reported that there were more than 5 million "persons of concern" (refugees or IDPs) on the African continent, representing more than one-quarter of the world's refugees.

Africa has seen several major refugee crises since the early 1990s. These crises are caused by a number of factors including natural disasters, drought and famine, civil war, political and economic instability, and ethnic conflict. Among the worst is the Great Lakes refugee crisis, which was brought about by a wave of ethnic cleansing in Rwanda in 1994 in which two ethnic groups, the Hutu and Tutsi, came into conflict. After the death of Rwandan president Juvénal Habyarimana, Hutu officials, police, and militia began a campaign to eliminate the minority Tutsi. When Tutsi forces retaliated and took over the Rwandan capital in April, Hutus, including many of those who had participated in the genocide, fled. By August more than two million people had left Rwanda, and one and a half million were internally displaced.

Between 1989 and 2003, civil war in Liberia spilled over into Sierra Leone, Guinea, and Cote d'Ivoire, leaving more than a quarter of a million people dead and 1.5 million uprooted. Hundreds of thousands of these refugees took **asylum** in Guinea, despite efforts of Liberian rebels and Guinean soldiers to prevent them from crossing the border.

Beginning in 2003 in Darfur, a region in western Sudan, attacks by a government-sponsored militia known as the Janjaweed forced 1.8 million residents to flee to neighboring countries, some of which were facing crises of their own. In 2007, civil war in the Central African Republic displaced more than 200,000 people, many of whom fled to Darfur. Some also escaped to Chad, which was embroiled in its own civil war. By some estimates, more than 2.5 million people in Darfur, Chad, and Central African Republic have been displaced.

In Zimbabwe, meanwhile, economic disaster caused human displacement on a massive scale. Inflation as high as 1200 percent led as many as 3 million people to flee to neighboring Mozambique, South Africa, Malawi, Namibia, and Botswana in search of work. Ironically, Mozambique also underwent a refugee crisis of its own in 2007. Flooding in that nation displaced more than 50,000 people.

Life in refugee camps in Africa can be almost unimaginably difficult for those people forced to live in them; people arrive with little more than the clothes on their backs and live in crowded, squalid conditions. Despite international aid, food and water are often scarce, sanitation is minimal, and crime and disease are rampant. Women and girls are often victimized in the camps, forced to trade sex for food. Refugees who escape civil war often find that the camps themselves are targeted by combatants, so that the bloodshed they tried to flee comes to them. Many refugees are unable return home—for a variety of reasons—and may end up living in camps for years, with no prospect of a better life or a way home.

*See also:* Civil Wars; Migration; Rwanda; Sudan; Tutsis and Hutus.

### FURTHER READING

Browne, Peter. *The Longest Journey: Resettling Refugees from Africa.* Sydney, Australia: UNSW Press, 2006.

Reader, John. *Africa: A Biography of the Continent.* New York: Vintage, 1999.

# Religion

In addition to providing moral guidance and helping explain the meaning of existence, religious beliefs and practices in Africa, as elsewhere, act as catalysts for social change.

Three major religious systems dominate the African continent: African traditional religions, Islam, and Christianity.

## TRADITIONAL RELIGIONS

There is no one African traditional religion; in fact, there are nearly as many religions as there are ethnic groups, because African traditional religions never became institutionalized as other religions did. They possess no written scripture like the Bible or Koran, and religious leaders tend to be tribal elders in each village. Nevertheless, some religious scholars insist that there are so many similarities among African traditional religions that they can be understood as one faith with many different expressions.

African traditional religions share a number of characteristics. For one thing, they are uniformly **monotheistic**, as are Christianity and Islam; that is, they are all based on a belief in a single supreme being who created the heavens and earth. In fact, this belief in one god made the conversion of many Africans to monotheistic religions easier than it might have been if they had been believers in many gods, or **polytheistic**. In African traditional religions, God is unknowable and mysterious. While he (or she—in some African cultures the supreme being is feminine) created everything, the supreme being is considered by most Africans to be, in the words of religious scholar John Mbiti, "completely other." God does not intervene in everyday life, as the Judeo-Christian deity does. Still, adherents pray to and express love for God. In various native religions, God is referred to as Friend, Father (or Mother), Giver of Children, God of Ancestors, Ruler of the Universe, Savior, Shepherd, the Everlasting, the Great Spirit, and the Just One. Africans never attempt to make images of the Supreme Being, as Western artists often do, because they do not conceptualize the deity as existing in a single form or as being like themselves. God is considered, in a sense, beyond human understanding.

African traditional religions also conceive of the Supreme Being as the source of all moral decisions; that is, they believe that God sees all and metes out rewards and punishments as appropriate.

Another common characteristic of African traditional religions is **animism**, a word from the Latin meaning *soul* that denotes the belief that everything has a spirit and that spirits are active in everyday life. Thus, many African traditional religions invest thunder, lightning, trees, mountains, and other natural phenomena with a spiritual dimension. An African hunter therefore might make a small sacrifice to the spirit of an animal he has killed, as an act of gratitude for the animal's sacrifice.

Adherents of African traditional religions believe that everything has a spirit or soul, and that death is not final. While the body dies, the spirit lives on. Africans believe that the spirits of dead ancestors are with them every day and actively involved in the lives of the living. Many rituals are connected with honoring or appeasing these spirits.

African traditional religions teach that everything that happens to an individual has meaning—that everything happens for a reason. If a person becomes ill, for example, adherents of native faiths do not attribute the cause of the illness to bacteria or viruses. Rather, they believe the illness is caused by offended spirits. The only way to cure the sufferer is to find out which spirit has been offended and why. Once the spirit's concerns have been dealt with, the illness should be cured.

Many Africans also believe in magic and sorcery. They believe that some people have a special connection to the spirit

## AFRICAN RELIGIONS, 1324–2005

**1324** Mansa Musa of Mali makes a hajj, or pilgrimage to Mecca

**15th Century** Portuguese missionaries come to the Kongo Kingdom

**1518** King Nzinga's grandson Henrique named first African bishop of the Catholic Church

**1830s** Sierra Leone and Liberia become centers for Christian missionaries

**1834** Abolition of the slave trade by Great Britain motivates missionaries from Europe and the United States to come to Africa to convert freed slaves

**1864** Samuel Ajayi Crowther named first black Anglican Bishop

**1928** Muslim Brotherhood, an organization that advocates making Egypt an Islamic state, founded

**1939** Two African Catholic bishops appointed

**2005** Muslim Brotherhood wins seventy-six seats in Egyptian Parliament

---

world and can intervene on behalf of others. Magic is generally considered good in African society, while sorcery is regarded as evil. When something bad happens to a person, for example, one of the causes may be that a sorcerer has cast an evil spell. A magician may be called on to counteract the spell.

Another common characteristic of African traditional religion is a strong sense of community. Because of the communal nature of African religion, there are many rites and ceremonies designed to bring people into the fold and keep them connected. Chief among these are initiation rites by which adolescents are transformed into adults. While some ethnic groups, such as the Krobo of Ghana, hold initiation rites for girls, most focus on boys. During the initiation rites, the boys learn what it is to be a man in their particular community.

Adherents of African traditional religions do not separate religion and daily life, as many Western people do. Every aspect of life is influenced and informed by religion.

### Vodun

Vodun, often referred to as "voodoo," comes from a word in the Fon language for "spirit." This African traditional religion was practiced by many West African ethnic groups and may be more than 6,000 years old. As practiced in Africa, vodun holds that there is a "god-creator," who does not interfere in human affairs, and several vodun, or "god actors," who govern the universe. Vodun came to the Americas with enslaved people and today is especially prevalent in Haiti. More than 60 million people practice vodun, which has been the official religion of Benin since 1989. During the colonial period, vodun was actively suppressed and many priests were killed.

### ISLAM

The first Muslims came to Africa in 615, during Mohammed's lifetime. This group had

In the town of Kosheh, about 500 miles (814.67 km) south of Cairo, Egypt, a mosque's minaret towers over the dome and spires of a Coptic Christian church. (Amr Mahmoud/AFP/Getty Images)

escaped persecution in Mecca and took refuge in Ethiopia. In 639, the Muslim Arab General Amr ibn al-Asi invaded Egypt, initiating the spread of Islam. Although he and his successors did not force Egyptians to convert, non-Muslims were taxed heavily, and many did adopt the new faith. In the seventh and eighth centuries, the Umayyads, a powerful Syrian Muslim dynasty, brought Islam to the Mediterranean coast of Africa. The Berbers, an ethnic group of northwest Africa, were among the first to convert to Islam. They, in turn, carried Islam throughout northwest Africa. Arab sailors who traded on Africa's east coast founded colonies on nearby islands, particularly Zanzibar, in the ninth century. From there, traders traveled into the interior, carrying their religion with them. Muslims typically did not force conversion but

## INTO THE 21ST CENTURY

### Islamic Politics in Africa

The Muslim Brotherhood, an organization founded to protest foreign domination in Egypt and other Islamic countries, was outlawed after an abortive assassination attempt against Gamal Abde Nasser, a government adviser who became Egyptian president in 1954. Since then, the brotherhood has helped to form a number of other Islamic **fundamentalist** organizations, including Hamas in Palestine. The brotherhood has renounced violence and is considered mainly a religious group, but it advocates making Egypt an Islamic **theocracy**. In 2005, the Brotherhood managed to win seventy-six seats in the Egyptian parliament, giving it the right to put forward a candidate in the 2011 elections, when longtime President Hosni Mubarak has said he will step down. Some experts believe that the Muslim Brotherhood might try to become an officially recognized political party, positioning itself to garner enough support to win in 2011.

Many Egyptians worry that if Egypt becomes an Islamic state, the country will be subject to Islamic law, known as Sharia. Sharia traditionally has applied only to Muslims. Many non-Muslims, however, are concerned that Sharia-inspired punishments might be imposed on them, including what is called "judicial amputation" for crimes. An armed robber, for example, would lose his right arm and left foot as punishment for his crime. Western leaders have expressed concern that Islamist states in Africa will become safe havens for Islamic terrorists, as Sudan once was for al-Qaeda's Osama bin Laden.

---

rather lived and intermarried with African people. Thus, conversion was a slow process, taking hundreds of years in some cases. Islam was easier for many Africans to accept than Christianity because it permitted a man to have more than one wife, a common practice in many African traditional religions. Christianity insisted that marriage be monogamous.

Islam spread quickly south of the Sahara. Mansa Musa (r. 1307–1332) of Mali was the first ruler to make Islam the state religion. In 1324, he made a famous hajj, or pilgrimage to Mecca, as all Muslims are supposed to do. Musa's hajj, however, included 100 camel-loads of gold, 500 slaves, each carrying a gold staff, thousands of subjects, and his wife with 500 attendants. Musa brought back religious scholars and an Arab architect who built the great mud mosques at Goa and Timbuktu. Songhai, a sixteenth-century empire centered in Mali, was also a powerful Islamic state. Its greatest king, Sonni Ali (r. 1464–1492), expanded the empire by military conquest and gained control of important cities along the trans-Saharan trade routes, such as Jenne and Timbuktu. He did not force those he conquered to convert to Islam and was tolerant of traditional African religions.

Today, nearly 40 percent of Africa's 750 million inhabitants are Muslim; most are of the Sunni sect. The populations of Algeria, Egypt, Djibouti, Libya, Mauritania, Senegal, Mali, Somalia, and Tunisia are all more than 90 percent Muslim. Half of Nigeria's 113 million people are also Muslim, and there are large Muslim populations in Niger, Sudan, Burkina Faso, Chad, Cote d'Ivoire, and Ethiopia.

In parts of Africa today, Islamic fundamentalists call on nations whose populations are largely Muslim to become **theocratic** Islamic states, much like Iran. In the 2005 elections in Egypt, the Muslim Brotherhood, an organization founded in 1928 that advocates making Egypt an Islamic state, won seventy-six seats in the nation's parliament.

## CHRISTIANITY

Christianity came early to Africa. By the first century, there were Christians in North Africa. Legend has it that Mark, one of the four Christian evangelists, arrived in Alexandria, Egypt, in C.E. 60 and began converting the inhabitants. The Egyptian Christian church founded by Mark split from the Roman Catholic Church after the Council of Chalcedon in 451 and is known today as Coptic Christianity. ("Copt" is the Arabic word for "Egyptian.") The dispute that caused the rift had to do with the nature of Christ and whether or not he was both human and divine. Coptic Christians believed that Christ had one nature only, intermingling humanity and divinity; Roman Catholics held that the two natures were separate. This rather esoteric theological difference created a schism that exists to this day between Coptic Christians and Roman Catholics.

From Egypt, Christianity spread to the west, where **indigenous** populations embraced the new religion as a way of protesting Roman rule. To the east, in the fourth century, King Ezana of Ethiopia made Christianity the official state religion. In 312, Constantine made Christianity the official religion of the Roman Empire.

Beginning in the seventh century, Christian populations began to shrink, while Islamic populations grew. By the end of that century, only Ethiopia remained primarily Christian. Then, in the fifteenth century, Christian missionaries came to Africa following in the footsteps of explorers. The first to arrive in sub-Saharan Africa were the Portuguese, who came at the behest of King Nzinga of the Kongo Kingdom. By 1500, Catholicism had become the official religion of the Kongo Empire, and King Nzinga's grandson, Henrique, became the first black African bishop in the Catholic Church in 1518.

By the beginning of the nineteenth century, there were very few Christians in Africa, except for some Coptic Christians in Egypt, Christians in Ethiopia, and people in the former Kongo Empire. In the 1800s, however, a renewed interest in converting Africans arose in both Catholic and Protestant denominations. The abolition of the slave trade by Great Britain in 1834 motivated many missionaries from Europe and the United States to come to Africa.

Christian missionary programs in Africa were successful largely because they offered education to the people. Missionaries taught Africans to read so that they could read the Bible. These same missionaries were often instrumental in creating the first alphabets for indigenous African languages in order to be able to translate the Bible for their new converts.

By the 1830s, Sierra Leone and Liberia, colonies established by freed slaves, became significant centers for Christian missionaries. J.R. Roberts, the first president of Liberia, was born in the United States and was himself a Christian. Both Protestant and Catholic churches began to ordain African priests and select African bishops. The first African to be made a bishop in the Anglican Church was Samuel Ajayi Crowther, a former slave. Crowther was ordained as a bishop in 1864. He once met Queen Victoria of England and read the Lord's Prayer to her in the Yoruba language.

In 1939, two African Catholic bishops were appointed—Joseph Kiwanuka of Uganda and Joseph Faye of Senegal.

In addition to Catholicism and various Protestant denominations, Africa is home to many African Initiated Churches. These organizations grew out of Protestant denominations as Africans became increasingly frustrated with the attitudes of some missionaries toward traditional African customs and practices. Some African Initiated Churches are only slightly different versions of the protestant denominations from which they derived, but many intermingle aspects of traditional religion—including the practice of **polygamy**—with aspects of Christianity.

Today there are about 360 million Christians in Africa, about half of whom are Roman Catholic. African countries with large Christian populations include Cape Verde, Ghana, Tanzania, and South Africa.

*See also:* Colonialism; Culture and Traditions; Society.

### FURTHER READING

Awolalu, J. Omosade. *Yoruba Beliefs and Sacrificial Rites.* New York: Athelia Henrietta, 1996.

Bediako, Kwame. *Christianity in Africa: The Renewal of Non-Western Religion.* Maryknoll, NY: Orbis, 1996.

Chidester, David. *Religions of South Africa.* London: Routledge, 1992.

Lawson, E. Thomas. *Religions of Africa: Traditions in Transformation.* Long Grove, IL: Waveland, 1998.

Magesa, Laurenti. *African Religion: The Moral Traditions of Abundant Life.* Maryknoll, NY: Orbis, 1997.

# Rwanda

A landlocked nation in east-central Africa, surrounded by the Democratic Republic of the Congo, Uganda, Tanzania, and Burundi. Although Rwanda is just two degrees south of the equator, its climate is **temperate** due to the high elevation of the land. The country has been plagued by shifts in power and wars of ethnic hatred.

Rwanda was a stable and unified society before the first European, German Count Gustave Adolf Von Goetzen, arrived there in 1894. The Hutu and Tutsi inhabitants had evolved a feudal society in which the ruling Tutsi herded cattle and the Hutu farmed the land. The two groups shared a language, culture, and regularly intermarried. In 1889, the Tutsi king, known as the *mwami*, peacefully allowed Rwanda to become a German **protectorate**. In 1915, Belgian troops from the Congo drove the Germans out of Rwanda and took control of the region.

After World War I, the League of Nations granted Rwanda and Burundi to Belgium as the territory of Ruanda-Urundi. Because the Belgians believed that the more European-looking Tutsis were superior to the majority Hutu, they allowed the Tutsis to administer the government on their behalf, which fueled resentment among the Hutu. In the 1950s, however, when the Belgians began to encourage the growth of democratic institutions, the Tutsis resisted the idea, preferring to retain their superior position. When Hutus rebelled against the Tutsi government in 1959, the Belgians supported the rebels. The rebels ousted the Tutsis in 1959 and, shortly thereafter, tens of thousands of Tutsis fled the country.

Rwanda was granted full independence by Belgium in 1962, and its first president was Gregoire Kayibanda, leader of the Party of the Hutu Emancipation Movement (PARMEHUTU). In 1973, accusing the Kayibanda government of corruption, Major

In 2007, Paul Kagame, president of the Republic of Rwanda, spoke before the United Nations General Assembly in New York. Kagame assumed the Rwandan presidency in 2000; in 2003, he went on to win a landslide victory in the first national elections since 1994. (Don Emmert/AFP/Getty Images)

General Juvénal Habyarimana, a Hutu, led a successful **coup** and installed himself as president. He was reelected in 1983 and again in 1988.

In 1990, an organization of Tutsi exiles called the Rwandan Patriotic Front (RPF) invaded Rwanda from its base in Uganda. The RPF accused the Habyarimana government of failing to bring democracy to Rwanda or to help the nearly half million Tutsis who had been forced to flee their native land. War continued for two years until the signing of the Arusha cease-fire in 1992.

On April 6, 1994, a plane carrying President Habyarimana and Cyprien Ntaryamira, the president of the neighboring nation of Burundi, was shot down while attempting to land at Kigali Airport. Both leaders were killed. Hutu officials suggested that the plane had been shot down under orders from the RPF, a suggestion that served as a trigger for a massacre of Tutsis and moderate Hutus by Hutu officials, civilians, and a newly formed Hutu militia called Interahamwe. More than 800,000 people were murdered before the carnage was halted by the RPF's capture of the capital city of Kigali. Fearing retaliation, nearly 2 million Hutus fled the country, many to neighboring Zaire (now the Democratic Republic of the Congo).

In 1994, in an attempt to heal the wounds of ethnic hatred, Paul Kagame, the Tutsi rebel leader, took the position of vice president in the new government and installed a Hutu, Pasteur Bizimungu, as president. Rwanda's involvement in the First and Second Congo Wars (1996–1997 and 1998–2003) stalled progress toward national unity and recovery. Hutu militia members who had escaped across the Rwandan border into Zaire began to attack Rwanda from their refugee camps there. In 1996, when Congolese rebel Laurent Kabila launched an offensive against Zaire's dictator Mobutu Sese Seko, Rwanda sent troops to support him in the hope of ending the Hutu threat. Kabila successfully deposed Mobutu, and Rwandan forces stayed in Zaire to help his government deal with hostile elements in the east, including the Hutu militia. In 1998, however, Kabila ordered all foreign troops out of Zaire. Rwandan and other troops refused to leave, igniting the Second Congo War, which cost the lives of 3.8 million people, making it the bloodiest conflict in the history of modern Africa. At the close of the four-year war in 2002, Rwanda agreed to pull its troops out of Zaire, and Zaire agreed to disarm the Hutu militia.

In 2000, President Bizimungu resigned and was succeeded by Paul Kagame, who became the first Tutsi president of Rwanda. In 2003, Kagame won the presidency in the first elections held in Rwanda since 1994. In the same year, Rwandans approved a new constitution that established a balance of power between Hutus and Tutsis by ensuring that neither group could hold more than half the seats in Parliament. The new constitution also forbids the incitement of ethnic hatred. Under Kagame's leadership, Rwanda has struggled to erase the legacy of ethnic hatred and to rebuild its economy, which is primarily based on the export of coffee and tea.

*See also:* Civil Wars; Colonization; Congo; Economic Development and Trade; Refugees; Tutsis and Hutus.

### FURTHER READING

Carr, Rosamond Halsey. *Land of a Thousand Hills: My Life in Rwanda.* New York: Plume, 2000.

Dallaire, Romeo. *Shake Hands with the Devil.* Lancashire, UK: Arrow, 2005.

Gourevitch, Philip. *We Wish to Inform You That Tomorrow We Will Be Killed with Our Families.* New York: Picador, 1999.

Harmon, Daniel E. *Central and East Africa.* New York: Chelsea House, 2001.

# S

# Slavery and the Slave Trade

From the sixteenth through most of the nineteenth centuries, some 12 to 15 million human beings were forcibly taken from their homes in West Africa and transported to the Caribbean and the Americas to work on plantations. From the ninth through the early twentieth centuries, Muslim slave traders took almost as many East Africans to parts of the Middle East, where they worked on clove plantations or as pearl divers, served in the army, or were used as sex slaves.

## EAST AFRICAN SLAVE TRADE

Muslim slave traders began taking slaves from eastern Africa and took them to places like modern-day Iraq, Iran, Kuwait, and Turkey sometime in the ninth century. Despite the horror and brutality of this trade in human beings, slavery in Muslim countries was governed by Islamic law and tradition. Under Islam, slaves were considered people, not property, and had some protection under the law. For example, slave owners were not allowed to take children away from their mothers and slaves could take their masters to court for offenses such as failure to provide adequate food and shelter. Under Islam, freeing slaves was considered a great virtue, and freed slaves ordinarily did not suffer discrimination. The eastern slave trade continued into the twentieth century. Slavery was outlawed in many Middle Eastern nations only when Western powers such as Britain and France applied economic and political pressure.

## ATLANTIC SLAVE TRADE

The Portuguese were the first Europeans to visit Africa and the first to take slaves, beginning in about 1440. These slaves were transported to the south of Portugal, where they worked primarily as household servants. As the Portuguese colony of Brazil grew, however, laborers were needed to work in its massive sugar cane plantations. In 1518, the first of thousands of ships tightly packed with slaves crossed the Atlantic destined for the Americas.

The slave trade became highly profitable for the Portuguese, a fact that was not lost on other European powers. After 1670, Spain, Britain, France, and the Netherlands began to compete for their share of the wealth. Over a period of about 300 years, slave traders made more than 50,000 voyages across the Atlantic, a journey of about 4,000 miles (6,400 km) that took about three months. Most of the slaves, about 42 percent, ended up working on plantations in the Caribbean; another 38 percent went to Brazil, and about 5 percent were brought to North America.

By all accounts, the crossing itself was hellish. People were kept below decks where the air was deadly and there was barely room to move. Many died of disease, malnutrition, or despair. Some committed suicide by banging their heads against the floor, refusing to eat, or jumping overboard. Food, while plentiful, was of poor quality and served in buckets, leading to fights as individuals struggled to get their share. Although slave traders had an economic investment in keeping their "property" alive, about 20 percent of Africans aboard the slave ships died before reaching their destination.

In general, the European slavers did not procure the slaves themselves. Slaves were captured in the interior by native traders and brought to ports along the west coast of Africa, in places such as Guinea and the Gold Coast, where they were sold to European traders. Many

**THE AFRICAN SLAVE TRADE, 1700–1810**

In the African slave trade, slave ships left Europe and sailed south to Africa, where they took slaves on board and sailed for the Americas. On the return trip to Europe, the ships were often laden with raw materials such as gold, silver, and sugar cane to be sold on the European market.

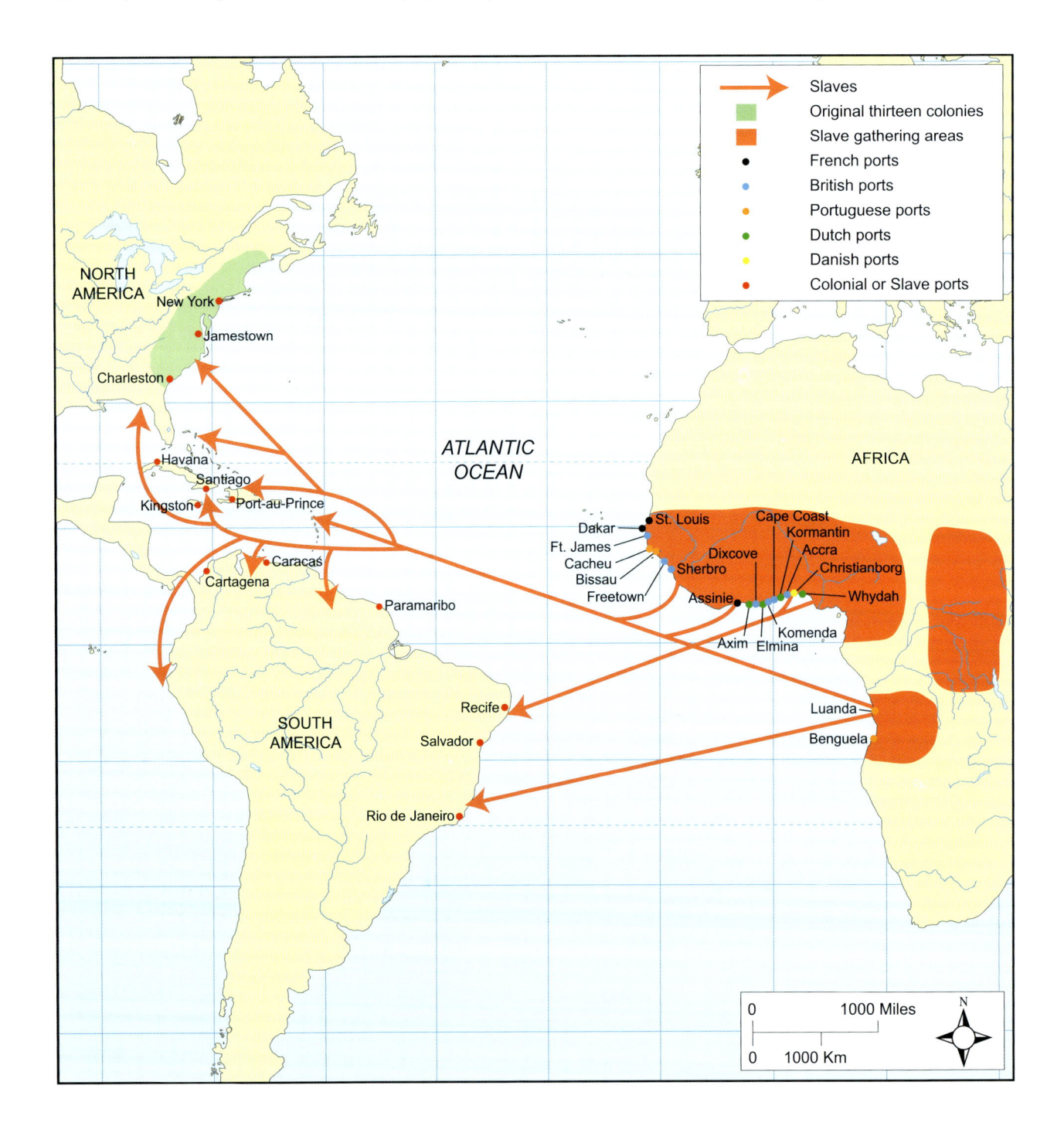

Africans grew rich not only by selling slaves, but also by trading in the supplies needed for the long sea journey. Indeed, when Britain banned the slave trade in 1807, many African traders and chiefs were angry, feeling that their livelihoods had been taken from them.

### ENDING THE SLAVE TRADE

Several factors contributed to the end of the slave trade. The first to outlaw the practice were the British, who put an end to slave trading in 1807 and outlawed slave ownership in 1834. Besides the efforts of British abolitionists such as Granville Sharp, Thomas Clarkson, and William Wilberforce, the **Industrial Revolution** itself contributed to the end of slavery because manufacturing processes, unlike plantations, worked better with free labor; people needed to be free to go where the work was. In addition, there was more wealth to be gained from industrial production than from agriculture. Furthermore, because the British had lost their American colonies in 1783, they no longer had a captive market for the slaves they transported; Americans were free to buy slaves from whomever they chose. The French Revolution, too, with its emphasis on liberty and equality, gave new impetus to those in Great Britain who opposed slavery. Ironically, Britain began to colonize Africa in part to try to *prevent* other nations from taking slaves. They began to move from the coastal areas of West Africa into the interior, for example, to prevent members of the Ashante ethnic group from continuing to capture and sell slaves.

Despite the French Revolution's impact on the British, it had little effect at first on the French slave trade. The French did not outlaw slave trading until 1818—almost thirty years after the revolution. Portugal outlawed the slave trade in 1830, but trading actually continued through the 1850s. The Dutch outlawed the slave trade in 1863. After the British banned the slave trade in 1807, more and more people began to think about the evils of slavery and in turn to pressure their governments to end the practice.

### CONSEQUENCES

The long-term effects of slavery on Africa can still be felt today. As the continent lost millions of people and many of its strongest men to slavery, industrial and agricultural development was slowed, even halted in some places. Much of the grinding poverty that one sees in Africa today can be attributed to this lack of development. Because slaves were often captured in wars between various African ethnic groups, armed conflict was sometimes initiated with the sole aim of taking slaves, creating a legacy of hatred between ethnic groups that might otherwise never have occurred. Because so many of the most fit men in African societies had been taken, when Europeans began their colonization efforts, there were many fewer warriors to fight back. In a sense, then, many of the evils of colonialism can be attributed to slavery, including the loss of identity and culture, political instability, corruption, and the failure of democratic institutions

*See also:* Agriculture; Civil Wars; Colonization; Culture and Tradition; Economic Development and Trade; Society.

### FURTHER READING

Cameron, Ann. *The Kidnapped Prince: The Life of Olaudah Equiano.* New York: Yearling, 2000.

Lovejoy, Paul E. *Transformations in Slavery: A History of Slaves in Africa.* Cambridge, UK: Cambridge University Press, 2000.

Newman, Shirlee P. *The African Slave Trade.* London: Franklin Watts, 2000.

Willis, John Ral. *Slaves and Slavery in Africa: Islam and the Ideology of Enslavement.* London: Routledge, 2006.

# Society

The traditional African extended family has always been, in many senses, the basis of all of African society, the shared culture and institutions that provide a common identity. Even today, many Africans do not think of themselves as Nigerian or Kenyan, but as members of particular clans or ethnic groups.

## FAMILY STRUCTURE

A variety of different kinship systems can be found in traditional African villages. For instance, the Ibo of Nigeria have a **patrilineal** system, in which all inheritance is passed through the father. When a woman marries, she leaves the family village and goes to live in her husband's village. Thus, nearly everyone in an Ibo village is related through their fathers.

On the other hand, the Akan of Ghana have a **matrilineal** system. They are divided into clans, with children becoming part of the mother's clan at birth. Inheritance among the Akan passes from the mother's brother to her sons.

The most important effect of the kinship structure in African society is the impact of the extended family on all aspects of life. It was said—before the AIDS epidemic hit the continent—that there are no orphans in Africa. This is because it is the duty of everyone in the village to care for children. If parents die, relatives raise children as their own. In some ethnic groups, particularly those that are matrilineal, in fact, children are routinely reared not by their parents but by members of the extended family, such as aunts or uncles. So important are kinship ties within some rural villages that children often refer to all women who are the same age as their biological mother as "mother," and to all men who are the same age as their biological father as "father." In addition, the extended family, not an individual, owns the land, and everyone pitches in to cultivate the crops. Land is never sold or inherited in the sense that it is in the West. It simply remains in the family.

Older members of the family or clan are revered for their experience and wisdom and they often function in place of a formal legal system, dispensing advice and justice to erring family members. There is no need for nursing homes or pension plans in most of rural Africa, because children care for their aging parents as a matter of course. As Africa becomes more urban, however, the old ways of doing things are being replaced by more Westernized systems, and age is less revered in the cities than in rural areas.

## GENDER ROLES

Throughout most of Africa, men are considered to be the breadwinners and heads of households, and women are considered to be subordinate to men. In many African nations, even though women do most of the farming, they are not allowed to own land, and children, in the event of divorce, usually "belong" to the father. Women receive significantly less education than men and generally are not prepared for work outside the home. Still, African women work hard, doing almost all of the agricultural work, building and maintaining homes, cooking, and rearing the children.

Many women's groups in Africa today are demanding Western-style equality—including the freedom to own property and the freedom to initiate divorce. While many nations have enacted such laws, they exist in conflict with customary laws, which are enforced by individual villages, clans, or ethnic groups.

## INTO THE 21ST CENTURY

### AIDS in Africa

AIDS has been a scourge on Africa like no other. In 2007, there were 22.5 million people in sub-Saharan Africa living with AIDS, with 2.8 million new cases that year. Of those infected, 13.3 million are women. There were also 2.1 million children living with AIDS in Africa, and 2.1 million people died of AIDS in 2006 alone. Since AIDS was first diagnosed in the late 1970s, nearly 22 million people worldwide have died from it, and 13 million children have lost one or both parents. About three-fourths of these deaths occurred in Africa, where AIDS is now the primary cause of death. In many African countries, 10 to 20 percent of all adults are infected with HIV.

In South Africa, where AIDS is the leading cause of death, the situation was made worse by the fact that President Thabo Mbeki for years denied that AIDS was a problem and even went so far as to question whether HIV and AIDS were actually related. He also questioned the safety and efficacy of the drugs used to treat the disease and diverted funds from AIDS treatment to combating crime. In 2003, health activists sued the government to force it to distribute AIDS drugs, but it was not until 2006 that the Mbeki government acknowledged the crisis.

Because so many in South Africa and other parts of sub-Saharan Africa are desperate, quacks have been able to make money selling dubious cures. Pharmacies in Johannesburg stock products with names such as "Life Extension" and "Ozone Rectal Treatment," which claim to treat AIDS, and the government has done nothing to regulate this practice. Even though South Africa has finally begun to use **antiretroviral** drugs to treat AIDS, many people prefer the alternative remedies, and people in rural areas are completely unaware of the treatment options.

The high cost of drugs to treat AIDS has also been a problem in Africa. With the proper treatment, HIV-positive patients in first-world countries can live long and healthy lives. However, for many years patients throughout Africa have died for lack of treatment because neither individuals nor governments could afford to pay for the drugs. Beginning in 2001, American and British pharmaceutical companies, including Bristol-Myers and Merck, agreed to cut the price of anti-AIDS drugs that are sold to Africa. Also in 2001, Cipla, an Indian pharmaceutical company, began to sell a generic anti-AIDS drug very inexpensively in Africa, providing patients themselves were not charged. In 2007, the William J. Clinton Foundation struck a deal with Cipla and another Indian pharmaceutical company, Matrix, to provide what are called "second-line" antiretroviral drugs (drugs that are used when a first treatment stops working) at a significantly reduced cost to Africa and other developing nations.

## LEGAL SYSTEMS

Most of Africa operates with a dual legal system that includes civil law—that which is enacted by the legislature—and customary law—the system of rules that governs traditional life in rural Africa. In many cases, those two systems are at odds, such as in the case of women's rights. For most Africans, the customary law is the more relevant of the two, but as it is not written down or subject to judicial review, abuses are possible if local chiefs choose to be unfair or arbitrary. Vivek Maru, founder of Timap for Justice, a non-profit organization that provides free legal services for the poor in his native Sierra Leone, recalls an instance in which a local chief imposed a large fine on a witness for answering a question before a very slow clerk had finished writing his answer to a previous question.

## CONTEMPORARY SOCIAL PROBLEMS

Africa today is in the grip of a number of thorny social issues. It is the poorest continent, and the effects of poverty permeate all aspects of African society today. The HIV/AIDS epidemic in Africa, which has devastated the continent, is directly related to poverty and the growth of a culture of poverty. Treatment for AIDS is expensive, and many African countries cannot afford to treat their infected populations. While most AIDS patients in Africa are heterosexuals, the fact that homosexuality is taboo in most of Africa also contributes to the spread of AIDS in part by discouraging treatment. Slavery still exists in parts of Africa. Moreover, rapid urbanization has created many problems, as people torn from traditional cultures struggle to survive in a modern environment.

### HIV/AIDS and Other Diseases

The spread of AIDS in Africa is unprecedented and has decimated the African population. As of the 2007, 22.5 million people in sub-Saharan Africa were living with HIV; one person there dies every thirteen seconds, and one person contracts HIV every nine seconds. The way in which AIDS is transmitted in Africa is different from the way it is transmitted in the rest of the world, and few strategies have been developed to deal with these differences. For example, there are several traditional rituals that may be spreading AIDS without sexual contact. HIV-positive mothers who nurse their babies may transmit the disease. Despite the warnings of African health professionals, infected women, who understand that they should not nurse their babies, may nevertheless do so as part of birth rituals—because it is expected of them. Circumcisions are frequently performed on large groups of boys at the same time, and the knife is not sterilized between uses. Very young girls are often married to much older men who have had many sexual partners and who may transmit the disease to their young wives. Mothers frequently transmit AIDS to infants through the birth process because they do not know about or cannot get the necessary medication to prevent the transmission. **Polygamy**, practiced in many parts of Africa, also contributes to the spread of the disease. Young people in urban areas, cut off from the traditional support systems of villages, may engage in unsafe sexual practices.

While condom use is clearly on the rise in Africa, many more people could benefit from consistent use. A study by ADVERT, an international AIDS charity, found that between 2001 and 2005, eight of eleven countries in sub-Saharan Africa reported increases in condom use. However, in many countries, condom use is limited by economic considerations. In Uganda, for example, where 120 to 150 million condoms are needed each year, only 40 million are available. In addition, in many countries, large numbers of people still do not understand that the disease is often sexually transmitted and do not, therefore, understand the importance of condom use.

Moreover, because discussion of sex is taboo in many African ethnic groups, people may not seek out the help that is available. People with AIDS are **stigmatized** in African society, so many attempt to hide their illness. Homosexuality is also taboo in most African cultures, and many gays will not seek help for fear of reprisals.

AIDS has wiped out entire families, and the traditional system of caring for children in Africa has broken down completely in many areas. With parents, aunts, uncles, and grandparents dead, young children, possibly also infected, are left to care for younger siblings, some of whom also have AIDS. These children barely survive, and few can afford an education, virtually guaranteeing impoverished adulthoods, assuming they survive that long.

HIV/AIDS is not the only disease to plague Africa. Many diseases are caused by unsanitary drinking water. More than one African child dies every minute from diarrheal diseases, such as typhoid fever, caused by bad water. One child also dies each minute from measles, a disease that is easily preventable by a vaccine costing less than $1 per child. Malaria kills 3,000 children a day and more than a million people each year. Sleeping sickness, a parasitic infection that spreads to the brain and covering of the spine, is caused by the bite of the tsetse fly. Untreated, the infection kills. Today, nearly 500,000 people in Africa are infected with sleeping sickness.

## Poverty

The reasons for poverty in Africa are many. The continent has not been successful in using the land that is suitable for farming to feed its people. Much **arable** land is in private hands and is not used to grow crops. Modern farming techniques, such as crop rotation, have not found their way into rural areas, where the majority of Africa's food is grown. Water, while plentiful on the continent, is often unavailable where it is needed to irrigate crops.

The legacy of colonialism also has contributed to poverty in Africa. For much of the nineteenth century, while Europe and America were benefiting from the **Industrial Revolution,** Africa was prized only for the raw materials it could provide, and colonial powers generally prevented the development of industry on the continent. Colonial powers also tended to build only the **infrastructure** that met their needs, with no thought to what the people of Africa might need to develop viable economies after the European colonizers left in the twentieth century.

Corruption of government officials is also a cause of poverty in Africa. Over the years, billions of dollars of aid money sent to Africa by governments and nongovernmental organizations (NGOs) have been appropriated by corrupt leaders, rather than being spent on the needs of the people. Corrupt governments also have caused the international business community to be hesitant about investing in Africa. Fearing that bribes will have to be paid at every step of the process, many multinational companies have decided to invest elsewhere in other regions of the world.

While the causes of poverty in African are many, the effects are devastating. One in six African children dies before the age of five of illnesses that are easily preventable in developed countries. One-third of all children in sub-Saharan Africa are underweight, and one-third of all Africans suffer from malnutrition. Only about half of all African children receive even a primary education. Half of all the people in sub-Saharan Africa survive on the equivalent of one U.S. dollar per day. Further, about 300 million Africans do not have access to safe water.

Many who migrated to Africa's cities live in grinding poverty. According to the UN-Habitat Executive Director, Anna K. Tibaijuka, urban "slums are places where hunger prevails, and where young people are drawn into anti-social behavior, including crime . . . for lack of better alternatives." Urban families live in shacks with no toilet facilities, no running water, and none of the basic services—such as trash removal—that people living in Europe or the United States take for granted.

There have been some successful programs to combat poverty. These include micro-loans, especially those given to women. A micro-loan is a small amount of money, sometimes only $200 or $300, which may allow a women to buy the seed and tools she needs to grow crops to feed her family, with some surplus to sell at market. In general, homegrown antipoverty programs in Africa have had greater success than many Western aid programs. For example, Ghanan Patrick Awuah runs a private university that saves half the spaces in its freshman class for students too poor to attend otherwise. Awuah feels strongly that education can be a major factor in easing poverty in Africa. In Western Kenya, a nongovernmental organization has been successful in ensuring that schoolchildren are well fed and have the textbooks they need, resulting in improved attendance and test scores.

### Slavery

Although the slave trade in Africa was banned in the early 1800s, forced labor is still practiced in parts of west and central Africa today. Many children from Benin and Togo, abducted by members of warring factions, are sold as **domestic** workers, agricultural laborers, or sex slaves to wealthier neighbors in countries such as Nigeria and Gabon. For instance, it was revealed in 2002 that almost half of all the chocolate produced in the United States was made from cocoa beans harvested by Ivorian children who were virtual slaves. Human trafficking is also prevalent in many parts of Africa. Trafficking occurs when people are forced, threatened, or deceived by others and then placed in a situation where they are treated like slaves. A report from the Women's Consortium of Nigeria notes that there are 10,000 - Nigerian women working as prostitutes in Italy, most of whom were initially victims of trafficking.

In Sudan, a twenty-year civil war has led to tens of thousands of ethnic Dinkas being captured and enslaved by government-supported tribal militias known as *mura-heleen*. A database compiled between 2001 and 2003 by the Rift Valley Institute, an NGO headquartered in Great Britain, listed 11,000 known abductees, only 500 of whom eventually found their way out of captivity. About 60 percent of those abducted were under the age of eighteen. Many have been subjected to forced conversion to Islam, branding, and rape.

Some Christian groups have begun a process known as "redemption," in which they buy slaves from the Arab slave traders and return them to their villages. While the intentions of these individuals are good, they have, at the same time, made the slave trade more profitable. Because slave traders can command top dollar from these "redeemers," it is believed that some engage in slave raids for the sole purpose of capturing slaves to sell to them. Although the government of Sudan has pledged to prosecute slave traders, no one has yet been brought to trial.

### Urban Life

Many African urban areas are growing so rapidly that by 2020, more than half of the continent's population will live in cities; in fact, the rate of urbanization in Africa is the highest in the world. Because many of those cities are burdened by overpopulation and inadequate infrastructure, migrants do not easily find work and must live in ramshackle housing on the edge of the city. Poor sanitation and insufficient drinking water lead to infection and disease, and because of overcrowding, disease spreads easily.

Young men without work, torn from their extended families, often turn to crime and violence. In South Africa, a serious crime is committed every seventeen seconds. Some have even begun to call South Africa the "crime capital of the world." Many people in Johannesburg have taken to living in walled, gated communities, and tourists are warned of the danger of armed robberies near hotels and banks.

In Accra, Ghana, the fastest growing slum—Fadama—is called Sodom and Gomorrah by the locals. Unsupervised children play in the streets, young men gamble, litter is everywhere, and frequent fires destroy what little residents own. Overall, sub-Saharan Africa has the world's highest rate of slum growth, and it has been estimated that 72 percent of all people who live in Africa's cities live in poverty, lacking many of the basic necessities of life.

While there is much to lament in the growth of Africa's cities, there is also much to celebrate. African cities, like cities the world over, are centers of education, culture, business, and technological innovation. It is in the city that the future of Africa's economic growth lies, particularly in the development of manufacturing and service industries.

*See also:* Agriculture; Culture and Traditions; Economic Development and Trade; Migration; South Africa; Slavery and the Slave Trade; Sudan.

## FURTHER READING

Chazen, Naomi, Peter Lewis, Robert Mortimer, Donald Rothchild, Stephen John Stedman. *Politics and Society in Contemporary Africa.* Boulder, CO: Westview Press, 1999.

Fox, Louise, and Robert Liebenthal, eds. *Attacking Africa's Poverty: Case Studies from a Global Learning Process.* Washington, D.C.: World Bank Publications, 2006.

Schraeder, Peter J. *African Politics and Society: A Mosaic in Transformation.* New York: Palgrave Macmillan, 1999.

Steady, Filomina. *Women and Collective Action in Africa: Development, Democratization, and Empowerment.* New York: Palgrave Macmillan, 2005.

# Somalia

A country in the Horn of Africa, bordered by Kenya, Ethiopia, and Djibouti. Somalia, which has the longest coastline of any nation in Africa, is bordered on the north by the Gulf of Aden and on the east and south by the Indian Ocean. The land was home to an ancient people known as Kushites.

Beginning in about C.E. 600, Arab traders from Yemen began making regular trips across the Gulf of Aden, leading the two populations to intermarry and develop a shared culture that included a common language and mutual devotion to Islam. Unified during the Middle Ages as the Sultanate of Adal, Somalia by 1500 had disintegrated into a number of small kingdoms and city-states.

In the nineteenth century, during the Scramble for Africa, Somalia was carved into three European territories: French Somaliland and British Somaliland in the north and Italian Somaliland in the south. After World War II, the United Nations granted southern Somalia as a **protectorate** to Italy to govern for ten years. This was done in order to allow Somalia time to prepare to govern itself. In 1960, Italy granted southern Somalia its independence, and Great Britain declared its holdings independent as well. British and Italian Somaliland agreed to form the United Republic of Somalia. French Somaliland, today the nation of Djibouti, remained under French control until it became independent in 1977.

When Somalia's second president, Abdirashid Ali Shermarke, was assassinated in 1969, General Mohammed Siad Barre led a **coup** and declared Somalia a **socialist** state to be governed by a twenty-member Supreme Revolutionary Council (SRC) with himself at the head. Barre allied himself with the Soviet Union and accepted military and other forms of aid from that nation.

In 1977, Somalia invaded Ogaden Province in Ethiopia, which in precolonial times had been Somali territory and was home to many displaced Somali people. In many African countries, European powers forced warring tribes and clans into an uneasy **coalition** and kept the peace only by exercising strong central authority. This was not the case in Somalia; it had once been a unified territory that was torn apart by colonialism. Thus, after independence, it was the policy of the Somali government to try to reunite its people and territories. During the assault on Ogaden Province, the Somali army succeeded in retaking it. Within a year, however, Ethiopian forces with the help of Cuba and the Soviet Union defeated and drove out the Somali army. Despite Somalia's alliance with the USSR, the Soviet Union chose to side with Ethiopia in this conflict, believing that a true **Marxist-Leninist** state was more likely to arise in Ethiopia than in Somalia.

After the war, various clan-based rebel groups, including the Isaaq, the Majeerteen, and the Hawiye, attacked the Barre government. Barre violently suppressed dissent. Rather than reduce opposition, however, Barre's attempts at suppression increased it. The 1980s saw the growth of a number of resistance movements, including the Somali National Movement (SNM), made up primarily of members of the Isaaq clan, and the United Somali Congress (USC). By 1988, the entire country was embroiled in a bloody civil war. In 1991, Barre was deposed by the United Somali Congress. Since then, there has been no effective central government in Somalia, and various factions continue to fight one another. The country descended into anarchy, leaving many people homeless, others starving, and the nation's **infrastructure** in disrepair.

In 1992, the United States and several other nations launched Operation Restore Hope, an effort to bring enough stability to Somalia to allow for the delivery of humanitarian aid to the people. Peacekeeping forces from the United States were sent to Somalia to try to quell the violence that had plagued the nation since Barre was deposed. In 1993, the United Nations mounted another effort to deliver aid. However, the situation was so chaotic, with various factions still battling one another, that both operations were forced to withdraw. As of 2007, there was no functioning government.

*See also:* Civil Wars; Colonization.

### FURTHER READING

Clarke, Walter, and Jeffrey Herbst, eds. *Learning from Somalia: The Lessons of Armed Humanitarian Intervention.* Jackson, TN: Westview Press, 1997.

Korn, Fadumo. *Born in the Big Rains: A Memoir of Somalia and Survival.* New York: The Feminist Press at CUNY, 2006.

Peterson, Scott. *Me Against My Brother: At War in Somalia, Sudan and Rwanda.* London: Routledge, 2001.

# South Africa

A nation on the southernmost tip of Africa, bordered on the north by Namibia, Botswana, Zimbabwe, Mozambique, and Swaziland. South Africa's economy is the most developed in all of Africa, and its **infrastructure** the most modern.

## SOUTH AFRICA, 1488–PRESENT

**1488** Portuguese explorer Bartholomew Dias becomes the first European to sail around the Cape of Good Hope at the southernmost tip of Africa

**1652** Dutch East India Company establishes a resupply station on the Cape of Good Hope that eventually becomes known as Cape Town

**1806** British take over Cape Town

**1836** Afrikaner farmers called Boers begin the "Great Trek" north and east of Cape Town to escape British rule

**1870** Diamonds discovered in Kimberly in Afrikaner territory

**1885** Gold discovered in Witwatersrand in Transvaal

**1899–1902** British forces defeat Afrikaners in the Boer War

**1910** Union of South Africa formed from Cape and Natal colonies, as well as the republics of Orange Free State and Transvaal

**1912** African National Congress (ANC) founded to obtain equal treatment for blacks

**1914** National Party founded by Afrikaner nationalists

**1948** First laws instituting the system of racial discrimination known as "apartheid" enacted

**1960** South African police fire on unarmed demonstrators in Sharpeville, provoking international outrage

**1986** South African government initiates secret talks with Nelson Mandela of the ANC in order to bring about an end to racial conflict

**1990** South African president F.W. de Klerk removes ban on ANC

**1991** Laws governing apartheid are repealed

**1994** Nelson Mandela elected president of South Africa in first elections in which blacks voted

**1999** Mandela steps down and Thabo Mbeki elected president of South Africa

**2004** Mbeki reelected president of South Africa for a second five-year term

South Africa is home to more than 47 million people. Major ethnic groups include the Zulu, Xhosa, Basotho, Bapedi, Venda, Tswana, Tsonga, Swazi, and Ndebele. All of these groups speak Bantu languages. The minority white population can be divided into descendents of the original Dutch and German settlers, whose native tongue is Afrikaans, and descendents of the original British settlers, who speak English. There is also a large Indian population, many of whom are descended from indentured servants brought to South Africa during the nineteenth century.

South Africa is diverse in religion as well, with Christians making up about 79 percent of the population. There are also significant numbers of adherents of African

## THE BOER WAR AND THE UNION OF SOUTH AFRICA, 1899–1910

Tensions grew between the original Dutch settlers of South Africa, known as Boers, and the British colonists who arrived later. The Boers feared that eventually the British government would deprive the Boer colonists of their independence. Fighting broke out in 1899. By the time the war ended in 1902, the Boer republics of Transvaal and Orange Free State were taken over by the British. In 1910, the British Crown unified all its South African colonies into the Union of South Africa.

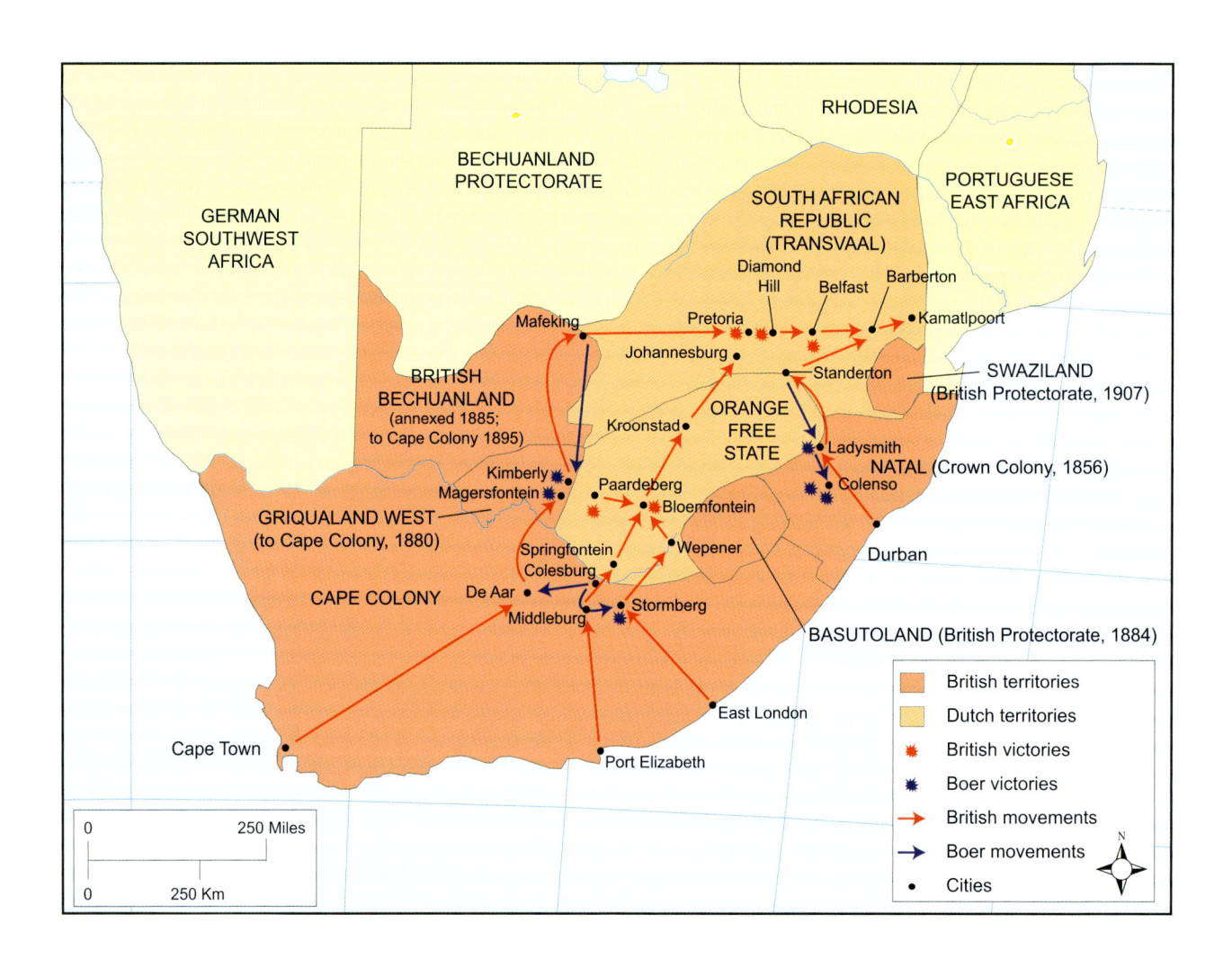

traditional religions, as well as Muslims and Hindus.

Although South Africa's economy is among the strongest in Africa, most of the development is based in four major urban areas—Johannesburg, Pretoria, Durban, and Cape Town. Rural parts of the country are significantly underdeveloped.

## THE SCRAMBLE FOR SOUTH AFRICA

In 1488, the Portuguese navigator Bartholomew Dias sighted what he called the "Cape of Storms" as he sailed around the African continent on his successful attempt to find a sea route to India. The cape was later renamed the Cape of Good

## MODERN WEAPONS

### Nuclear Testing

South Africa is a nation rich in uranium, one of the major components of nuclear weapons. The nation has admitted that it began its first nuclear research project in 1959 with the stated goal of building a nuclear reactor. Although the South African government initially claimed to be developing peaceful nuclear explosives (PNEs), by 1982 it had built its first bomb and was working to develop missiles to deliver it. Because of its policy of apartheid, South Africa was isolated from the international community, and the development of nuclear weaponry was part of a strategy the government believed was necessary to protect itself from potential threats. The arrival of Cuban forces in Angola in the mid-1970s only increased South Africa's sense that its very existence was threatened.

By 1989, South Africa reportedly had six nuclear devices. In the same year, Cuban forces left Angola and F.W. de Klerk was elected president of South Africa. De Klerk immediately embarked on a plan to end apartheid and bring South Africa back into the international community. In 1991, South Africa signed the Nuclear Nonproliferation Treaty and dismantled its nuclear arsenal, the only nation ever to voluntarily give up nuclear weapons.

---

Hope by his patron, Henry the Navigator of Portugal, because it became the gateway to the riches of India—the only sea route until the opening of the Suez Canal in 1869. In 1652, the Dutch East India Company established a station on the Cape where its ships could stop and resupply. Over the next century, French Huguenot refugees and Dutch and German immigrants arrived and settled the area around the Cape and eastward to the Great Fish River. (Huguenots are French Protestants who suffered religious persecution at the hands of French Catholics.) Descendents of this group are today referred to as Afrikaners.

In 1806, during the Napoleonic Wars, Britain took the colony from the Dutch East India Company in an attempt to protect its trade with India. The Afrikaner settlers were not happy with British rule and particularly disliked that the British abolished slavery in 1834, because they did not want to give up the option of owning slaves. In 1836, many Afrikaner farmers, also called Boers, began what has come to be called the "Great Trek," a northern and northeastern migration to escape British rule. Along the way, they encountered several African groups hostile to them, especially the Zulu, led by the powerful Shaka Zulu.

The Boers prevailed over the hostile natives and created two independent **republics**, the Transvaal and the Orange Free State. Already shaky relations between the Afrikaners and the British were further strained when diamonds were found in Kimberly in 1870 and gold was discovered in the Witwatersrand region of the Transvaal in 1885, both Boer-controlled areas. When the Boers attempted to place restrictions on British immigration and investment, the British struck back. The Boer War began in 1899 and ended in 1902 with a British victory. In 1910, Transvaal, the Orange Free State, and the British colonies of

In 1990, then African National Congress leader Nelson Mandela was released from prison after spending 27 years in jail. With fist raised in victory, he is joined by his wife, Winnie Mandela. In 1994, Nelson Mandela became the first democratically president of South Africa. (Alexander Joe/AFP/Getty Images)

Cape Town and Natal united to form the Union of South Africa. Although the population of the new nation was primarily African, whites held all of the political power; blacks were not allowed to vote and were restricted in terms of where they could live and what jobs they could hold. In 1912, the African National Congress (ANC) was founded to work for legal and political rights for Africans.

## THE ERA OF APARTHEID

In 1914, Afrikaner nationalists founded the National Party. It first gained power electorally in 1924, with J.B.M. Herzog as the nation's prime minister. In 1948, with the National Party again at the helm, the South African legislature began passing laws to enforce a policy of racial domination and separation known as apartheid. (*Apartheid* —pronounced apart-ate—is the Afrikaner word for "separateness.") As the South African economy grew and its white population prospered, the policy of apartheid guaranteed that the African population would not share in the prosperity. Africans suffered from widespread discrimination in every aspect of their lives, forced to live in less desirable areas, carry identification cards, use separate facilities, and take the least desirable jobs.

On March 21, 1960, a group of between 5,000 and 7,000 protesters converged on the police station in Sharpeville in northeastern South Africa, protesting legislation that required blacks to carry identification passes. Police fired on the unarmed protesters, killing sixty-nine people, including

## TURNING POINT

### 1994 Free Elections

For the first time in its history, on April 27, 1994, South Africa held free elections in which all of its people were allowed to vote for the National Assembly, provincial legislatures, and president. Until that time, blacks had been completely excluded from the electoral process.

The voting took three days, with more than 22 million South Africans casting their ballots. The nation chose Nelson Mandela to head a coalition government, which included the top three vote-getting parties: Mandela's African National Congress, the Afrikaner National Party of former president F.W. de Klerk, and the Inkatha Freedom Party headed by Zulu leader Mangosuthu Buthelezi. A total of nineteen parties participated in the election.

As many as 16 million of those who cast their ballots in the election had never voted before. The Independent Electoral Commission (IEC) that supervised the election did not require formal voter registration, but allowed people to vote if they had proof of citizenship. Even so, about 2.5 million voters did not have proof and were issued temporary identification cards to allow them to participate.

---

women and children. The Sharpeville Massacre, as the incident came to be called, sparked riots and protests throughout the country, prompting the government to declare a state of emergency and to arrest more than 18,000 people. The ANC was banned and forced underground. International reaction was swift and clear; many nations and the United Nations (UN) condemned South Africa.

South Africa became progressively more isolated from the rest of the world and believed that its national security was threatened. In 1979, a blast over the Indian Ocean detected by an American satellite was believed to be the result of a South African nuclear test, but this could not be proven.

Despite the government's ban of the ANC, protests and popular uprisings continued—as did international pressure, including boycotts of South African products—leading the South African government to begin secret talks with Nelson Mandela, the jailed leader of the ANC, in 1986. In 1990, F.W. de Klerk, who had been elected president of South Africa the previous year, lifted the ban on the ANC and other anti-apartheid groups and freed Mandela from prison. In 1991, the South African government repealed the most oppressive apartheid laws and created a new constitution. In the same year, South Africa signed a nuclear nonproliferation treaty and banned the manufacture of nuclear weapons. Then, in 1994, the first election in which blacks were allowed to participate was held, and Nelson Mandela was elected president of South Africa.

Mandela served as president of South Africa for five years. During his tenure, he worked to resolve the many problems that had arisen from decades of neglecting the majority black population's needs. Among these were unemployment, housing shortages, and crime. Mandela also tried to bring South Africa back into the global marketplace with an economic plan known as Growth, Employment and Redistribution (GEAR). In 1995, Mandela attempted to heal the wounds of apartheid and unify the nation. He appointed South African Anglican archbishop Desmond Tutu to head the Truth and Reconciliation Commission (TRC), a body charged with gathering testimony from both the victims and the perpetrators of violence during the period of apartheid. The TRC heard more than 7,000 petitions for amnesty from those who had committed acts of violence, and it granted amnesty to 849 individuals. Although the TRC was widely criticized for not being harsh enough, it brought peace and closure to many individuals.

In 1999, Nelson Mandela's term as president ended and he did not seek reelection. He was succeeded by Thabo Mbeki, who was elected to a second five-year term in 2004. Mbeki's primary goal has been to focus the government's efforts on improving South Africa's economic situation. He has worked hard to increase foreign investment in South Africa and has advocated free-market **capitalism** over socialism, even though that policy has not been popular with poor blacks. Mbeki has contended that economic prosperity must precede any kind of redistribution of property, as advocated by many **socialists**. Many black South Africans still live in dire poverty, and the nation faces one of the world's largest AIDS epidemics. By the end of 2005, about 5.5 million South Africans were infected with HIV, the virus that causes AIDS, and as many as 1,000 people were dying from AIDS every day. The government has been widely criticized for its slow response to the epidemic.

South Africa is a place of many contradictions. It is at once the wealthiest country in Africa and the home to many very poor people. South Africa is the continent's most industrialized nation and one of Africa's few successful democracies.

*See also:* Apartheid; Boer War; British Colonies; Colonization; Technology and Inventions.

### FURTHER READING

Deegan, Heather. *The Politics of the New South Africa.* New York: Longman, 2000.

Hamilton, Janice. *South Africa in Pictures.* Minneapolis: Lerner, 2003.

Mandela, Nelson. *Long Walk to Freedom: The Autobiography of Nelson Mandela.* New York: Holt & Rinehart, 2000.

Roberts, Martin. *South Africa, 1948–1994: The Rise and Fall of Apartheid.* New York: Longman, 2001.

Schiff, Ben. *Heart of Whiteness: Afrikaners Face Black Rule in the New South Africa.* New York: Scribner, 1995.

# Sudan

The largest country in Africa, with an area of more than 2.5 million square miles (6.5 million sq km), and one of the most ethnically diverse. Located directly south of Egypt along the Nile River, Sudan comprises hundreds of ethnic and language groups. It is bordered on the north by Egypt and Libya; on the west by Chad, Central African Republic, and Democratic Republic of the Congo; on the south by Uganda and Kenya; and on the east by Ethiopia and Eritrea, as well as the Red Sea.

Until being conquered by Egypt in 1821, Sudan was a collection of small kingdoms. The new Egyptian leadership was able to unify the northern part of the country, but the south remained under tribal rule. In 1881 a Muslim religious leader named Muham-

## INTO THE 21ST CENTURY

### Darfur

Just as the civil war in Sudan was winding down, another conflict broke out in a region of Western Sudan known as Darfur. In 2003, rebel groups, including the Sudan Liberation Movement (SLM) and the Justice and Equality Movement (JEM), began attacking government targets.

The rebels were motivated by a belief that the largely Arab Sudanese government ignored the needs of the black farmers of Darfur and actively discriminated against them. The Sudanese government retaliated with air strikes against the rebels. The conflict worsened when local militias, known as the Janjaweed, began attacking villages in coordination with the air strikes. The Janjaweed, a term that means "devils on horseback," represent Arab **pastoralists** who want Dinka farmland and water sources for their herds. In the past, Arab herders and Dinka farmers had lived peacefully side by side in Darfur. However, as populations increased, the groups came into more frequent conflict over scarce natural resources. Thus, the Janjaweed appear to be using the Darfur rebellion as an occasion to pursue their own desire to gain more land.

The conflict in Darfur came to international attention because of the brutality of the Janjaweed attacks on the civilian population. The Janjaweed have regularly carried out raids against farming villages, killing, raping, and kidnapping women as sex slaves. No one knows for sure how many people have died, but some estimates are as high as 400,000. More than 2 million have fled their homes and are living in refugee camps in Sudan and Chad. The international community has labeled what is happening in Darfur "genocide."

Although the Sudanese government claims to support neither side in the conflict, there is evidence from official documents that the government has, in fact, armed and recruited for the Janjaweed. Despite cease-fires, peace agreements, and numerous UN resolutions, no end to the fighting was in sight as of 2007. In overcrowded refugee camps, millions of people lacked sufficient food or water. Children starved to death while families waited for the conflict to end.

---

mad ibn Abdalla declared himself the Mahdi, or "expected one," and led a successful rebellion against the Egyptians that ended with the fall of the capital city, Khartoum, in 1885. Thanks to the Madhi's rebellion, Sudan was again an independent nation. Although he died shortly after the rebellion, his successor, Abd Allah, was able to rule an independent Sudan until 1898. In that year, the territory was reconquered, this time by an Anglo-Egyptian force led by the British general, Lord Kitchener.

Sudan was then ruled jointly by Egypt and Great Britain. After Egyptian independence in 1952, Britain and Egypt agreed to allow Sudan self-government. In 1954, the first parliament was inaugurated. Then, in 1956, with the consent of both Great Britain and Egypt, Sudan was granted full independence. The leaders of the new nation (a five-person Sovereignty Council) promised to create a federal system in which the south had equal representation with the north in Parliament. When the

More than 4 million people have been displaced by the civil war in Sudan. Most refugees are from Sudan's Christian south, but another one-half million refugees have come to Sudan fleeing famine and strife in neighboring countries. (Mustafa Ozer/AFP/Getty Images)

Sovereignty Council, made up primarily of northern Arabs, failed to keep their promise, southern soldiers rebelled, beginning a seventeen-year civil war.

The differences between north and south Sudan have been, and remain, pronounced. The north is primarily urban and populated by Arabic-speaking Muslims, while the south is rural and populated largely by poor farmers, many of whom are black Africans. Throughout the civil war (1955–1972), the Sudanese government continued to advocate domination by Arab Muslims and to deny self-determination to the south.

In 1969, a group of communist and **socialist** officers led by Colonel Gaafar Muhammad Nimeiry took over the government. Nimeiry proclaimed a socialist state and, in so doing, affronted both Islamists and his communist allies. His Islamic allies expected him to declare an Islamist state; his communist friends expected him to declare a communist state. Having alienated these two powerful groups and, in the process, the Soviet Union, Nimeiry looked to rebel forces in the south for support. In 1972, he signed an agreement to grant autonomy to that region. However, when oil was discovered in the south in 1979, Nimeiry went back on his agreement, declared Arabic the national language, and returned control of the southern military to the central command. Nimeiry also changed the nation's legal code to follow Sharia, or Islamic law, which was opposed by non-Muslims in the south.

In 1985, Nimeiry was overthrown and replaced by a civilian government—a fifteen-person council that took steps to reconcile the north and south by exempting the south from Islamic law. This action angered Islamists in the north, who formed their own party, the National Islamic Front led by General Umar al-Bashir, which overthrew the government. Having taken over several political offices, including that of chief of state and the prime ministry, Bashir aligned Sudan with international Islamic terrorist movements and provided safe haven for militant groups, including the international terrorist group al-Qaeda.

Throughout the 1990s, a number of regional organizations tried to find a way to end the civil war. Finally, in July 2002, the Sudanese government and the major rebel organization, the Sudan People's Liberation Movement/Army (SPLM/A), reached a historic agreement. The agreement established a government of national unity and called for the north and south to share both power and wealth. Umar al-Bashir was sworn in as president of Sudan in July 2005, with SPLM leader John Garang as his first vice president. Garang was killed in a helicopter crash three weeks after his inauguration. Officially, the crash was caused by bad weather, but some of Garang's supporters believe the crash was not accidental. There was rioting after Garang's death, but the peace has held nevertheless.

***See also:*** British Colonies; Civil Wars; Communist Movements; Language; Religion.

## FURTHER READING

Deng, Benson, Alephonsion Deng, Benjamin Ajak, with Judy A. Bernstein. *They Poured Fire on Us from the Sky: The True Story of Three Lost Boys from Sudan.* New York: Public Affairs, 2007.

# Suez Canal

A large artificial waterway west of the Sinai Peninsula in Egypt that connects the Mediterranean Sea with the Red Sea. The canal allows ships to travel between Europe and Asia without having to sail all the way around the African continent. This, in turn, allows for trade between Europe and the Middle and Far East. At 101 miles (163 km) in length, the canal is the longest in the world without locks.

The modern Suez Canal is not the first Suez Canal. Pharaoh Necho of Egypt, who reigned during the sixth century B.C.E., is believed to have built a canal that connected the Nile River with the Red Sea. Engineers working for Napoleon Bonaparte, who occupied Egypt from 1798 to 1801, suggested that a canal be dug through the narrow neck of land that separated the Mediterranean and the Red Sea. However, they miscalculated the water levels of the two bodies of water and incorrectly concluded that the difference would cause large tracts of land to be flooded. They thus abandoned the idea.

In the 1850s, a retired French diplomat, Ferdinand de Lesseps, who had read about Napoleon's idea for a canal, proposed the project to Egypt's viceroy (similar to a governor), Said Pasha, who supported the plan. De Lesseps then sought financial support from many sources, including the British government, and finally managed to secure the money he needed from French emperor Napoleon III and others. Construction began in 1859, and the canal was opened in 1869. Said Pasha granted De Lesseps's La Compagnie Universelle du Canal Maritime de Suez permission to run the canal for ninety-nine years after its completion. In 1875, the next viceroy, Ismai'l Pasha, sold Egypt's shares of the canal to the British. France, however, remained the majority shareholder. The Convention of Constantinople (1888), signed by Great Britain, Germany, Austria-Hungary, Spain, France, Italy, Russia, and the Ottoman Empire—but not Egypt—declared that the Suez Canal was a neutral zone under British protection. The treaty also guaranteed right of passage for all ships through the canal.

In 1956, Egypt's first president, Gamal Abdel Nasser, announced his intention to **nationalize** the Suez Canal. He made this decision after British, French, and American leaders refused to lend Egypt the money to build the Aswan Dam across the Nile River. Nasser intended to use revenue from the canal to pay for the construction of the dam. France, Britain, and Israel all invaded Egypt in October of that year to protect their access to the canal, resulting in the 1956 Suez Crisis. When the Soviet Union threatened to intervene on behalf of Egypt, the United Nations sent a peacekeeping force to the region and the United States pressured the invaders to withdraw.

During the 1967 Six-Day War, the Israelis captured and held the Sinai Peninsula. Egypt, in turn, closed the canal to trade. As tensions between the two nations lessened, Egypt's President Anwar Sadat presided at the canal's grand reopening in 1975. Today, more than 20,000 ships pass through the canal annually. Since it was constructed in 1867, the canal has been deepened and widened several times in order to accommodate ever larger ships.

*See also:* Aswan High Dam; Egypt.

## FURTHER READING

Karabell, Zachary. *Parting the Desert: The Creation of the Suez Canal.* New York: Vintage, 2004.

Varble, Derek. *The Suez Crisis 1956.* Oxford, UK: Osprey, 2003.

# T-U

# Technology and Inventions

While ancient Africa was home to many important inventions (scientists believe that the very first tools used by humans were made in Africa 70,000 years ago, for example), a number of factors has left modern Africa far behind other parts of the world in technological and scientific development. In many ways, Africa has been the victim of modern Western technology.

## EARLY EUROPEAN CONTACT

The Portuguese were the first Europeans to visit Africa, arriving in 1441. They were aided in their explorations by a new kind of ship, known as the caravel, which could withstand long sea voyages. Thanks to the caravel, the Portuguese were able to establish trading ports in West Africa. During the sixteenth century, having sailed around the Cape of Good Hope, the Portuguese conquered regions of East Africa as well.

During the years of the Atlantic slave trade, from the beginning of the sixteenth century to the beginning of the nineteenth century, Europeans bribed African kings to help enslave their own people, offering them European-produced goods, which were superior in many ways to locally produced goods. Kings acquired jewelry, cloth, and weapons—including guns—in return for slaves. The impact of the slave trade has echoed through the centuries. Africa's population was decimated and hundreds of thousands of young, able-bodied workers were lost to the continent. African slaves helped to create the economic system known as **capitalism** in the West, which in turn led to the Industrial Revolution. As people grew rich from the labor of slaves, they had more money to invest. Much of the capital was invested in factories and new technologies for the mass production of goods.

## SCRAMBLE FOR AFRICA

Western technology also led to the colonization of Africa in the nineteenth century. The race to colonize Africa, known as the Scramble for Africa, began with the 1884–1885 Berlin Conference, in which the European powers divided Africa among themselves. The Industrial Revolution created a need for raw materials that were plentiful in Africa, such as palm oil, which was used to lubricate machines, as well as rubber, various metals, wood, and cotton. Africa also became a market for manufactured materials. In fact, during the period of heavy colonization, Africans were forbidden to compete with their European colonizers; they were not allowed to manufacture the same goods as the European powers. This, in turn, meant that during the years of colonization, African nations did little or nothing to develop the technology and skills needed for an industrial economy, leaving them far behind the rest of the world.

Also during the nineteenth and early twentieth centuries, modern weapons, modes of transportation, and medicines allowed Europeans to continue their colonization of Africa, moving from coastal areas into the interior. The invention of the steamboat in 1803 by the American inventor Robert Fulton was a crucial step that led to the European penetration of Africa. Because the steamboat could travel easily both upstream and downriver, it allowed Europeans to navigate Africa's great internal waterways. According to historian David Headrick, steamboats "carried the power that European ships had possessed on the high seas for centuries" into Africa. "Indeed,

## TECHNOLOGY IN AFRICA

**70,000 B.C.E.** Earliest tools made by humans in Africa

**1441** Portuguese sailors arrive in Africa aboard caravels, ships built to be able to withstand long sea voyages

**18th Century** Beginning of Industrial Revolution

**19th Century** Design of the breech-loading rifle is perfected; Europeans use this weapon effectively to conquer Africa

**1820s** Scientists discover an effective method to extract quinine from the bark of the chinchona tree; quinine is used to treat malaria

**1880s** Scientists discover that malaria is transmitted by mosquitoes

**1885** Scramble for Africa begins; Europeans conquer Africa easily because of modern weapons

**1897** Railroad from Kimberly, South Africa, to Northern Rhodesia completed

**1960–1970** Construction of the Aswan High Dam in Egypt

**1970s** Worldwide recession slows Africa's progress in developing new technology

**2001** Africa becomes first region of the world in which cell phones outnumber landlines

---

no single piece of equipment is so closely associated with imperialism as is the armed shallow draft steamer." (A shallow draft steamer is one designed to navigate inland rivers, as opposed to oceangoing steamers.) The steamer was particularly useful in bringing the Congo under the domination of Belgium's King Leopold II. Steamboats could easily navigate the Congo River, and their armed crews could easily defeat any native people who tried to stop their progress. In the mid-1880s, the invention of the inflatable rubber tire by John Boyd Dunlop in Belfast, Ireland, helped make Leopold's rubber plantations valuable. Before that invention, rubber had not been widely used and was a less desirable commodity.

European colonists in Africa also set about building railroads to link various parts of the continent—to bring raw materials out and people and manufactured goods in. South Africa's Cecil Rhodes dreamed of a railroad linking Cape Town to Cairo, Egypt, and in 1897 saw a railroad built from Kimberley in South Africa to Northern Rhodesia.

One of the great barriers to exploring the interior of Africa was disease, especially malaria. Many Europeans died of the disease. Although it had been known for hundreds of years that the bark of the chinchona tree, which contains quinine, was effective in treating malaria, it was not until the 1820s that the active ingredient was extracted from the bark. In the 1880s, scientists discovered that malaria was caused by a protozoan and then that the disease was transmitted by mosquitoes. This new knowledge allowed Europeans to explore the interior of the continent with a greater degree of safety.

TECHNOLOGY AND INVENTIONS | 135

In 1901, British soldiers landed on the southern coast of Nigeria to defeat the Aro people. With their superior weapons, the British easily defeated the Aros by early 1902. (Hulton Archive/Stringer/Getty Images)

Although breech-loading rifles were used as far back as the fifteenth century, it was only in the nineteenth century that the mechanism was perfected, making widespread use possible. Before the breech-loading rifle, most weaponry was muzzle-loaded; that is, the powder and shot were loaded into the barrel of the gun from the front. With breech loading, the shot was loaded into the back, or breech, of the gun, making reloading much quicker. In Africa, battles between Europeans and Africans pitted these new rifles against spears and swords, making it very difficult for Africans to defend their lands. In essence, then, the colonization of the continent was facilitated by superior European technology.

### POST-INDEPENDENCE AFRICA

Immediately after independence—which for most of the continent came in the 1960s—Africa seemed to have a bright future with respect to technology and innovation. The **Cold War** between the United States and the Soviet Union led both powers to finance various development projects in Africa. The Soviet Union, for example, provided much of the financing for the construction of the Aswan High Dam in Egypt, a multimillion-dollar construction effort designed to help control and direct the annual flooding of the Nile River. Construction began in 1960 and was completed in 1970. As the years passed, however, that future grew dimmer. Along with development funding, there were billions to be made in weapons sales to Africa. The United States alone sold more than $1.5 billion in weapons to Africa. The nations that bought most of the weapons—Liberia, Somalia, Sudan, and Zaire (later known as the Democratic Republic of the

Congo)—were also the nations most disrupted by armed civil conflict in the years since independence.

Among the factors that prevented African development of technology since the latter part of the twentieth century has been civil conflict. Other factors are the worldwide recession of the 1970s, the failure of democratic institutions, and the many corrupt dictators—such as Idi Amin of Uganda, Charles Taylor of Liberia, and Robert Mugabe of Zimbabwe—who pilfered government treasuries for their own enrichment while neglecting economic and technological development.

In the early part of the twenty-first century, Africa was in desperate need of improved technology in a number of areas. A 2007 UNESCO report, "Science in Africa," outlines several kinds of scientific and technological initiatives that are needed to help the continent develop economically. One of Africa's great treasures, its **biodiversity**, is rapidly disappearing, and methods must be developed to preserve what is left. There are today seventy-one biosphere reserves in Africa, protected areas that are designed to preserve biodiversity. As many of these reserves cross national boundaries, they also assist African nations in finding ways to develop cooperative preservation efforts.

Also under way are efforts to bring electricity to parts of the continent that are without it. In sub-Saharan Africa, nearly 92 percent of rural Africans and about half of urban Africans lack access to modern energy services. UNESCO has been active in creating "solar villages" in rural areas in Burkina Faso and Mali, using solar technology to provide enough electricity for a village's basic needs. While solar energy is expensive to install, the cost to operate such systems is relatively low. Much work in this area remains to be done, especially in research and development to find ways to bring costs down.

Lack of water is another problem facing Africa today that will require innovative solutions. More than 300 million Africans have no access to safe drinking water. By 2025, for example, some scientists estimate that half the capacity of Africa's reservoirs will be lost to sedimentation. (Sedimentation happens when rain causes dirt and other particles to run off the land into rivers and streams.)

Africa also lacks the means by which to educate young people in science and technology. According to UNESCO's 2005 Science Report on Africa:

> Universities that once served as beacons of hope, including the universities of Ibadan in Nigeria, Dakar in Senegal, Dar-es-Salaam in the United Republic of Tanzania and Khartoum in Sudan, have been turned into shells of their former selves. Buildings are poorly maintained, modern laboratory equipment is rarely available, and faculty and staff go underappreciated and sometimes unpaid.

In addition, many African engineers, scientists, and doctors leave the continent and emigrate to Europe and the United States, creating a "brain drain" that leaves Africa without the talent and training to solve many problems that could be solved by improved technology.

One technological bright spot in Africa today is the spread of the cell phone. In 2001, Africa became the first region of the world in which cell phone users outnumbered those with landlines, with more than 2 million subscribers; experts estimate that the number could reach more than 140 million before 2010. According to a British study, economic growth rates tend to be higher in countries with greater cell-phone use. Among the other benefits brought to developing countries by cell phones are a means for poor rural families to stay in contact with relatives who live in urban areas.

*See also:* Agriculture; Aswan High Dam; Colonialism; Imperialism; Society; Suez Canal.

## FURTHER READING

Schneegans, Susan, and Anne Candau, eds. "Science in Africa: UNESCO's Contribution to Africa's Plan for Science and Technology to 2010." New York: UNESCO, 2007.

Zeleza, Paul Tiyambe, and Ibulaimu Kakoma. *Science and Technology in Africa.* Lawrenceville, NJ: Africa World Press, 2004.

# Tools and Weapons

The development of tools and weaponry in Africa has a long history. As Europeans established colonies across the continent, they brought with them their tools and, most significantly, their advanced weaponry, giving them a notable military advantage over African natives. Until the twentieth century, most African weapons were not mechanized and were designed for African warfare, which involved hand-to-hand combat at close range.

### IRON TOOLS

In Africa, ironworking has a long and venerable tradition, beginning sometime before 900 B.C.E. Many scholars believe that knowledge of how to smelt iron arose independently in several parts of Africa, including Egypt and the Great Lakes Region of East Africa. Other scholars believe that the technology was brought to Africa by the Phoenicians when they founded the North African city of Carthage in 814 B.C.E. Regardless of how the technology arrived, African smiths made it their own. Some of the pre-colonial techniques used in Africa to smelt iron are so specialized that they cannot now be duplicated, even with modern techniques. Museums around the world have magnificent collections of African ironwork, often as functional as it is beautiful. Major collections can be found at the Museum of International Folk Art, in Santa Fe, New Mexico, at the Field Museum of Natural History in Chicago, and at the University of Iowa Museum of Art and Project for the Advanced Study of Art and Life in Africa. Objects in these collections include everything from knives and swords to coins and musical instruments.

Ironworking was such an important part of many African cultures that it took on symbolic significance. The process of iron smelting was often associated with procreation, because when very high heat is applied to the iron ore, a "bloom," or mass of iron free from other elements, appears to grow out of the ore, much as a child grows in the mother's womb and is then born. Among many African ethnic groups, such as the Bassari of western Togo, iron furnaces were designed to look like women. Because iron smelting is difficult and unreliable, the process is sometimes associated with magic, and blacksmiths themselves are often considered to have supernatural powers. Blacksmiths often associate elaborate rituals with the process of iron smelting and lead prayers and dances to ensure the success of the process. Among the Bassari, when a site for the furnace is chosen, it is marked with a branch to keep away evil spirits, then the iron maker prays and pours *chakpa* (beer made from millet) as an offering to the ancestors. As the furnace is built, offerings and potions are added to the construction materials. When the furnace is complete, the master smelter and his workers share a celebratory meal. Everyone associated with

## MODERN WEAPONS

### The Military Innovations of Shaka Zulu

Shaka Zula was a great military leader of South Africa. He expanded his territory in the early years of the nineteenth century and, by the time of his death in 1828, ruled over more than 250,000 people and could command as many as 50,000 warriors.

Part of Shaka Zulu's military success came from his unusual tactics. At the time, most African warfare was a simple matter of two groups attacking each other head on, throwing spears, with little maneuvering or planning. Shaka Zulu trained his soldiers, making them run without shoes to toughen their feet. Eventually, his force could run 50 miles (80 km) in a day, which allowed them to attack swiftly and without warning. Zulu also introduced a larger, heavier shield made of cowhide and replaced light spears with heavier, shorter thrusting spears. He commanded his forces from high ground, using a formation known as the "buffalo" or "bull horn," in which a large central force, flanked by "horns"—two quicker flanks—would surround the enemy and cut off any means of escape as the central force continued to advance. Zulu drilled his army regularly and simply killed those who would not obey, with the result being a highly disciplined fighting force.

the process must abstain from sexual intercourse before and during smelting.

Iron throwing-knives are among the most distinctive and beautiful objects made by African weapons makers from several ethnic groups, including the Azande of north central Africa, the Sara of Chad, and the Marghi and Kapsiki of Cameroon. These knives, meant to be thrown overhand, have several cutting surfaces; no matter their orientation when they strike the target, they cut. The multiple blades allow for all sorts of design options, and many have a curved and birdlike shape. Ornamental tools—including knives, adzes, and axes—were often signs of status kept by higher-ranking or wealthier individuals. Among the Shu of the Congo, blacksmiths crafted razor-sharp claws that were used in **guerrilla** warfare against colonists. The wounds they left led many to assume the victims had been killed by animals.

Iron was so valuable in pre-colonial African societies that tools often served as money in tribal communities of western and central Africa. The hoe in many sub-Saharan societies is among the most important tools, as it is used to till the hard earth, scrape the soil, and hack weeds. It is also used during the harvest to chop down stalks and dig up sweet potatoes and other tubers. Because of its many uses, the hoe symbolizes agricultural work in general. It is this symbolic connection that gives it value as currency. In many cultures, such as that of the Afo people of northern Nigeria, bundles of hoe-like objects served as currency. Real hoe blades were often given as the bride price when a man decided to marry.

Many iron tools were also used to honor the gods. Ceremonial swords, in particular,

## MODERN WEAPONS

### NeoStead 2000

The NeoStead 2000 is a shotgun developed in early 1990s by two South African engineers, Tony Neophytou and Wilmore Stead. In 1991, they patented a pump-action shotgun with forward-sliding barrel, and later modified it for a dual feed tube magazine. Production began in 2001, and it became known as one of the most technologically advanced shotguns ever developed.

It is a lightweight weapon designed primarily for handling civil disturbances. Although it is built like a shotgun with a 22.5-inch (57-cm) barrel, the weapon itself is only 27 inches (68.5 cm) long, meaning that the NeoStead 2000 can be used in situations where there is not a great deal of room.

The NeoStead has a switch that allows the shooter to switch from bullets to baton rounds, a kind of shotgun shell that is not lethal. It is a pump-action shotgun, meaning it has a sliding mechanism that ejects the spent round while cocking the gun for the next shot. The United States does not allow importation of the NeoStead 2000.

---

were dedicated to particular deities, such as Ogun among the Yoruba. An umbrella-shaped object known as an *asen*, elaborately decorated, adorns the tombs of the Fon and Nago people of southern Benin.

### SHIELDS

Until the coming of the Europeans, most warfare in Africa was conducted at close quarters, on the ground, with spears, clubs, and knives. Thus, shields were a very important part of any warrior's suite of equipment. Shields came in many different shapes and sizes—round, oblong, some as large as a person. The Dinka, an ethnic group from what is now southern Sudan, used objects that looked like bows as a kind of shield, deflecting and parrying blows from clubs and sticks.

Shields were made of many different materials. Large animals with thick hides, such as buffalo, rhinoceros, elephant, and giraffe, were the most prized for making shields. The hides of smaller animals, such as zebra, wildebeest, and antelope, were stitched together to form shields. The Zulu people of South Africa used the hides of cows, wildebeest, and kudus to make their shields. Besides leather, shields were made of wicker and wood. The Musgu of central Africa carried wicker shields, while the Songye, also of central Africa, carried carved wooden shields. Shields were often elaborately decorated, carved, or painted. Maasai warriors of Kenya often had their war exploits depicted on their shields. The backs of shields had handles and were often grooved to hold an extra lance or spear. Like iron weapons, some African shields were intended as ornaments, symbols of a king or warrior's status.

Despite the relative primitiveness of African weapons in comparison with European guns, colonial military forces did not win every battle. African warriors were brave, and many were excellent tacticians. Shaka Zulu, a South African chief, expanded territory with innovative battle tactics, such as the buffalo formation, and new weapons, such as a short stabbing spear.

## WEAPONS TODAY

One of the reasons that Europeans were able to make inroads into Africa during the period of colonization is superior weapons technology. In an ironic twist of fate, however, much of contemporary Africa is awash in modern small weapons, including guns, grenade launchers, and portable anti-tank and anti-aircraft weapons. With weak governments unwilling or unable to stem the flow of weaponry into the hands of thugs, rebels, warlords, and gang members, many nations have a populace that is better armed than the police. Violent crime has been a growing problem in South Africa since free elections began in 1994; one of the weapons in the hands of many criminals is a local invention—a small pump-action shotgun called the NeoStead 2000.

*See also:* Colonization; Congo; Religion; South Africa; Sudan.

## FURTHER READING

Westerdijk, Peter. *African Metal Implements*: *Weapons, Tools, and Regalia.* New York: C.W. Post, 1984.

# Tutsis and Hutus

African ethnic groups located in present-day Rwanda and Burundi. The original inhabitants of Rwanda and Burundi were the Twa, a tribe of hunter-gatherers. Beginning in the eleventh century, the Bantu-speaking Hutus arrived in the territory and gradually came to dominate. The Hutus were agriculturalists who cleared the land for farming and grazing. Sometime during the sixteenth century, the Tutsis, a group of cattle-herding warriors, arrived from Ethiopia. As the Hutu dominated the Twa, so the Tutsis came to dominate the Hutu. Theirs was a stable, feudal society, with the Tutsis as lords and the Hutu and Twa as serfs. The three groups developed a shared culture, spoke the same language—Kinyarwanda—and lived peacefully together for hundreds of years.

## COLONIAL ERA

When the Belgians colonized the area beginning in 1916, they made sharp distinctions between the minority Tutsis and the majority Hutus. They favored the Tutsis because they apparently looked more "European," with thinner noses, lighter skin, and taller stature than the Hutus. In fact, the line dividing the group was not racial; a person born a Hutu might be classified as a Tutsi if he or she had the "right" physical characteristics. During the colonial period, those classified as Tutsis got better jobs and better education than their Hutu neighbors.

## AFTER INDEPENDENCE

Hutus came to resent this system and in 1959 precipitated a series of riots in Rwanda, during which more than 20,000 Tutsis were slaughtered. Many Tutsis fled Rwanda and settled in the neighboring nations of Burundi, Tanzania, and Uganda. In 1962, when Rwanda was granted independence, Hutus dominated the political system.

Exiled Tutsis in Uganda and Burundi formed the Rwandan Patriotic Front (RPF), which invaded Rwanda in 1990. During three years of fighting, both Hutus and Tutsis committed atrocities, including the murders of thousands of civilians. In

A government soldier oversees Tutsi refugees in Rwanda. By July 1994, the genocide in Rwanda left more than one million Tutsis and moderate Hutus dead. (Scott Peterson/Getty Images)

August 1993, however, Rwanda's President Juvénal Habyarimana and RPF commander Paul Kagame signed an agreement to end the war. In April of the same year, a plane carrying Habyarimana and Burundi's President Cyprien Ntaryamira was shot down while landing in Rwanda's capital city of Kigali. No one knows who was responsible for the crash, but some suspect that radical members of Habyarimana's own government were behind the attack, believing that the president's death would serve as a convenient excuse for ethnic cleansing.

Indeed, almost immediately, the presidential guard attacked members of the opposition party and then began a systematic campaign to rid the nation of Tutsis and moderate Hutus. An unofficial militia comprised of more than 30,000 men, called the Interhamwe ("those who attack together"), also carried out attacks on Tutsis across the nation. Soldiers, police, and government radio all encouraged civilians to exterminate their Tutsi neighbors, sometimes offering them bribes of food or Tutsi land as encouragement. Civilians were also forced by the military to help with the killing. Hutu officials distributed lists of people to be killed and provided weapons to civilians. As many as 800,000 people were slaughtered in about 100 days of violence lasting from early April to mid-July 1994—and more than a quarter of a million women were raped, according to United Nations estimates.

The slaughter ended in July 1994, when RPF forces captured the Rwandan capital city of Kigali. Fearing for their lives, 2 million Hutus fled to Zaire, including many who were responsible for the atrocities.

Shortly after the fall of Kigali, a new multi-ethnic government was established with Pasteur Bizimungu, a Hutu, as president and former members of the RPF as cabinet members. Even though many of the leaders of the Hutu death squads escaped justice, more than 500 people have been tried and sentenced to death for their role in the violence, and 100,000 are in prison.

### INTERNATIONAL INACTION

The international community did little to stop the carnage in Rwanda, and the United Nations has since apologized for its inaction. When ten UN soldiers were killed early in the conflict, the UN withdrew most of its troops and did not provide those that remained with the necessary equipment or a mandate to stop the violence. In 1999, UN Secretary-General Kofi Annan issued a statement expressing "deep remorse" for the inaction of the body. In 1998, President Bill Clinton apologized for the United States's failure to act. He told the Rwandan people, "All over the world there were people like me sitting in offices who did not fully appreciate the depth and the speed with which you were being engulfed by this unimaginable terror."

Violence between Tutsis and Hutus in Burundi has flared as well. As in Rwanda, the Tutsis are the minority but, unlike Rwanda, Tutsis run the Burundi government. In 1965, a Hutu rebellion was put down and 5,000 Hutus were executed by Tutsi officials. In 1972, 100,000 Hutus were killed in a civil war, and between 1994 and 2006, more than 300,000 died in conflicts between the two groups. Peace talks between the government and the rebels ended the civil war in 2006.

*See also:* Civil Wars; Colonization; Rwanda; Uganda.

### FURTHER READING

Hatzfeld, Jean. *Machete Season: The Killers in Rwanda Speak.* New York: Farrar, Straus and Giroux, 2005.

Khan, Shaharyan M. *The Shallow Graves of Rwanda.* London: I.B. Tauris, 2001.

Mjuawiyera, Eugenie. *The Rwandan Tutsis: A Tutsi Woman's Account of the Hidden Causes of the Rwandan Tragedy.* London: Adonis & Abbey, 2006.

Semujanga, Josias. *Origins of Rwandan Genocide.* Amherst, NY: Humanity Books, 2003.

# Uganda

A landlocked nation located in east-central equatorial Africa. Uganda is populated by Bantu speakers, who form the majority of the population and live in the southern and western parts of the country, and non-Bantu speakers, including the Lani, Acholi, and Madi, who live in the eastern and northern regions. The Bantu-speaking Buganda are the largest ethnic group in the country. In fact, "Uganda" is the Swahili name for "Buganda." About 85 percent of Ugandans are Christian.

In the 1860s, British explorers searching for the source of the Nile River first entered the area. By 1894, Britain had declared the region a **protectorate**. After **annexing** a number of nearby territories, Britain unified them in 1894 and named the resulting colony "Uganda."

Britain granted Uganda its independence in 1962. The first president of the new nation was Edward Muteesa, leader of the Buganda people, with politician Milton Obote serving as his prime minister. In 1966, Obote overthrew the government and proclaimed himself president. He, in

## GREAT LIVES

### Idi Amin

One of the most infamous and brutal dictators in the modern world, Idi Amin was born in about 1925 near Koboko in what is now Uganda. He was a member of the Kakwa ethnic group, a small Muslim tribe in a majority Christian nation.

In 1946, Amin joined the King's African Rifles (KAR), African troops under British command, as an assistant cook. He became an army private, slowly advancing through the KAR's ranks. Amin also gained a reputation for cruelty. Sent to suppress cattle theft by Turkana tribesmen from Kenya, for example, Amin's troops beat, tortured, and buried the thieves alive. Nevertheless, he continued to rise through the ranks, eventually being named major general. In January 1971, while Ugandan president Milton Obote was in Singapore at a Commonwealth meeting, Amin took over the government in a military **coup**. He began releasing political prisoners, many of whom were his supporters, and established "killer squads" to track down Obote supporters, including members of the Acholi and Lango ethnic groups. Over the years, Amin's killer squads are believed to have been responsible for between 300,000 and 500,000 deaths. Amin personally ordered the execution of Uganda's Anglican archbishop, its chief justice, the chancellor of Makerere College, the governor of the Bank of Uganda, and a number of members of Parliament. He even is believed to have murdered and dismembered one of his six wives.

In 1978, when Amin tried to annex Kagera, a province of Tanzania, Tanzanian president Julius Nyerere counterattacked. Aided by Ugandan rebels, Tanzanian forces captured the Ugandan capital of Kampala and drove Amin into exile in Libya. Ten years later, Amin relocated to Saudi Arabia where he lived until his death in August 2003. Protected by the Libyan and Saudi Arabian governments, Amin was never tried for his crimes against humanity.

---

turn, was overthrown in 1971 by Idi Amin, who ruled Uganda until 1979. Amin was a brutal dictator, responsible for 300,000 to 500,000 deaths of his own people. In 1979, Amin invaded Tanzania, which retaliated and eventually forced Amin into exile. He was succeeded by Milton Obote, who was deposed six years later by General Tito Okello. Okello ruled for only six months, until his government was felled by the National Resistance Army (NRM), led by Yoweri Museveni. Museveni rose to power in 1986 and remained president into the early 2000s. He put an end to the human rights abuses of his predecessors, allowed freedom of the press, and instituted economic reform, but his government has also been accused of corruption and embezzlement of public funds.

Beginning in 1986, Uganda was besieged by the Lord's Resistance Army (LRA), a cult-like organization led by Joseph Kony, who claims to be a medium (someone who can receive messages from the spirit world). The LRA, whose goal has never been clear, has murdered, mutilated, and kidnapped thousands of people, including children, who have been forced into armed combat. More than 1.7 million people have been displaced by LRA violence. In July

2006, the Ugandan government began peace talks with the LRA, and a peace treaty was signed the following month.

There are more than forty ethnic groups in Uganda with no group forming a majority. There are also forty different languages spoken by its people, with Luanda being the most prevalent. Uganda is primarily a Christian nation, with about 85 percent of the population practicing some form of Christianity. About 12 percent of the population is Muslim.

Although Uganda is a country blessed in natural resources, including extensive fertile land for agriculture (coffee is a major export crop) and large stores of copper, cobalt, oil, and natural gas, years of misrule have left the country poor. In 2004, the International Monetary Fund estimated Uganda's per capita **gross dometic product (GDP)** at $300, only half of that of most sub-Saharan countries.

*See also:* British Colonies; Civil Wars; Colonization.

## FURTHER READING

Harmon, Daniel E. *Central and East Africa.* New York: Chelsea House, 2001.

Ingram, Scott. *History's Villains—Idi Amin.* Chicago: Blackbirch Press, 2003.

Ofcansky, Thomas P. *Uganda: Tarnished Pearl of Africa.* Jackson, TN: Westview Press, 1996.

Otiso, Kefa M. *Culture and Customs of Uganda.* Westport, CT: Greenwood Press, 2006.

# Glossary

## THE HISTORIAN'S TOOLS

These terms and concepts are commonly used or referred to by historians and other researchers and writers to analyze the past.

**cause-and-effect relationship**  A paradigm for understanding historical events where one result or condition is the direct consequence of a preceding event or condition

**chronological thinking**  Developing a clear sense of historical time—past, present, and future

**cultural history**  *See* history, cultural

**economic history**  *See* history, economic

**era**  A period of time usually marked by a characteristic circumstance or event

**historical inquiry**  A methodical approach to historical understanding that involves asking a question, gathering information, exploring hypotheses, and establishing conclusions

**historical interpretation/analysis**  An approach to studying history that involves applying a set of questions to a set of data in order to understand how things change over time

**historical research**  An investigation into an era or event using primary sources (records made during the period in question) and secondary sources (information gathered after the period in question)

**historical understanding**  Knowledge of a moment, person, event, or pattern in history that links that item to a larger context

**history of science and technology**  Study of the evolution of scientific discoveries and technological advances

**history, cultural**  An analysis of history in terms of a people's culture, or way of life, including investigating patterns of human work and thought

**history, economic**  An analysis of history in terms of the production, distribution, and consumption of goods

**history, political**  An analysis of history in terms of the methods used to govern a group of people

**history, social**  An analysis of history in terms of the personal relationships between people and groups

**patterns of continuity and change**  A paradigm for understanding historical events in terms of institutions, culture, or other social behavior that either remains consistent or shows marked differences over time

**periodization**  Dividing history into distinct eras

**political history**  *See* history, political

**radiocarbon dating**  A test for determining the approximate age of an object or artifact by measuring the number of carbon 14 atoms in that object

**social history**  *See* history, social

## KEY TERMS FOUND IN A TO Z ENTRIES

The following words and terms appear in context in **boldface type** throughout this volume.

**animism**  A belief that spirits inhabit natural objects, including animal life and land formations

**annex**  To attach or incorporate a territory into another existing political entity

**antiretroviral**  A type of drug used to treat viral infections, such as AIDS

**arable**  Fit for cultivation

**asylum**  Protection or sanctuary, particularly political immunity granted to a refugee

**autocratic**  Characterized by having unlimited power

**bas-relief**  A kind of sculpture that is not free-standing and is only slightly raised from its background

**biodiversity**  Biological variety in an environment, relating to the number of different organisms within an area

**bureaucracy**  Administration or management of a government or business through a network of departments

**capitalism**  An economic system based on private ownership, investment of profits, and free or unregulated trade

**coalition**  An alliance of people, groups, or nations, particularly for purposes of leadership

**Cold War**  The period between the end of World War II and 1989 when the United States and the Soviet Union coexisted in a state of political and military tension

**communism**  An economic system based on communal ownership of resources and the use of those resources for the good of the community

**coup**  (coup d'état) A takeover of military or leadership power; often describes a transfer of political power using military force

**desertification**  The transformation of previously fertile land into desert

**disenfranchised**  Not having the right to vote

**domestic**  On a private level, relating to a family or household; on a national level, relating to affairs within the country rather than outside exchanges

**elite**  A group or class of people enjoying superior social or economic status

**emir**  A Middle-Eastern term for a prince or governor of a territory

**fascist**  Relating to fascism, a system of government involving a strict central authority, typically intolerant of opposition, using tactics of terror or censorship, and often based on nationalism or racism

**federation**  A joining together of states into a larger league or political union

**fundamentalist**  A person upholding a religious movement or point of view characterized by strict adherence to certain principles, often attended by intolerance of other points of view

**genre**   A type, as of literature, sculpture, or art

**gerrymandering**   To divide up an area into voting districts in a manner that gives an unfair advantage to one party over another in an election

**glottochronologist**   Someone who studies how languages evolved from a common "parent" language

**gross domestic product (GDP)**   The total market value of all goods and services produced in a country in a given year

**guerrilla**   Describing a type of irregular, unofficially organized warfare, typically involving surprise attacks

**hydroelectric power**   Electricity generated by the power of running water

**ideology**   A set of beliefs that form a political or economic system

**imperialist**   One who advocates a policy of extending a nation's power and wealth by acquiring territory and/or ruling other nations

**indigenous**   Originating within or native to an area

**Industrial Revolution**   A period of time from the mid-1800s to about 1930 during which the manufacture of goods went from a process of making one object at a time to mass production

**infrastructure**   Basic facilities necessary to connect or serve a community or society, such as transportation, communication, and supply systems

**Marxist-Leninist**   A person that holds to the political and economic doctrine of Karl Marx, Fredrich Engels, and Vladimir Lenin involving the evolution of a capitalist society into a classless socialist society

**matrilineal**   Tracing descent through the maternal or mother's line

**monotheistic**   Characterized by belief in one deity or god

**nationalization**   Takeover by government, as in the case of resources, industry, or other assets

**pagan**   A term used to describe native or traditional religions

**pastoralist**   Describes an economic or social system based on herding of livestock

**patrilineal**   Tracing descent through the paternal or father's line

**polygamy**   Referring to a social arrangement in which a husband may take more than one wife or (less often) a wife more than one husband

**polytheistic**   Characterized by the belief in several deities or gods

**protectorate**   A colony or region under the partial control and protection of a powerful nation

**referendum**   A public measure or action offered for popular vote

**republic**   A political order in which voting citizens elect their representatives and their head of state

**rule of law**   The concept that no person is above the law and that all people are subject to the law

**secede**  To withdraw formally from an organization, association, or alliance

**socialist**  Relating to socialism, the stage between capitalism and communism characterized by control by a centralized government rather than ownership by a collective

**sovereignty**  Supreme authority or power to rule

**stigmatized**  Identified or marked with something considered disgraceful, such as a disease

**subordinate**  A person secondary to or subject to the control of another person

**subsistence**  A level sufficient to merely sustain life, without extra comfort or commodities

**tariff**  Tax on imported goods

**temperate**  Referring to climate, characterized by moderate temperatures

**textiles**  Woven fabrics or cloth

**theocratic**  Of or relating to a theocracy

**theocracy**  A government subject to religious, rather than secular, authority

**totalitarian**  Having a form of government in which one central authority exercises total control over all aspects of citizens' lives

**ultimatum**  A final statement of terms

**utopian**  Characterizing an ideal society

# Selected Bibliography

Africana Encyclopedia. www.africanaencyclopedia.com.

Albright, David E. *Africa and International Communism*. New York: Macmillan Education, 1980.

Arnold, Guy. *Historical Dictionary of Civil Wars in Africa*. Lanham, MD: Scarecrow Press, 1999.

Asante, Molefi Kete, ed. *African Culture: The Rhythms of Unity*. Lawrenceville, NJ: Africa World Press, 1989.

Asihene, Emmanuel. *Traditional Folk Tales of Ghana*. Lewiston, NY: Edwin Mellen Press, 1997.

Awolalu, J. Omosade. *Yoruba Beliefs and Sacrificial Rites*. New York: Athelia Henrietta PR, 1996.

Baldwin, James. *Perspectives: Angles on African Art*. New York: Harry N. Abrams, 1987.

Basden, George T. *Among the Ibos of Nigeria*. Dublin: Nonesuch, 2006.

Bediako, Kwame. *Christianity in Africa: The Renewal of Non-Western Religion*. Maryknoll, NY: Orbis, 1996.

Bowden, Rob. *Kenya*. New York: Chelsea House, 2003.

Buckles, Daniels, and Albert Eteka, eds. *Cover Crops in West Africa: Contributing to Sustainable Agriculture*. Ottawa: IDRC, 1998.

Cameron, Ann. *The Kidnapped Prince: The Life of Olaudah Equiano*. New York: Yearling, 2000.

Carr, Rosamond Halsey. *Land of a Thousand Hills: My Life in Rwanda*. New York: Plume, 2000.

Christiaensen, Luc J., and Lionel Demery. *Down to Earth: Agriculture and Poverty Reduction in Africa*. Washington, DC: World Bank, 2007.

Clark, Nancy L., and William H. Worger. *South Africa: The Rise and Fall of Apartheid*. White Plains, NY: Longman, 2004.

Clarke, Walter, and Jeffrey Herbst, eds. *Learning from Somalia: The Lessons of Armed Humanitarian Intervention*. Jackson, TN: Westview Press, 1997.

Collier, Paul, and Nicholas Sambanis, eds. *Understanding Civil War: Evidence and Analysis*, *Vol. 1—Africa*. World Bank Publications, 2005.

Davidson, Basil. *Africa: History of a Continent*. New York: Macmillan, 1972.

Deegan, Heather. *The Politics of the New South Africa*. New York: Longman, 2000.

Edgerton, Robert. *The Troubled Heart of Africa: A History of the Congo*. New York: St. Martin's Press, 2002.

Efiong, Philip. *Nigeria and Biafra: My Story*. New York: Seaburn Books, 2007.

El-Ayouty, Yassin. *The Organization of African Unity After Thirty Years*. Westport, CT: Praeger, 1993.

Enwezor, Okwui, and Chinua Achebe, eds. *The Short Century: Independence and Liberation Movements in Africa*. New York: Prestel, 2001.

Farwell, Byron. *The Great Anglo-Boer War*. New York: Norton, 1990.

———. *The Great War in Africa, 1914–1918.* New York: Norton, 1989.

Finley, Carol. *The Art of African Masks: Exploring Cultural Traditions.* Minneapolis: Lerner, 1999.

Fremont-Barnes, Gregory. *The Boer War 1899–1902 (Essential Histories).* Oxford: Osprey, 2003.

French, Howard W. *A Continent for the Taking: The Tragedy and Hope of Africa.* New York: Vintage, 2005.

Gillon, Werner. *A Short History of African Art.* New York: Penguin, 1991.

Goldschmidt, Arthur. *Modern Egypt: The Formation of a Nation State.* Boulder, CO: Westview Press, 2004.

Gourevitch, Philip. *We Wish to Inform You That Tomorrow We Will Be Killed with Our Families.* New York: Picador, 1999.

Guest, Robert. *The Shackled Continent: Power, Corruption, and African Lives.* Washington, DC: Smithsonian, 2004.

Habeeb, William Mark. *Civil Wars in Africa.* Broomall, PA: Mason Crest, 2006.

Haile, Rebecca G. *Held at a Distance: My Rediscovery of Ethiopia.* Chicago: Academy Chicago, 2007.

Harris, Gordon. *The Organization of African Unity.* Somerset, NJ: Transaction, 1994.

Hatzfeld, Jean. *Machete Season: The Killers in Rwanda Speak.* New York: Farrar, Straus and Giroux, 2005.

Hintz, Martin. *Algeria.* San Francisco, CA: Children's Press, 2006.

Hochschild, Adam. *King Leopold's Ghost: A Story of Greed, Terror, and Heroism.* New York: Mariner Books, 1999.

Horne, Alistair. *A Savage War of Peace: Algeria 1954–1962.* New York: NYRB Classics, 2006.

Ingram, Scott. *History's Villains—Idi Amin.* Chicago: Blackbirch Press, 2003.

Karabell, Zachary. *Parting the Desert: The Creation of the Suez Canal.* New York: Vintage, 2004.

Korn, Fadumo. *Born in the Big Rains: A Memoir of Somalia and Survival.* New York: The Feminist Press at CUNY, 2006.

Lawson, E. Thomas. *Religions of Africa: Traditions in Transformation.* Long Grove, IL: Waveland, 1998.

Lewis, Suzanne Grant. *Education in Africa.* Broomall, PA: Mason Crest, 2006.

Louw, P. Eric. *The Rise, Fall, and Legacy of Apartheid.* Westport, CT: Praeger, 2004.

Lovejoy, Paul E., and Toyin Falola, eds. *Pawnship, Slavery, and Colonialism in Africa.* Trenton, NJ: Africa World Press, 2003.

Magesa, Laurenti. *African Religion: The Moral Traditions of Abundant Life.* Maryknoll, NY: Orbis, 1997.

Mandela, Nelson. *Long Walk to Freedom: The Autobiography of Nelson Mandela.* New York: Holt & Rinehart, 2000.

Marcovitz, Hal. *Islam in Africa.* Broomall, PA: Mason Crest, 2007.

Mathabane, Mark. *Kaffir Boy: The True Story of a Black Youth's Coming of Age in Apartheid

*South Africa.* Topeka, KS: Tandem Books, 1999.

Meredith, Martin. *The Fate of Africa. From the Hopes of Freedom to the Heart of Despair: A History of 50 Years of Independence.* New York: Public Affairs, 2005.

Mitchell, Peter, ed. *Peoples and Cultures of North Africa.* New York: Chelsea House, 2006.

Mungazi, Dickson A. *The Last British Liberals in Africa: Michael Blundell and Garfield Todd.* Portsmouth, NH: Praeger, 1999.

Murithi, Timothy. *The African Union: Pan-Africanism, Peacebuilding and Development.* London: Ashgate, 2005.

Mwanki, Angela. "Achieving Food Security in Africa: Challenges and Issues." www.un.org/africa/OSAA/reports

Mwaura, Mdirangu. *Kenya Today: Breaking the Yoke of Colonialism.* New York: Algora, 2005.

Obadina, Elizabeth. *Ethnic Groups in Africa.* Broomall, PA: Mason Crest, 2006.

Ofcansky, Thomas P. *Uganda: Tarnished Pearl of Africa.* Jackson, TN: Westview Press, 1996.

Ogunjimi, Bayo, and Abdul-Rasheed Na'Allah. *Introduction to African Oral Literature and Performance.* Lawrenceville, NJ: Africa World Press, 2005.

Oppong, Joseph R. *Africa South of the Sahara.* New York: Chelsea House, 2005.

Otiso, Kefa M. *Culture and Customs of Uganda.* Westport, CT: Greenwood Press, 2006.

Pallangyo, E.P. *Environmental Concerns and the Sustainability of Africa's Agriculture in the 1990s and Beyond.* New York: Vantage, 1995.

Panford, Martin Kwamina, ed. *Africa's Development in the Twenty-first Century: Pertinent Socio-economic and Development Issues.* London: Ashgate, 2006.

Parks, Peggy J. *Aswan High Dam (Building World Landmarks).* Farmington Hills, MI: Blackbirch Press, 2004.

Paulos, Milkias. *Haile Selassie, Western Education, and Political Revolution in Ethiopia.* Youngstown, NY: Cambria Press, 2006.

Perry, Glenn E. *The History of Egypt.* Westport, CT: Greenwood Press, 2004.

Pham, John-Peter. *Liberia: Portrait of a Failed State.* New York: Reed Press, 2004.

Rea, William. *African Art.* New York: Chelsea House, 1996.

Reader, John. *Africa.* Washington, DC: National Geographic Press, 2001.

———. *Africa: A Biography of the Continent.* New York: Vintage, 1999.

Reynolds, Jonathan T. and Erik Gilbert. *Africa in World History: From Prehistory to the Present.* Upper Saddle River, NJ: Pearson Education, 2004.

Roberts, Martin. *South Africa, 1948–1994: The Rise and Fall of Apartheid.* New York: Longman, 2001.

Roberts, Russell. *The Role of the African Union.* Broomall, PA: Mason Crest, 2007.

Rockman, Hazel. *Somehow Tenderness Survives: Stories of Southern Africa.* New York: HarperTeen, 1990.

Rosenberg, Anne. *Nigeria—The Culture.* New York: Crabtree, 2000.

Said, Edward. *Culture and Imperialism.* New York: Vintage, reprint 1994.

Sayre, April Pulley. *Africa.* Minneapolis: Lerner Books, 1999.

Schiff, Ben. *Heart of Whiteness: Afrikaners Face Black Rule in the New South Africa.* New York: Scribner, 1995.

Sellström, Tor, and Lennart Wohlgemuth. "The International Response to Conflict and Genocide: Lessons from the Rwanda Experience." *Journal of Humanitarian Assistance*, March 1996.

Semujanga, Josias. *Origins of Rwandan Genocide.* Amherst, NY: Humanity Books, 2003.

Shah, Anup. *Helping Africa Help Itself: A Global Effort.* Broomall, PA: Mason Crest, 2006.

Soyinka, Wole. *Myth, Literature and the African World.* Cambridge, UK: Cambridge University Press, 1990.

Tayler, Jeffrey. *Facing the Congo: A Modern-Day Journey into the Heart of Darkness.* New York: Three Rivers Press, 2002.

Uzokwe, Alfred Obiora. *Surviving in Biafra: The Story of the Nigerian Civil War.* Media, PA: Writer's Advantage, 2003.

von Braun, Joachim. *Famine in Africa: Causes, Responses, and Prevention.* Washington, DC: International Food Policy Research Institute, 2000.

Waldemeir, Patt. *Anatomy of a Miracle: The End of Apartheid and the Birth of a New South Africa.* New York: Norton, 1997.

Westerdijk, Peter. *African Metal Implements*: *Weapons, Tools, and Regalia.* New York: C.W. Post, 1984.

Williams, Trevor I. *The History of Invention.* New York: Facts On File, 1987.

Wrong, Michael. *I Didn't Do It for You: How the World Betrayed a Small African Nation.* New York: Harper, 2000.

# Index

## A

Abacha, Sani, 46, 99
Abiola, Moshood, 46
Achebe, Chinua, 92, 92p
Addis Ababa, Treaty of, 81
Adulthood, 41–42
Adwa, Battle of, 81
Africa Association, 22
African Democratic Rally, 76–77
African Growth and Opportunity Act, 7
African National Congress, 11, 13, 14, 44–46, 79–80, 126–127
African Party for the Independence of Guinea & Cape Verde, 79
African socialism, 34
African Union, 1–4, 2p
Afrikaners, 10, 125–126
Afro-Asiatic language family, 84
Afwewerki, Isaias, 62
Agriculture, 4–8, 6p
   cash *vs.* food crops, 67, 119
   climate change, 7–8
   colonialism's effect on, 75
   **desertification**, 60–61
   economic sector, 52
   pesticides, 60
   poor yields, 5–7, 67
   poverty and, 119
   *See also* Water
AIDS. *See* HIV/AIDS
Air pollution, 58–60
Aksum Obelisk, 83
Al-Bashir, Umar, 131
Al-Qaeda, 89
Algeria, 9–10, 31, 33, 70, 78
Ali Pasha, Muhammad, 55, 56
Amharic language, literature written in, 92
Amin, Idi, 143
ANC. *See* African National Congress
Ancestors, 40
Angola
   civil war, 27, 103
   colonization, 102
   independence movements, 78–79, 103
   socialist government, 36, 79
Animal masks, 15–16
Animal tricksters, 91
Animals, xii
   poaching, 60p
**Animism**, 105
Apartheid
   end of, xiv, 14–15, 127
   healing from, 128
   literature about, 94
   origins, 10–11, 126
   resistance, 11–14, 44–45, 126–127
   timeline, 12t
   world reaction, 14
Arab socialism, 57
Architecture, 16t, 17–19
   *See also* Art
Art
   characteristics of, 15
   painting, 19
   sculpture, 15–17
   **textiles**, 17, 18p
   timeline, 16t
   *See also* Architecture
Ashante **federation**, 22
Ashante palace, 17–18
Aswan High Dam, 19–20, 20p
   effect on water quality, 61
   funding for, 135
**Asylum**, 97
Atlantic Charter, 76

## B

Babangida, Ibrahim, 46, 99
Bantu, 86, 90
Bantu Authorities Act, 11
Bantu Homelands Citizens Act, 11
Barre, Mohammed Siad, 121–122
**Bas-relief**, 17
Bassari, iron furnaces, 137–138
Battle of Adwa, 81
Battle of Waterberg, 72
Belgium, Rwanda and, 110
Ben Bella, Ahmed, 9
Bendjedid, Chadi, 9
Benin Bronzes, 17
Benin Palace, 18
Berbers, 9
Berlin Conference, 31, 32m, 33, 74
Beti, Mongo, 95
Biafra, 98
Biafran War, 99
Biko, Steve, 13
**Biodiversity**, 136
Biosphere reserves, 136
Birth, 41, 118
Bismarck, Otto von, 31, 33
Biya, Paul, 47–48
Bizimungu, Pasteur, 112, 142
Blacks, discrimination of. *See* Apartheid
Blood diamonds. *See* Diamonds
Bluefin tuna, 61
Boer War, 11, 21–22, 124m, 125
Boers, 21–22, 125
Bokero, 72
Botha, Louis, 11
Botha, P.W., 11
Botswana, 24m, 44
Boudiaf, Mohamed, 9
Boumarafi, Lembarek, 9
Boumédienne, Houari, 9
Bouteflika, Abdelaziz, 10
Brain drain, 96, 136
Buganda, 142
Burkina Faso, agriculture, 8
Burundi, 140, 142

## C

Cameroon
   agriculture, 8

Cameroon (*continued*)
   colonization, 23, 73
   democratic movements, 47–48
Camp David Accords, 57
Canary Islands, 96
Cape Town, colonization, 23
**Capitalism**, 133
Carnation Revolution, 79, 103
Cell phones, 136
Central African Republic, 104
Central Orange Free State. *See* Orange Free State
Ceremonies. *See* Rites & rituals
Chad, refugees in, 104
Chemical weapons, 82
Children
   diseases affecting, 119
   forced labor, 120
   initiation rites, 41–42, 42*p*, 106
   marriage, 40
   role of, 40, 41
Christianity, 84, 109–110
Churches, 107*p*, 110
Circumcision, 42, 118
Civil Concord Policy, 10
Civil rights, 102
Civil wars
   effect on economy, 50
   map of, 29*m*
   migration and, 96
   reasons for, 27–30
   refugee crisis and, 104
Clean Diamond Trade Act, 28
Click languages, 85
Climate change, xii, 7–8, 49
Climate map, 59*m*
Climate zones, xii
**Coalitions**, democratic movement, 46
Coastal erosion, 61
Coetzee, J.M., 94–95
**Cold War**, xiv, 35
   Angola and, 79
   Mobutu Sese Seko and, 37–38
   technology & innovations, 135
   *See also* **Communism**
Colonization, xiii, 21, 32*m*
   apartheid and, 10
   British, 22–26, 30–31, 33, 62, 97–98, 115
   civil war and, 27
   direct rule, 33, 70
   Dutch, 125
   effects of, 33–34, 50, 75, 119
   French, 9, 31, 68–71, 69*m*
   German, 31, 71–73
   indirect rule, 23, 33
   Italian, 80–83, 121
   literature about, 95
   motive for, 30–31
   Portuguese, 78–79, 102–103
   Scramble for Africa, 24*m*, 31, 74–75, 133–135
   technology and, 133–135
   types of, 31–33
   *See also* Imperialism; Independence
**Communism**, 34–36, 64
   Angola, 103
   Mozambique, 103
   Sudan, 130
   *See also* **Cold War**
Community, sense of, 106
Concentration camps, 21
Condom use, 118
Congo. *See* Democratic Republic of the Congo; Republic of Congo
Congo Wars, 112
Coptic Christianity. *See* Christianity
Cote d'Ivoire, 71
Cotton, Egyptian, 56
Creation stories, 90
Creole language, 87–88
Crime, 120
Crowther, Samuel Ajayi, 109
Cultural superiority, 74
Culture & tradition
   colonialism's effect on, 75
   family life, 40–43, 116
   urban life, 43, 120–121
   *See also* Rites & rituals
Currency, 138

## D

Dams, 19–20
   *See also* Aswan High Dam
Darfur, 104, 129
De Gaulle, Charles, 78
De Klerk, F.W., 14, 46, 80, 127
Death, 43
DeBeers diamonds, 25
Defiance Campaign, 44, 79–80
Delegates, African Union, 2*p*
Democratic movements
   Cameroon, 47–48
   Congo, 48
   Egypt, 46–47
   Nigeria, 46
   South Africa, 44–46
   timeline, 45*t*
Democratic Republic of the Congo, 27, 36–39
Denmark, slave trade, xii
Derg, 64
**Desertification**, 60–61
Diagne, Ahmadou Mapaté, 95
Diamonds, 23, 27, 28
Dictators, xiii–xiv, 27, 47, 143
Dictator's club, 3
Direct rule, 33, 70
Disease, xiv, 118–119
   climate change and, 8
   colonization and, 134
   effect on agriculture, 7
   effect on economy, 53
   HIV/AIDS, xiv, 7, 53, 67, 117, 118–119
Divorce, 40
Doe, Samuel K., 89
Dogon, use of masks, 15–16
Drilling, 53
Drought, 8, 48–49, 52, 67
Drums, talking, 86
Du Bois, W.E.B., 101
Dube, John, 11
Dutch colonialism, 125

## E

East Africa
   colonization, 23
   German, 72–73
   slave trade, 113
Economy, xiv
   civil war and, 27, 50
   economic sectors, 52–53
   future developments, 53–54
   **gross domestic product**, 51*m*, 52, 54, 96
   influences on, 50–52, 53
   migration and, 96–97
   **socialist**, 50, 70
   *See also* Trade
Education, 136
Egypt, 54–58
   Christianity, 109
   colonization, 23, 24*m*, 31, 55
   cotton, 56
   democratic movements, 46–47, 58
   Islam and, 108
   Nile River delta, 6*p*
   relations with Israel, 55–57
   resort hotel/pyramids, 55*p*
   Sudan and, 129
   Suez Crisis, 55–56, 132
Elders, 41, 116
Elections
   Cameroon, 47–48
   democratic, 10, 44, 46–47
   Egypt, 46–47, 58
   Eritrea, 62
   Ethiopia, 66
   Ghana, 78
   Liberia, 89
   Nigeria, 46, 98–99
   Rwanda, 111, 112
   South Africa, 14, 46, 127–128
   *See also* Democratic movements
Electricity, 136
English language, 87
   literature written in, 92–95
Environmental issues, 58–61
Eritrea, 62–63, 81
Eritrean Liberation Front (ELF), 62
Eritrean People's Liberation Front (EPLF), 62
Ethiopia, 63–66
   Aksum Obelisk, 83
   Christianity, 109
   **communism**, 35
   Eritrea and, 62, 65
   famine, 67
   independence, 81, 82–83
   Italy's invasion of, 62, 63, 64, 81, 82
   Somalia's invasion of, 122
Ethnic hatred, 27, 30, 112
   slavery and, 115
Everything But Arms (EBA), 7
Exploitation colonies, 31–33
Extended family, 116

## F

Family life, 40–41, 116
Famine, 67–68, 68*p*
Farms. *See* Agriculture

**Federations**, Nigeria, 98
Figurines, 16
First Congo War, 112
FIS. *See* Islamic Salvation Front
Folk tale, 90
France
   colonialism, 9, 31, 68–71, 69*m*
   slave trade, 115
   *See also* French language
Freetown, 22
French language, 87
   literature written in, 95
French West Africa. *See* West Africa
Fru Ndi, Ni John, 47
Funeral customs, 43
Fuze, Magema ka Magwaza, 91

## G

Gandhi, Mahatma, 75
Garang, John, 131
Gender roles, 116
Genetically modified crops, 8
Genital mutilation, 42
Genocide, 129
Geography, xii
Germany, colonialism, 31, 71–73
**Gerrymandering**, 14
Ghana (Gold Coast)
   colonization, 22, 24*m*
   independence movements, 25, 77–78
   slums, 121
   **socialist** economy, 50
Global warming. *See* Climate change
**Glottochronologists**, 85
Gold, 21, 22
Gold Coast. *See* Ghana
Gordimer, Nadine, 94
Gowon, Yakubu, 98
Great Britain
   Boer War, 11, 21–22
   colonialism, 22–26, 24*m*, 30–31, 32*m*, 33, 97–98, 115
   imperialism, 74
   slave trade, xii–xiii, 115
   soldiers, 135*p*
   Ultimatum of 1890, 103
Great Lakes refugee crisis, 104
Great Mosque, 18
Great Trek, 10
Great Zimbabwe, 17
Green revolution, 5
**Gross domestic product (GDP)**, 51*m*, 52, 54, 96
Groud, Gilbert, 19
Group Areas Act, 11
**Guerrilla** warfare
   Algeria, 9, 78
   Angola, 78
   apartheid-based, 13
   Eritrea, 62
Guinea, 71, 104
Guinea-Bissau, 79, 103

## H

Habyarimana, Juvénal, 111, 141
Hausa language, literature written in, 91
Heligoland-Zanzibar Treaty, 72

Herero Wars, 72
HIV/AIDS, xiv, 7, 53, 67, 117, 118–119
Hoe, 138
Homelands, 11
Homosexuality, 118
Hotels, 55p
Houphouët-Boigny, Félix, 71, 76, 76t
Human capital, xiii
Human trafficking, 120
Human waste, 61
Hutu, 38–39, 104, 110–112, 140–142
**Hydroelectric power**, 19, 61

**I**
Idia's Mask, 16
Imperialism, 73–75
  See also Colonization
**Imperialists**, 25, 75
Independence, xiii–xiv, 23–26
  Algeria, 9, 78
  Congo, 36
  economic development after, 50–52
  Eritrea, 62
  Ethiopia, 81, 82–83
  French West Africa, 71
  Nigeria, 98
  Rwanda, 110
  Sudan, 129
  technology & inventions after, 135–136
  Uganda, 142
  See also Independence movements
Independence movements
  African Democratic Rally (RDA), 76–77
  Angola, 78–79, 103
  Ghana, 77–78
  Guinea-Bissau, 79, 103
  influences on, 75–76
  Mozambique, 79
  South Africa, 79–80
  timeline, 76t
  See also Independence
Indirect rule, 23, 33
Industrial emissions, 58
**Industrial Revolution**, slave trade and, 115
**Infrastructure**, lack of, 5, 50
Initiation rites, 41–42, 42p, 106
Interhamwe, 38, 111, 141
Inventions. See Technology & inventions
Iron tools, 137–139
Irrigation. See Water
Islam
  depicted in art, 18
  **fundamentalists**, 108, 109
  Muslim law, 100, 108, 130–131
  slavery, 113
  spread of, 106–109
Islamic Salvation Front (FIS), 9
Israel, relations with Egypt, 55–57
Italy
  colonialism, 80–83, 121
  invasion of Ethiopia, 62, 63, 64, 81, 82
  **sovereignty** over Eritrea, 62
Ivory tusks, 60p

**J**
Jameson Raid, 25
Janjaweed, 104, 129

**K**
Kabila, Joseph, 39
Kabila, Laurent-Desiré, 38–39, 112
Kagame, Paul, 111p, 112, 141
Kano literature, 91
Kasavubu, Joseph, 36–37, 38
Kayibanda, Gregoire, 110
Kente, 17, 18p
Kenya
  colonization, 24m
  literature & writing, 94
Khoisan language family, 84–86
Kifaya, 47
Kimberly Process Certification Scheme, 28
Kinship, 116
Kipling, Rudyard, 74
Kitchener, Herbert, 23
Kleptocracy, 38
Knives, throwing, 138
Kony, Joseph, 143
Kwangware, Peter, 19

**L**
Lagos
  British annexation of, 97
  colonization, 23
Lake Nasser, 20
Land, ownership of, 116
Language
  Bantu, 86
  characteristics, 86
  classifications, 84–86
  click, 85
  European, 86–87
  extinction of African, 88
  map of, 85m
  pidgins & creoles, 87–88
  See also Literature & writing
Legal system, 117–118
Leopold II, 31, 33, 36
Lettow-Vorbeck, Paul Emil von, 73
Liberia, 88–90
  Christianity, 109
  refugees from, 104
Libya, colonization, 82
Literature & writing
  in African languages, 91–92
  in English, 92–95
  in French, 95
  landmarks in, 93t
  oral, 90–91
Livingstone, David, xiii
Lobengula, 25
London Manifesto, 101
Lord's Resistance Army (LRA), 143–144
Lüderitz, Adolf, 72
Lugard, Frederick, 23
Lumumba, Patrice, 36, 37, 38
Lusaka Accord, 39

## M

Magic, 105–106
Maji Maji Rebellion, 73
Malaria, 7, 8, 119, 134
Malawi, agriculture, 8
Malcom X, 102
Mali, Islam, 108
Malnutrition, 4, 119
Mandela, Nelson, xiv, 13, 92p, 126p, 128
    arrest of, 12, 80
    elected president, 14, 46, 127
    release of, 14, 127
Mandela, Winnie, 126p
Manufacturing, 53, 54, 58
Maponya Mall, 52p
Marriage, 40–41, 43
Masks, 15–16
**Matrilineal** systems, 116
Mauritius, democracy in, 44
Mbeki, Thabo, 117, 128
McCarthy, Sir Charles, 22
Measles, 119
Menelik II, 63, 66, 81
Mengistu Haile Mariam, 64–65
Micro-loans, 119–120
Migration, 96–97
Migration, illegal, 96
Military tactics, 138
Mineral resources, xiii
Mining, 53, 60
Missionaries, Christian, 109, 110
Mkumba, 19
Mobutu, Joseph-Désiré. *See* Mobutu Sese Seko
Mobutu Sese Seko, 37–38, 37p, 44, 48
Mofolo, Thomas, 91
**Monotheistic** religions, 105
Morocco, Organization of African Unity and, 2
Mosques, 18, 107p
Mozambique
    civil war, 103
    colonization, 102
    **communism**, 36
    independence movements, 79
    refugees crisis, 104
Mozambique Liberation Front (FRELIMO), 79
Mqhayi, Edward Krune Loliwe, 91
Mubarak, Hosni, 46–47, 58
Muhammed, Murtala, 98
Musa, Mansa, 108
Museveni, Yoweri, 143
Muslim Brotherhood, 108
Muslim law. *See* Islam
Mustard gas, 82
Muteesa, Edward, 142
Mythology, 90

## N

Names, 41
Nasser, Gamal Abdel, 46, 55–56, 57
National Democratic Coalition (NADECO), 46
National Liberation Front, 9, 78
National Liberation Front of Angola (FNLA), 78, 79
National Party, 126
National Union for the Total Independence of Angola (UNITA), 79

Natural resources
    civil war and, 27–28
    depletion of, 5
    an economic sector, 53
Négritude, 71
NeoStead 2000, 139
New Rice for Africa (NERIC), 8
New Testament, 84
Ngugi wa Thiong'o, 91, 94
Niger-Congo language family, 86
Nigeria
    civil war, 98, 99
    colonization, 23, 24m, 97–98
    democratic movements, 46
    elections, 98–99
    independence, 98
    literature & writing, 92–94
    migration & economy, 96
    sectarian violence, 99–100
    slavery & slave trade, 97
    soldiers in, 135p
Nile River, 6p
    Aswan High Dam, 19–20, 20p
Nilo-Saharan language family, 84
Nimeiry, Gaafar Muhammed, 130
Nkrumah, Kwame, 77–78, 77p, 101
Nour, Ayuman, 47
Nuclear testing. *See* Weapons

## O

Obasanjo, Olusegun, 98, 99
Obelisk, Aksum, 83
Obote, Milton, 142–143
Obsanjo, Olusegun, 46
Ogot, Grace, 94
Oil, 53
    Nigeria, 98, 98p, 99
    spills, 60
Ojukwu, Odumegwu, 99
Okello, Tito, 143
Okri, Ben, 94
Oral traditions, 90–91
Orange Free State, 10, 21, 124m, 125
Organization of African Unity, 2–4, 77p, 102
    *See also* African Union
Oyono, Ferdinand, 95

## P

**Pagan** religions, 74
Painting, 19
Palaces, 17–18
Pan African Congresses, 80, 101, 102
Pan-African Movement, 3, 75–76, 101–102
Pan-Africanist Congress, 12, 45, 46, 80
Pass laws campaign, 45, 80
**Pastoralists**, 129
Paton, Alan, 95
**Patrilineal** systems, 116
Pesticides, 60
Petroleum. *See* Oil
Pidgin language, 87
Plaatje, Sol, 11
Poaching, 60p
**Polygamy**, 40
    AIDS and, 118

**Polygamy** (continued)
   Islamic, 108
   in literature, 91
Popular Movement for the Liberation of Angola, 79
Portugal
   colonialism, 78–79, 102–103
      slave trade, 102, 113, 115
Poverty, 27, 119–120
Praise songs, 90
Principle of Effectivity, 33
Privatization, 50
Proverbs, 91

**R**
Rabat Plan, 96
Racial discrimination. *See* Apartheid
Racial superiority, 74
Red Terror, 64
Redemption, 120
**Referendum**, 10
Refugees, 103–104, 130*p*, 141*p*
Religion, xii, 104–110
   Christianity, 84, 109–110
   conversion, 74
   Islam. *See* Islam
   literature, 92
   **pagan**, 74
   timeline, 106*t*
   traditional, 105–106
   *See also* Rites & rituals
Republic of Congo, **communism**, 35
Rhodes, Cecil, 23, 25
Rhodesia, 23, 24*m*, 25
Riddles, 91
Rites & rituals
   art and, 15–16
   birth, 41
   death, 43
   initiation, 41–42, 42*p*, 106
   ironworking, 137–139
   marriage, 43
Robert, Shaaban, 92
Rwanda, 110–112
   civil war, 27
   Hutu/Tutsi conflict, 38–39, 104, 110–112, 140–142
   international inaction, 142
Rwandan Patriotic Front, 111, 140

**S**
Sadat, Anwar, 46, 56–58
Salim, Salim Ahmed, 3
Salisbury, Robert, xiii
Saro-Wiwa, Ken, 93–94
Schreiner, Olive, 94
Science in Africa, 136
Scramble for Africa, 24*m*, 31, 74–75, 133–135
Second Congo War, 112
Sékou Touré, Ahmed, 70, 71
Selassie, Haile, 1, 62, 64, 64*p*, 65, 82
Senegal, 69, 69*m*, 71
Senghor, Léopold, 71, 95
Separate Amenities Act, 11
Settlement colonies, 31–33
Shagari, Alhjai Shehu, 98–99
Sharia. *See* Islam, Muslim law

Sharpeville massacre, 12, 45, 80, 126–127
Shields, 139
Shonekan, Ernest, 99
Shopping malls, 52*p*
Shotguns, 139
Sierra Leone
   Christianity, 109
   civil war, 27, 29*m*
   colonization, 22, 24*m*
Sirleaf, Ellen Johnson, 89–90
Six-Day War, 56, 132
Slavery & slave trade, xii–xiii, 113–115
   **capitalism** and, 133
   effect on economy, 50, 115
   Nigeria, 97
   Portugal, 102, 113
   present day, 120
   shipping routes, 114*m*
Sleeping sickness, 119
Slums, 121
Socé, Ousmane, 95
Social Democratic Front, 47
Social problems, xiv–xv, 118
Socialism, 34–36, 57
**Socialist** economies, 50, 70
Soil depletion, 5
Soil Fertility Management Unit (UGFS), 8
Solar energy, 136
Somalia, 121–122
   colonization, 24*m*, 121
   literature & language, 92
Sorcery, 105–106
Sotho language, literature written in, 91
South Africa, 122–128
   agriculture, 8
   AIDS, 117
   apartheid. *See* Apartheid
   Boer War, 11, 21–22, 124*m*, 125
   colonization, 23, 24*m*, 124–125
   crime, 120
   democratic movements, 44–46
   economy, 52, 124, 128
   ethnicity & religion, 123–124
   free elections, 127
   independence movements, 79–80
   literature & writing, 91, 94–95
   Maponya Mall, 52*p*
   nuclear testing, 125, 127
   Organization of African Unity and, 3
South African Party, 11
Southern African Development Community, 8
Southwest Africa, German, 72
Sovereign National Conference, 48
Soviet Union, xiv, 35, 122
   *See also* **Cold War**
Soweto uprising, 14
Soyinka, Wole, 93, 93*t*
Spear of the Nation, 13, 45, 80
Stanley, Henry Morton, xiii
Steamboats, 133–134
Sudan, 128–131
   civil war, 27, 130–131
   colonization, 23, 24*m*, 31
   famine, 68*p*
   Islam, 130–131

refugees, 68p, 130p
slavery, 120
Suez Canal, 23, 31, 55–56, 131–132
Swahili language, literature written in, 92, 93t

## T
Taboo, 118
Talking drums, 86
Tani, Shine, 19
Taxes, corruption and, 28
Taylor, Charles, 89
Technology & inventions, 133–137
**Textiles**, 17, 18p
Throwing-knives, 138
Togoland, 23, 73
Tolbert, William, 89
Tonal languages, 86
Tools, 137–138
    See also Weapons
**Totalitarian** rule, 64
Toxic waste, 58, 60
Trade
    agricultural, 7, 8
    geographic limitations, 53
    See also Economy; Slavery & slave trade
Tradition. See Culture & tradition
Transvaal, 10, 21, 25, 124m, 125
Treaty of Addis Ababa, 81
Treaty of Vereeniging, 21–22
Treaty of Wuchale, 81
Tshisekedi, Étienne, 48
Tshombe, Moise, 37
Tubman, William, 89
Tutola, Amos, 92–93
Tutsi, 38–39, 104, 110–112, 140–142
    refugees, 141p
Tutu, Desmond, 14–15, 128

## U
Uccaile, Treaty of. See Treaty of Wuchale
Uganda, 142–144
    colonization, 23, 24m, 142
Uhuru decade, xiii
Ultimatum of 1890, 103
UNESCO, 20, 136
United Gold Coast Convention, 77
United Nations
    on blood diamonds, 28
    Organization of African Unity and, 3
    reaction to apartheid, 14
    Trust Territories, 62
United States
    African Growth and Opportunity Act, 7
    civil rights, 102
    Clean Diamond Trade Act, 28
    Liberia and, 88
    weapons sales, 135
    See also **Cold War**
Urban life, 43, 120–121

## V
Vereeniging, Treaty of, 21–22
Vodun (voodoo), 106

## W
**Waste**
    human, 61
    toxic, 58, 60
Water
    drought, 8, 48–49, 61
    irrigation, 5–6, 119
    pollution, 60, 61
    unsanitary, 61, 119, 136
Waterberg, Battle of, 72
Weapons 135p
    chemical, 82
    iron, 138
    modern, 134t, 140
    NeoStead 2000, 139
    nuclear, 125, 127
    rifles, 134t, 135
    sale of, 135
    shields, 139
    See also Tools
West Africa
    British, 22–23
    French, 68–71, 76–78
    German, 72
Williams, Henry Sylvester, 101
Women
    and agriculture, 7, 8, 67
    AIDS and, 67, 117, 118
    genital mutilation, 42
    human trafficking, 120
    marriage, 40–41, 43, 116
    micro-loans, 119–120
    rights of, 43, 116, 117
    role of, 43, 116
World Diamond Council, 28
World War II, independence movements and, 76
Writing. See Literature & writing
Wuchale, Treaty of, 81

## X
Xasan, Sayyid Maxamed Cabdulle, 92
Xhosa language, literature written in, 91

## Y
Yar'Adua, Umaru, 46
Yom Kippur War, 56
Yoruba language, literature written in, 91, 92–93t

## Z
Zaire, 37, 38, 39, 135
    Hutu refugees in, 111, 112, 142
Zambia, agriculture, 8
Zanzibar, 25, 72, 107
Zenawi, Meles, 65
Zewditu, 64, 65
Zimbabwe
    architecture, 17
    economy, 52
    refugee crisis, 104
Zula, Shaka, 90, 125, 138, 139
Zulu language, literature written in, 91, 93t

MATAWAN-ABERDEEN PUBLIC LIBRARY
165 MAIN STREET
MATAWAN, NJ 07747
(732) 583-9100

# Modern World Time Line

| AFRICA | MIDDLE EAST AND SOUTHWEST ASIA |
|---|---|
| **1952** King Farouk of Egypt overthrown | **1947** UN recommends dividing Palestine into two states—one Jewish and one Arab |
| **1954** National Liberation Front (FLN) begins guerrilla war against French in Algeria | **1948** Nation of Israel founded; first Arab-Israeli War |
| **1956** Gamal Abdel Nasser becomes president of Egypt | **1950** Jordan annexes the Bank |
| **1957** Ghana become first sub-Saharan nation to achieve independence | **1959** Restoration of the Church of the Holy Sepulchre in Jerusalem begins |
| **1960** Sharpeville Massacre in South Africa; Belgium grants Congo independence | **1960** Organization of Petroleum Exporting Countries (OPEC) founded |
| **1961** South Africa becomes a republic | **1964** Palestine Liberation Organization (PLO) formed |
| **1962** Algeria gains independence | **1967** Six-Day War between Israel and Arab neighbors |
| **1963** Organization of Africa Unity (OAU) formed | **1969** Yassir Arafat becomes chairman of the Palestine Liberation Organization (PLO) |
| **1967** Nigerian Civil War begins | **1970** General Hafez al-Assad seizes control of Syria |
| **1970** Aswan High Dam in Egypt completed | **1973** Yom Kippur War between Israel and neighboring Arab nations |
| **1974–1991** Angolan Civil War | **1978** Camp David Accords; Iranian Revolution begins |
| **1976** Soweto Uprising in South Africa | **1979** Israel-Egypt Peace Treaty signed; Iran declared Islamic state |
| **1979** Zimbabwe becomes independent nation | **1980–1988** Iran-Iraq War |
| **1981** Egyptian president Anwar Sadat assassinated | **1982** Israel invades Lebanon to stop guerrilla attacks |
| **1990** Namibia becomes independent | **1987** First *intifada* uprising in Gaza Strip |
| **1993** Eritrea declares independence | **1990** Iraq invades Kuwait |
| **1994** Apartheid ends; first free, multi-racial elections in South Africa | **1991** Persian Gulf War |
| **1998** War breaks out between Eritrea and Ethiopia | **1992** Saudi King Fahd introduces the Basic Law of Governance |
| **2000** Senegal and Gambia hold democratic elections | **1993** Oslo Accords establish a roadmap for peace in Middle East |
| **2002** African Union (AU) formed, replacing OAU | **1994** Israel-Jordan Peace Treaty |
| **2003** Civil war begins in Sudan | **2003** Iraq War begins |
| **2004** Algeria holds first democratic election | **2005** Israeli settlers withdraw from Gaza Strip |
| **2005** Democratic Republic of the Congo holds democratic elections | **2007** Hamas takes control of Gaza Strip |

MATAWAN-ABERDEEN PUBLIC LIBRARY
165 MAIN STREET
MATAWAN, NJ 07747
(732) 583-9100